VSAM

The Macmillan Database/Data Communications Series

Jay Ranade, Series Editor

Available
Cave/Maymon   *Software Lifecycle Management*
Fadok   *Effective Design of CODASYL Data Base*
Ha   *Digital Satellite Communications*
Ranade/Ranade   *VSAM: Concepts, Programming, and Design*
Singer   *Written Communication for MIS/DP Professionals*
St. Amand   *A Guide to Packet-Switched, Value-Added Networks*
Towner   *The ADS/Online Cookbook*

Forthcoming
Azevedo   *ISPF: The Strategic Dialog Manager*
Emanuel   *CICS: Designing for Performance*
Girard/Carrico/Jones   *Expert Systems*
McGrew/McDaniel   *In-House Publishing in a Mainframe Environment*
Piggott   *CICS Performance*
Potter   *Local Area Networks: Applications and Design*
Samson   *MVS Performance Management*
Towner   *Automate Plus*
Towner   *IDMS/R™ Cookbook*
Turban   *Expert Systems*
Wipfler   *CICS: Application Development and Programming*

VSAM Performance, Design, and Fine Tuning

Jay Ranade
Assistant Vice President
Merrill Lynch, Pierce, Fenner & Smith, Inc.

McGraw-Hill Book Company

New York St. Louis San Francisco Auckland
Bogotá Hamburg London Madrid Milan Mexico
Montreal New Delhi Panama Paris São Paulo
Singapore Sydney Tokyo Toronto

Copyright © 1987, Jay Ranade

Printed in the United States of America

All rights reserved. No part of this book may be reproduced or transmitted in any form or by any means, electronic or mechanical, including photocopying, recording, or by any information storage and retrieval system, without permission in writing from the Publisher.

McGraw-Hill Book Company

ISBN 0-07-583963-6

Library of Congress Cataloging-in-Publication Data

Ranade, Jay.
   VSAM, performance, design, and fine tuning.

  (The McGraw-Hill database/data communications series)
  Bibliography: p.
  Includes index.
  1. Virtual computer systems. 2. Virtual storage
(Computer science) I. Title. II. Series.
QA76.9.V5R365   1987   004.5'6   87-12391
ISBN 0-07-583963-6

To my mother

Mrs. Krishna Rani Ranade

Contents

Preface — xvii
Acknowledgments — xx

PART ONE CONCEPTS AND THEORY OF FINE TUNING — 1

chapter 1 Concepts of Fine Tuning — 3

1.1 Introduction — 3
   1.1.1 What is Fine Tuning? — 4
1.2 Different Views of Fine Tuning — 4
   1.2.1 Batch Jobs — 4
   1.2.2 On-Line (CICS/VS) Systems — 5
   1.2.3 Buffer and Virtual Storage Management — 5
   1.2.4 DASD Space Utilization — 6
1.3 Flow of an On-Line (CICS/VS) Transaction — 7
1.4 The Basis of VSAM Fine Tuning — 9
1.5 Fine Tuning—an Ongoing Process — 9
1.6 Significance of an Application Design — 10
1.7 Understanding Different Environments — 11
   1.7.1 VSAM, DF/EF, and DFP — 11
   1.7.2 VSAM Catalogs and ICF Catalogs — 11

chapter 2 VSAM File Architecture and I/O's — 13

2.1 Control Intervals and Control Areas — 13

		2.1.1	Data CIs and CAs	14
		2.1.2	Index CIs and CAs	15
	2.2	Key-Sequenced Data Set (KSDS)		16
		2.2.1	Levels of Index	18
		2.2.2	Index Set and Sequence Set	18
		2.2.3	File Requests and I/O's	19
	2.3	Entry-Sequenced Data Set (ESDS)		21
	2.4	Relative Record Data Set (RRDS)		22
	2.5	Alternate Indexes		22
		2.5.1	Levels of Index	23
		2.5.2	Upgrade Set	23

chapter 3 Control Interval and Control Area Splits — 24

	3.1	The Problem of CI and CA Splits		24
	3.2	Control Interval Split		24
		3.2.1	How Does a CI Split Take Place?	24
		3.2.2	I/Os in a CI Split	30
	3.3	Control Area Split		33
		3.3.1	How Does a CA Split Take Place?	33
		3.3.2	I/Os in a CA Split	33
		3.3.3	Points of Failure in a CA Split	36
		3.3.4	Shareoption 4 and CA Split	37
	3.4	Techniques to Minimize CI and CA Splits		37
		3.4.1	Fixed Free Space Allocation	37
		3.4.2	Variable Free Space Allocation	37
		3.4.3	Internal Formatting	38
		3.4.4	Premature CA Splits	38
		3.4.5	KSDS vs ESDS with Alternate Index	38
	3.5	CI and CA Splits and File Sharing		38
		3.5.1	The CICS Environment	39

chapter 4 Glossary and Features of Fine Tuning — 44

	4.1	Definitions		44
		4.1.1	Strings	44
		4.1.2	Index Buffers and Data Buffers	44
		4.1.3	Buffer Space	46

		4.1.4	Buffer Look-Aside	47
		4.1.5	Buffer Refresh	47
		4.1.6	NSR Buffers	47
		4.1.7	LSR Buffers	48
		4.1.8	Read-Ahead	49
		4.1.9	Control Blocks	50
	4.2	Some Important Features of VSAM		50

PART TWO HARDWARE AND PERFORMANCE   55

chapter 5 Internals of an Input/Output   57

	5.1	A DASD Configuration		57
		5.1.1	Disk Drives	57
		5.1.2	DASD Control Unit	58
		5.1.3	Channels	59
	5.2	Path of an "Ideal World" I/O		60
	5.3	Path of a "Real World" I/O		63
	5.4	Serializing I/O's		65
		5.4.1	Reserve Macro	66
		5.4.2	Global Resource Serialization (GRS)	67
	5.5	Techniques for Faster and Fewer I/O's		68

chapter 6 Physical Storage Media   70

	6.1	What Does a DASD Look Like?		70
		6.1.1	Conceptual Architecture	70
		6.1.2	Physical Architecture	71
	6.2	I/O Delays		73
		6.2.1	Seek Time Delay	73
		6.2.2	Rotational Delay	73
		6.2.3	Data Transfer Delay	74
		6.2.4	Reducing the Delays	74
		6.2.5	Fixed-Head Cylinders	75
	6.3	DASD Storage Capacity		76
	6.4	Control Intervals, Physical Blocks, and Logical Records		76
		6.4.1	Physical Block Size	76
		6.4.2	Interblock Gaps	77
		6.4.3	Conserving DASD Space	79

chapter 7 Cache DASD Controllers   80

	7.1	What is Cache?	80

7.1.1	Configuration of a Cache DASD Controller	81
7.1.2	I/O with a Cache DASD Controller	83
7.2	Cache Management Modes	84
7.3	AMS Commands Used with Cache	85
7.3.1	SETCACHE	85
7.3.2	BINDDATA	87
7.3.3	LISTDATA	92
7.4	Cache Ratios	93
7.4.1	Read/Write Ratio	93
7.4.2	Read-Hit Ratio	93
7.5	Summary	96

chapter 8 Expanded Memory, Mass Storage System, and Solid State Devices — 97

- 8.1 Expanded Memory — 97
- 8.2 Mass Storage System (MSS) — 97
  - 8.2.1 DESTAGEWAIT Parameter — 99
  - 8.2.2 STAGE, BIND, and CYLINDERFAULT — 100
  - 8.2.3 Recommendations — 101
- 8.3 Solid State Devices (SSDs) — 101
  - 8.3.1 Comparison of SSDs and DASDs — 102
  - 8.3.2 SSD and Cache — 103
  - 8.3.3 SSD and Expanded Memory — 104

PART THREE ACCESS METHOD SERVICES PARAMETERS — 105

chapter 9 CI Size and Record Size — 107

- 9.1 Data CI Size — 107
  - 9.1.1 Type of Processing — 108
  - 9.1.2 Record Size and Insert Activity — 109
  - 9.1.3 DASD Type and Physical Records — 109
  - 9.1.4 Virtual Storage Constraint — 110
- 9.2 Index CI Size — 110
  - 9.2.1 Implications of a Small Index CI — 112
  - 9.2.2 Testing for Index CI Utilization — 112

	9.2.3 Recommendations	124
9.3	Record Size	125
	9.3.1 Support for Spanned Records	125

chapter 10 Space Allocation Parameters   126

10.1	Cylinders, Tracks, and Records	126
	10.1.1 Data CA Size	127
10.2	Index Space Allocation	128
10.3	FBA Devices (DOS/VSE Only)	131
10.4	UNIQUE vs. SUBALLOCATION	132
	10.4.1 First Available vs Best Fit Algorithms	132
	10.4.2 Recommendation	135
10.5	Secondary Extents	136
10.6	KEYRANGES	137
10.7	Summary	139

chapter 11 IMBED and REPLICATE   140

11.1	IMBED and NOREPLICATE	141
	11.1.1 Increased DASD Space Requirement	143
	11.1.2 Effect on I/O Performance	143
	11.1.3 Summary	146
11.2	IMBED and REPLICATE	146
	11.2.1 DASD Space Requirement	147
	11.2.2 I/O Performance	147
	11.2.3 Summary	150
11.3	NOIMBED and REPLICATE	150
11.4	NOIMBED and NOREPLICATE	153
	11.4.1 Cache DASD Controllers	153
11.5	IMS/DB and REPLICATE	153
11.6	Alternate Indexes	155

chapter 12 Techniques for Using Freespace   156

12.1	Factors Affecting Free Space	158
12.2	Fixed Free Space Allocation	161
	12.2.1 CI vs CA Free Space	161
12.3	Variable Free Space Allocation	162
12.4	Reorganization of Files	167

		12.5	Preformatting Data Sets	167
		12.6	Alternate Indexes and Free Space	171

chapter 13 Other Performance-Related Parameters — 172

- 13.1 SPEED vs RECOVERY — 172
- 13.2 ERASE vs NOERASE — 175
- 13.3 WRITECHECK vs NOWRITECHECK — 176
- 13.4 SHAREOPTION 4 — 176
- 13.5 SPANNED Records — 176
- 13.6 BUFFERSPACE — 177
- 13.7 GDGs and VSAM Catalogs (MVS Only) — 179
- 13.8 REUSE — 180
- 13.9 BLDINDEX — 180
- 13.10 UPGRADE vs NOUPGRADE — 183

chapter 14 Space Estimation for Data Sets — 184

- 14.1 Estimating for a KSDS — 185
  - 14.1.1 Estimating Space for Fixed-Length Records — 185
  - 14.1.2 Estimating Space for Variable-Length Records — 189
- 14.2 Estimating for an Alternate Index — 189
- 14.3 Estimating for an ESDS — 193
- 14.4 Estimating for an RRDS — 194
- 14.5 HURBA and HARBA — 196

PART FOUR BUFFER MANAGEMENT — 199

chapter 15 Batch Environment — 201

- 15.1 What are Buffers? — 201
- 15.2 How to Specify Buffers — 202
- 15.3 Index Buffers — 204
  - 15.3.1 Random Access — 204
  - 15.3.2 Sequential Access — 207
  - 15.3.3 Mixed Mode Access — 207
- 15.4 Data Buffers — 207
  - 15.4.1 Random Access — 208

	15.4.2	Sequential Access	208
	15.4.3	Mixed Mode Access	209
15.5	Alternate Index Considerations		210
	15.5.1	Dynamic Open via Path	210
15.6	DOS/VSE Considerations		212
15.7	Backup and Reorganization		212

chapter 16 CICS Environment—NSR 213

16.1	Where Do the Buffers Reside?		214
16.2	File Control Table and the LSRPOOL Operand		214
16.3	VSAM Strings (STRNO) Allocation		216
	16.3.1	How Many Strings Are Needed?	216
	16.3.2	Duration of a String	218
16.4	Index Buffers (BUFNI)		219
	16.4.1	Excess Index Buffers	223
16.5	Data Buffers (BUFND)		224
	16.5.1	Excess Data Buffers	224
16.6	STRNO, BUFNI, BUFND Interrelationship		225
16.7	Alternate Index Considerations		225
	16.7.1	BASE Parameter	226

chapter 17 CICS Environment—LSR 228

17.1	What is LSR?		228
17.2	LSR Characteristics		230
	17.2.1	Buffers Shared by Index and Data Components	230
	17.2.2	Less Virtual Storage	230
	17.2.3	Buffer Look-Aside	231
	17.2.4	Sequence Set in Core	231
	17.2.5	MVS/XA Environment	232
	17.2.6	No Read-Ahead in Browses	232
	17.2.7	Alternate Index Support	232
17.3	LSR Problems		233
	17.3.1	Lockout Possibility	233
	17.3.2	Browses Monopolize Buffers	234
	17.3.3	Slow CA Splits	235
	17.3.4	Increased Path Length	235
17.4	How to Define LSR in CICS		235
	17.4.1	DFHFCT TYPE = SHRCTL Macro	237

17.4.2	Effect of Default Allocation	238
17.4.3	LSR Guidelines	239
17.5	LSR Recommendations	239
17.5.1	Monitor via Statistics	239
17.5.2	Use Multiple LSR Pools	240
17.5.3	Use IMBED and REPLICATE	241
17.5.4	Keep Index and Data CI Sizes Separate	241
17.5.5	Use LSR for Files with Heavy Look-Asides	241
17.5.6	Combine Files with Nonuniform Activity	242
17.5.7	Use LSR Buffers for Low-Activity Files	242
17.5.8	Define Buffer Pools for All CI Sizes	242
17.5.9	Keep Buffer Pools on a 4K Boundary	243

appendix A **VSAM Terminology Glossary** 245

appendix B **Access Method Services Command Summary for Cache DASD Controllers** 252

appendix C **File Requests and I/O's** 254

appendix D **CI/CA Splits and I/O's** 256

appendix E **Seek Time, Rotational Delay, and Data Transfer Delay for Selected DASDs** 257

appendix F **"Ideal World" I/O Times for Selected DASDs** 259

appendix G **DASD Storage Capacity** 260

appendix H **CI Sizes, Physical Block Sizes, IBGs, and DASD Utilization** 261

	15.4.2 Sequential Access	208
	15.4.3 Mixed Mode Access	209
15.5	Alternate Index Considerations	210
	15.5.1 Dynamic Open via Path	210
15.6	DOS/VSE Considerations	212
15.7	Backup and Reorganization	212

chapter 16 CICS Environment—NSR 213

16.1	Where Do the Buffers Reside?	214
16.2	File Control Table and the LSRPOOL Operand	214
16.3	VSAM Strings (STRNO) Allocation	216
	16.3.1 How Many Strings Are Needed?	216
	16.3.2 Duration of a String	218
16.4	Index Buffers (BUFNI)	219
	16.4.1 Excess Index Buffers	223
16.5	Data Buffers (BUFND)	224
	16.5.1 Excess Data Buffers	224
16.6	STRNO, BUFNI, BUFND Interrelationship	225
16.7	Alternate Index Considerations	225
	16.7.1 BASE Parameter	226

chapter 17 CICS Environment—LSR 228

17.1	What is LSR?	228
17.2	LSR Characteristics	230
	17.2.1 Buffers Shared by Index and Data Components	230
	17.2.2 Less Virtual Storage	230
	17.2.3 Buffer Look-Aside	231
	17.2.4 Sequence Set in Core	231
	17.2.5 MVS/XA Environment	232
	17.2.6 No Read-Ahead in Browses	232
	17.2.7 Alternate Index Support	232
17.3	LSR Problems	233
	17.3.1 Lockout Possibility	233
	17.3.2 Browses Monopolize Buffers	234
	17.3.3 Slow CA Splits	235
	17.3.4 Increased Path Length	235
17.4	How to Define LSR in CICS	235
	17.4.1 DFHFCT TYPE = SHRCTL Macro	237

17.4.2	Effect of Default Allocation	238
17.4.3	LSR Guidelines	239
17.5	LSR Recommendations	239
17.5.1	Monitor via Statistics	239
17.5.2	Use Multiple LSR Pools	240
17.5.3	Use IMBED and REPLICATE	241
17.5.4	Keep Index and Data CI Sizes Separate	241
17.5.5	Use LSR for Files with Heavy Look-Asides	241
17.5.6	Combine Files with Nonuniform Activity	242
17.5.7	Use LSR Buffers for Low-Activity Files	242
17.5.8	Define Buffer Pools for All CI Sizes	242
17.5.9	Keep Buffer Pools on a 4K Boundary	243

appendix A   VSAM Terminology Glossary   245

appendix B   Access Method Services Command Summary for Cache DASD Controllers   252

appendix C   File Requests and I/O's   254

appendix D   CI/CA Splits and I/O's   256

appendix E   Seek Time, Rotational Delay, and Data Transfer Delay for Selected DASDs   257

appendix F   "Ideal World" I/O Times for Selected DASDs   259

appendix G   DASD Storage Capacity   260

appendix H   CI Sizes, Physical Block Sizes, IBGs, and DASD Utilization   261 *appendix I* **Storage Characteristics of FBA Devices (DOS/VSE Only)**   **263**

Index   **265**

Preface

"Thou shalt not skip the preface"

AUTHOR

This is a sequel to *VSAM: Concepts, Programming, and Design* (Macmillan, 1986). The success of that book proved that the "real-life-examples" approach in presenting the subject matter was effective and well received. That style has been retained in this volume, and I hope that it will be as useful to you as before.

The subject of VSAM fine tuning has always fascinated me. It has probably had more than its share of my attention because the vendors' manuals do not tell you how to use VSAM effectively. Once a student of mine remarked, "How can vendors sell you more hardware if they teach you to use the current environment more effectively?" Although I do not agree with the cynicism of this remark, it has always puzzled me that there is no systematic way to learn fine tuning from IBM manuals. Anyway, that remark forced me to start researching the subject in greater depth. The result of that research is in your hands.

For Whom This Book Was Written

This text is advanced enough to be used by MVS systems programmers, CICS systems programmers, data base administrators, systems designers, and systems analysts. At the same time, it has been kept simple enough to be easily understood by application programmers with sufficient knowledge of VSAM to be able to understand Access Method Services commands. If you have already read the earlier book on VSAM, you should have more than enough knowledge to understand this volume. Data base administrators, especially those dealing with IMS/DB, will find quite a few tips and hints to make more effective use of their data bases. CICS systems programmers and designers will find the chapters on buffer management useful and effective. MVS systems programmers and capacity management personnel will learn about the relationship between

VSAM and hardware, the internals of I/O's, performance guidelines, cache controllers, solid state devices, and much more. Wherever applicable, performance guidelines have been presented in terms that can be easily understood by COBOL programmers.

The book has been structured in such a way that it can be used as *a self-teaching guide without additional guidance*. At a reasonable pace, it should take you about 35 hours to finish the book. It may also be used as a textbook for a 2- to 3-day seminar on VSAM fine tuning. Although the format and writing style are similar to those of a textbook, the numerous tables and practical examples can continue to be used for guideline and reference purposes.

Operating System Environment

This book has been written primarily for *OS/MVS*, *MVS/XA* and *DOS/VSE* environments, but since most of the concepts are similar, DOS/VS, OS/VS1, and VM/CMS users will also be able to benefit from it.

If You Do Not Know VSAM

An assumption has been made that you are already familiar with VSAM. This book is not intended to teach you how to use VSAM; its purpose is to teach you how to use VSAM *well*. If you are not very familiar with VSAM, it would be advisable for you to read *VSAM: Concepts, Programming and Design* first.

A Word on the Style Used

The style of the book has purposely been kept simple. I understand the complexity of the data processing environment and the limited amount of time one can spare to learn new concepts in a constantly changing environment. I have worked hard to make reading this book a pleasant experience rather than a strenuous mental exercise. The reading material is supported with an ample supply of diagrams, illustrations, and examples.

Why This Book Is Complete

VSAM has been discussed in reference to numerous pieces of hardware and software. The book contains discussions on almost all available DASDs, which include the IBM 9335 and IBM 9332 announced with the IBM 9370 series of computers. Cache DASD controllers, i.e., IBM 3880 Models 13 and 23, are included, and the new releases of CICS, including CICS 1.7 and CICS 2.1, have been incorporated. There are tips and hints on the use of VSAM files for IMS/VS including IMS 1.3, IMS 2.1, and IMS 2.2. In fact, I made some last-minute changes to the text when IBM announced some new hardware that affected the use of the IMBED and REPLICATE parameters. In a nutshell, the book is complete in all respects, and I believe that there is no other literature currently available that incorporates all these features in a single volume.

VSAM Fine Tuning Knowledge Gap

It is surprising to learn that the improper use of VSAM is usually the major cause of poorly performing batch jobs and on-line systems. Only a handful of people know how to tune it well. This doesn't mean that it is difficult to learn—merely that nobody has put it together in an easily understandable format. You may find that after using the techniques discussed in this book, you can run the same batch jobs in half the time or less. You may also cut CICS I/O's in half and thus improve transaction response time.

How Your Installation Benefits

If you can run your batch jobs and on-line systems more efficiently with the currently available resources, it may make a planned hardware upgrade unnecessary. This could save your installation anywhere from a few thousand to several million dollars. In fact, I am eager to hear how you benefit from the use of the techniques learned from this book. Please drop me a line c/o Sci-Tech Editor, Professional Books Division, Macmillan Publishers, 866 Third Ave., New York, NY 10022.

What Is Included

Part I discusses the concepts and theory of fine tuning VSAM and lays the foundations for understanding the rest of the book. It includes VSAM file architectures, I/O's, CI and CA splits, and a few important definitions.

Part II includes a detailed discussion of hardware and how it affects VSAM performance. It discusses almost all the CKD and FBA DASDs, cache DASD controllers, expanded memory, mass storage systems, solid state devices, and much more.

Part III provides extensive coverage of some important AMS commands and how their parameters affect VSAM performance. It includes CI size, record size, space-allocation parameters, IMBED, REPLICATE, FREESPACE, and about half a dozen other lesser known parameters.

Part IV encompasses a detailed discussion on VSAM buffer management in the batch and CICS environments. The CICS environment has further been subdivided into files using NSR and LSR buffering techniques. Buffer management in a virtual storage constrained situation is given due coverage.

Summary

After finishing this book, you should know all the hitherto unrevealed secrets of VSAM fine tuning in batch, CICS, and IMS environments. You should be able to design new systems and determine how they will perform when implemented. You should also be able to fine tune current systems and extract better performance without the need for additional resources. I believe that after finishing this book, you should be able to design and fine tune VSAM-based systems with a high degree of confidence and competence.

Acknowledgments

And now the pleasant job of acknowledging the people who helped me in my current endeavor. First and foremost, I am grateful to Kyungjoo Suh, who spent her valuable time in planning, reviewing, typing, and criticizing all the chapters. Her excellent suggestions on the layout were very helpful, and it is a pleasure to acknowledge this debt. I am also grateful to Carol Lehn, Assistant Vice President of Merrill Lynch, Pierce, Fenner & Smith, Inc. for her suggestions on style, language, and contents. She made sure that I do not overlook the interests of application programmers.

I wish to express my appreciation to Neelam Ranade and Nidhi Ranade for helping me with the manuscript. I gratefully acknowledge the assistance of my sister, Chander Ranade, and brother Jagmohan Ranade, who reviewed, proofread, and compared the various versions of the manuscript. Joseph Marrone deserves my thanks for his encouragement and his unending patience. I am indebted to Mr. Charles Vamossy, Vice President of Merrill Lynch and Company for his support and encouragement. My thanks are also due to Sunita Engira for all her assistance.

I especially want to thank my editor Jack Repcheck for his constant encouragement, and Robert J. Axelrod, his assistant, for taking care of numerous details. Steve Bedney, production supervisor, deserves my thanks for expediting the production cycle. I express my sincerest thanks to the numerous readers of the previous VSAM book for calling me to compliment me on the work and then sneaking in a few questions on VSAM fine tuning that forced me to finish this work early. My thanks are due to my mother-in-law Mrs. Raj Rani Singha for supplying me with innumerable cups of tea to keep me awake. My wife deserves my thanks for everything else.

Jay Ranade

one

CONCEPTS AND THEORY OF FINE TUNING

A basic understanding of the file architecture and internals of the file I/O of the Virtual Storage Access Method (VSAM) is essential to the proper design of VSAM-based systems. Part 1 will lay the foundations of the theory and the internals upon which the rest of the text is based. Chapter 1 introduces some of the fundamental concepts of fine tuning. The architecture of VSAM data sets and internals of an I/O, the understanding of which is the focal point of performance analysis, are discussed in Chapter 2. Control interval (CI) and control area (CA) splits, well known for their role in performance degradation, are the subject matter of Chapter 3. Some of the essential VSAM terminology is defined in Chapter 4, and lesser known but important facts about VSAM are also discussed in that chapter. At the end of Part 1 you will be well aware of the underlying principles of VSAM and AMS. As the tips, tricks, and techniques of fine tuning are discussed in subsequent parts, you will be able to relate them to your own environment.

chapter 1
Concepts of Fine Tuning

1.1 INTRODUCTION

VSAM-based file structures (KSDS, ESDS, and RRDS) are common data set architectures for batch as well as on-line application systems. VSAM is also IBM's strategic access method for MVS/SP, MVS/XA, DOS/VS, DOS/VSE, OS/VS1, and VM/CMS systems. KSDS and ESDS are commonly used as the underlying file structures for data base management systems such as IMS/DB and DB2. Although VSAM is the most widely used access method, neither the vendor's manuals nor other textbooks discuss its performance, design, and fine tuning. When you apply the design and tuning methodologies discussed in this text, you will be surprised to see how fast your batch jobs and on-line transactions can execute. Even a planned hardware upgrade may become unnecessary because you will be able to squeeze more work out of the available resources.

You will learn that VSAM fine tuning is not complex. However, you must thoroughly understand the underlying principles and the numerous variables that should affect your decisions. Most of the techniques discussed here are straightforward and are applicable to any environment. Others may have to be adjusted to suit your particular environment. In either case, it can be an interesting and rewarding experience in which the results of your efforts are immediately apparent.

1.1.1 What is Fine Tuning?

Fine tuning is the art (or science) of achieving optimum performance with the use of available resources, such as CPU cycles, direct access storage devices (DASDs), memory, cache storage for paging and application data sets, and virtual storage. Depending upon the installation, there may be a shortage of a particular resource and/or an abundance of another. Desirable performance levels may be achieved by manipulating the existing resources. For example, if virtual storage is an available resource, the system may be tuned by keeping as many index buffers in core as possible. However, if you have a virtual storage constraint problem, almost comparable results can be achieved by using the IMBED and REPLICATE parameters of Access Method Services. In the latter case, some additional DASD space may be required.

Sometimes it is impossible to manipulate the currently available resources for purposes of fine tuning. This may result in the need to acquire additional resources. We will also learn that it is sometimes more appropriate to *reduce* resource allocation and consumption to achieve better results.

1.2 DIFFERENT VIEWS OF FINE TUNING

Fine tuning can have different meanings for different installations. It may relate not only to performance, but also to the conservation of critical resources such as DASD and virtual storage. The four most common areas subject to fine tuning are discussed in the following sections.

1.2.1 Batch Jobs

The fine tuning of batch jobs involves (1) reducing the run time of a program and (2) reducing the number of CPU cycles consumed. Except in very rare circumstances, most performance goals are attainable without modifying the application. You should use all other fine tuning techniques before suggesting changes in the current application code or logic. Also, remember that application redesign and modification is the most expensive alternative and should therefore be entered into only as a last resort.

When the various techniques discussed in this volume are employed, it is not unusual to halve the run time of a batch program. Batch jobs include the backup of VSAM files, reorganization of KSDS files, restoration of damaged data sets from their previous backups, faster building of alternate indexes, etc. Inefficiently run batch jobs may also affect on-line (CICS/VS or IMS/DC) systems. If a batch job is not finished within its own time window, it may cause a delay in bringing up an on-line system.

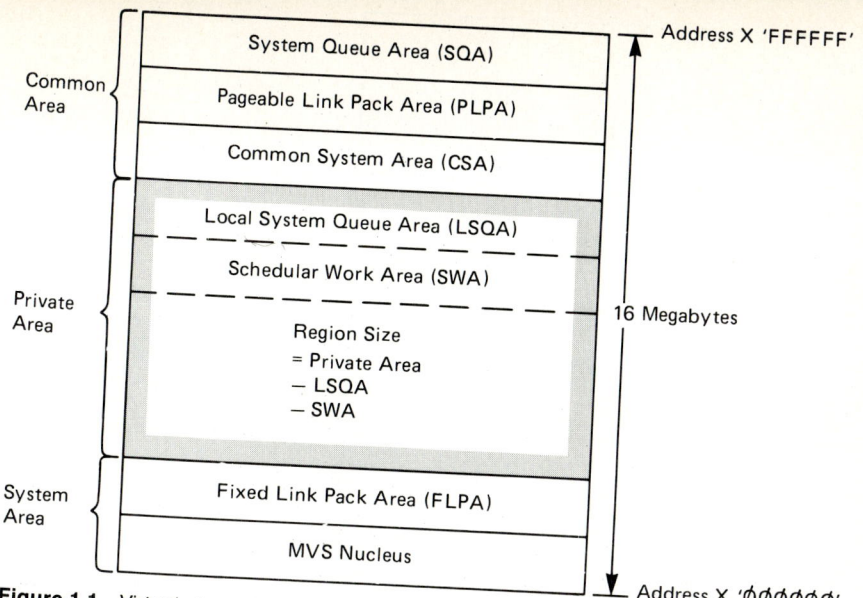

Figure 1.1 Virtual storage allocation within a non-MVS/XA System.

1.2.2 On-Line (CICS/VS) Systems

Badly tuned on-line systems result in poor end-user response time at the terminal, and this in turn results in the loss of user time and productivity. Although there may be many reasons for poor performance in an on-line system, one of the major causes is the *improper or inefficient use of VSAM*. By using the proper buffering techniques, as discussed in subsequent chapters, you will experience reduced response times.

1.2.3 Buffer and Virtual Storage Management

If you are working in a non-MVS/XA environment, you have only 24-bit addressability, which means that you can address a maximum of 16 megabytes. A major portion of the 16 megabytes is used by system software and common areas like the nucleus, Pageable Link Pack Area (PLPA), Fixed Link Pack Area (FLPA), System Queue Area (SQA), and Common Service Area (CSA) (Fig. 1.1). Depending upon your installation, you may have only 6 to 7 megabytes left for private use. The Private Area is the addressability within which your applications may run. MVS system programmers refer to this limitation as the *virtual storage constraint* (VSC) problem. You may not have a REGION (coded in the job or the step card) larger than the size of the private area. Running a CICS/VS region within the constraints of these boundaries may not leave you

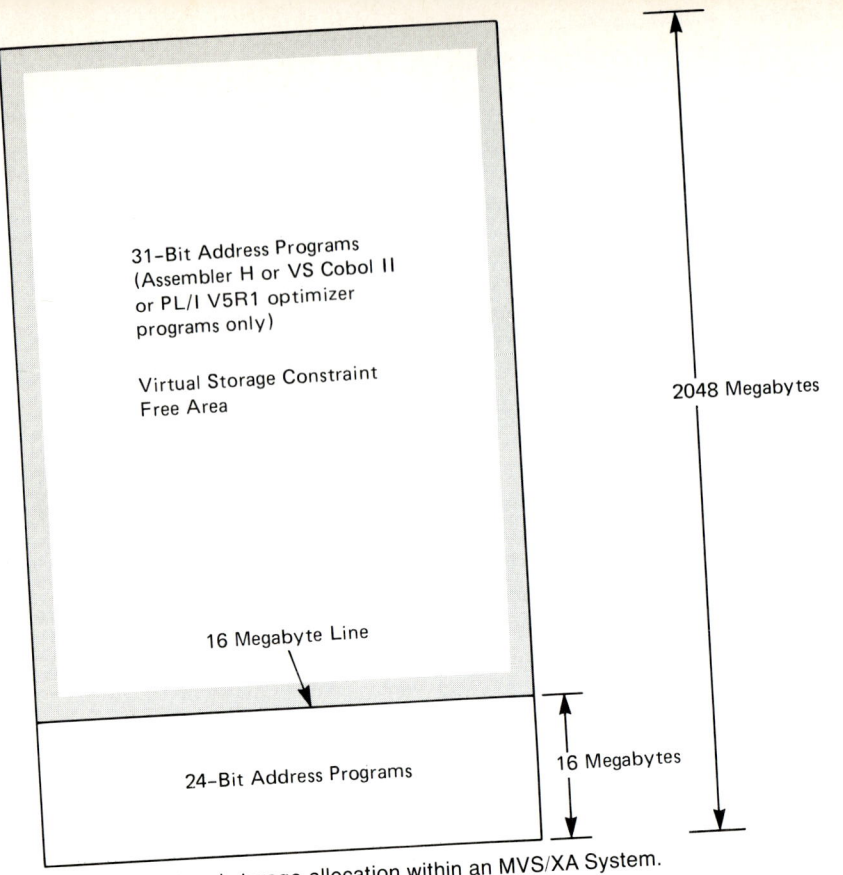

Figure 1.2 Virtual storage allocation within an MVS/XA System.

with much freedom to optimize your buffer allocation. Under these circumstances, you must make less use of buffers (virtual storage) and use other VSAM fine tuning techniques to achieve performance.

MVS/XA provides *virtual storage constraint relief* (VSCR) by providing 31-bit addressability, i.e., 2048 megabytes of virtual storage (Fig. 1.2). However, you are still limited to versions and release levels of software that can make use of this extra virtual storage. The imaginary 16-megabyte line between the 24-bit and 31-bit addressability is commonly referred to as "the line." Programs eligible to run above the 16-megabyte line must be written in Assembler H or compiled using VS Cobol II compiler or PL/I V5R1 optimizer. More on this later.

1.2.4 DASD Space Utilization

Many installations have restrictions on the use of DASD space. Often, one has to go through a justification procedure to have DASD space allocated for new application systems or to change the requirements for existing applications. Most of the time, the reasons for such restrictions are financial rather than technical. Use of some of the techniques discussed later (e.g., IMBED, REPLICATE, FREESPACE) may increase DASD space requirements. We must keep in mind that DASD is relatively less expensive than it has been in the past. A few extra dollars to achieve optimum performance can more than justify the increase in end-user productivity for many on-line systems. In most shops, one can determine few systems that are using more DASD space than necessary. For example, one could be allocating FREESPACE for data sets that have no add/update activity. Such DASD space can be reclaimed and allocated to the applications that need it. Surprisingly, overallocation of space can have as bad an effect on performance as underallocation. This will be discussed in greater detail later.

1.3 FLOW OF AN ON-LINE (CICS/VS) TRANSACTION

Although VSAM is not involved in every step of the flow of a task from terminal to CICS and back, it is important to understand where it fits into the whole picture. Figure 1.3 shows the steps involved. Remember that each step of the flow is a potential bottleneck.

1. Terminal operator causes an interrupt at the terminal (return, PF, or PA).
2. Screen data gets moved to the cluster controller (Terminal Control Unit). It is waiting to be polled by the Network Control Program (NCP). A cluster controller, depending upon the model, can control anywhere from 8 to 32 terminals.
3. Data moves from the cluster controller to the communications controller (37×5 running NCP). Synchronous modems at either end determine the speed at which data will be transmitted over the telecommunication lines. For example, a 9600 kilobits/s (KBS) modem will transmit at twice the speed of a 4800 KBS modem.
4. Data will sit in the NCP buffers waiting to be transferred to the telecommunication access method buffers (TCAM or VTAM).
5. Once the data is in the VTAM/TCAM buffers, it is in the host mainframe.
6. The CICS/VS region receives the data in the terminal I/O area (TIOA). A CICS task is waiting to be attached and dispatched subject to Max Task limits.
7. A CICS task is dispatched after allocation of the appropriate control blocks and other storage areas.
8. At some point, the CICS program issues a data base I/O request (e.g., IMS/DB call) or a native VSAM I/O request. A channel command word and start I/O are issued. The request goes to the channel, moves on to the DASD controller, and is eventually ex-

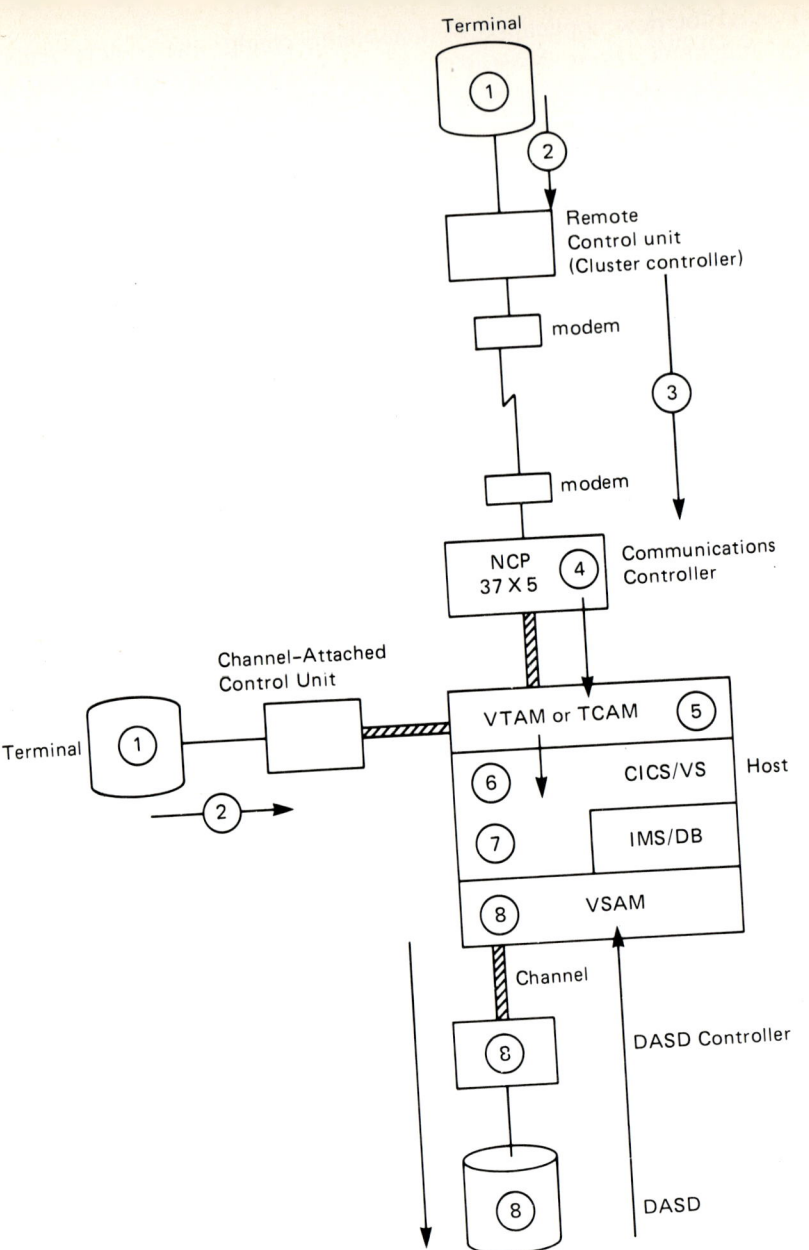

Figure 1.3 Flow of an on-line (CICS/VS) transaction from terminal to the host and back.

ecuted on the disk. An I/O takes place, and the data moves to the buffers via the DASD controller and the channel.

9. A program can issue multiple data base and/or VSAM requests. It can also request more storage. Eventually it is going to send a map or screen back to the terminal via VTAM or TCAM, NCP, the modem, and the cluster controller. Note that a cluster controller does not have to be remotely attached to a host. It can be channel-attached[1] provided that it is located within the physical distance specified by the hardware vendor. In this case, it does not go through the modems and NCP; it goes directly to the cluster controller.

Any of these nine points discussed can be a potential bottleneck and can significantly affect the end-user response time. Most of the time, the major bottleneck lies in the processing of the I/O request (item 8). The rest of this text is devoted to fine tuning in this area.

1.4 THE BASIS OF VSAM FINE TUNING

VSAM fine tuning is based on three very simple principles:

1. Keep frequently used data (especially index buffers) in core. Processing in real storage, which is done in microseconds, is more than a 1000 times as fast as a disk I/O, which is done in milliseconds.
2. Reduce the I/O's needed to satisfy a file request (read, write, delete etc.).
3. Make the I/O's faster.

None of these three principles should require modifications to existing application programs or system design.

1.5 FINE TUNING—AN ONGOING PROCESS

Many installations fail to understand that *fine tuning is an ongoing process* whose strategy changes with changes in the environment. A few examples will make this clearer.

1. *Change in the type of resource:* An installation was getting optimum performance from their on-line systems by putting the index components of highly active KSDS files on the fixed-head cyliner areas of IBM 3350s. Because the seek time for fixed-head cylin-

---

[1] Channels are very high speed (millions of bits per second) I/O media that connect a locally attached device to the CPU. They are discussed in greater detail in Chap. 5.

ders is zero, the I/O's were very fast, but when the installation upgraded to IBM 3380s, they had to change their fine tuning strategy because 3380s do not have fixed-head cylinders.

2. *System software evolution:* In a CICS/VS 1.5 and MVS/XA environment, virtual storage constraints still existed because VSAM buffers could not reside in the constraint-free "above-the-line" zone. Since the introduction of CICS/VS 1.6.1 and subsequent releases, non-IMS/DB-related VSAM buffers can reside above the line. This could mean reconfiguration of buffer allocation strategy for better performance.

3. *Evolution of new techniques:* Data collection KSDS files that initially contain a dummy record at the start of the on-line system are subject to a number of CI/CA splits as records are added to them randomly. Excessive CA splits not only cause performance problems but can also render a file unusable if the system goes down during a split. With the evolution of the KSDS internal preformatting technique (discussed in Chap. 12), such CA splits can be minimized or eliminated.

4. *Future technologies:* Most of the VSAM-related performance issues stem from the electromechanical characteristics of modern DASDs. After completing a data seek, the read-write arm has to wait for the disk to rotate to the proper location before the data can be transferred to the buffers. The future holds the introduction of high-speed inexpensive solid state memories that may render the current DASDs obsolete. Fine tuning strategy in its entirety changes with the introduction of such hardware, because no electromechanical moving parts are involved in a solid state memory. Although solid state DASDs are currently available from various non-IBM hardware vendors, they are very expensive, and it is not anticipated that they will be widely used in the very near future.

1.6 SIGNIFICANCE OF AN APPLICATION DESIGN

The most expensive (hence undesirable) way to fine tune an existing VSAM-based system is to alter the basic system and file design. Such changes necessitate the modification or even rewrite of the application programs. Since this is time-consuming, it should be considered only as a last resort.

In some cases, however, it may not be possible to extract better performance without changing the basic infrastructure of an application system. Therefore, the initial design of a system is of paramount importance. Usually, the file and application design is done with the end deliverable in mind. Many designers and analysts, however, do not even consider performance implications when going through the basic design, and the performance problems surface when the system goes into production. It is recommended that performance considerations be kept in mind during the initial design.

1.7 UNDERSTANDING DIFFERENT ENVIRONMENTS

It is important that you understand VSAM, DF/EF, DFP, VSAM user and master catalogs, and ICF user and master catalogs. If you are not already thoroughly familiar with them, it would be wise to learn more about them by referring to the appropriate IBM manuals. You can also become familiar with these topics by reading Chap. 4 of Ranade and Ranade, *VSAM: Concepts, Programming, and Design* (Macmillan, 1986). The fundamentals of these environments are discused here briefly.

1.7.1 VSAM, DF/EF, and DFP

VSAM, DF/EF, and DFP are program products of IBM. VSAM was the first product to support KSDS, ESDS, and RRDS file structures. Data Facility/Extended Function (DF/EF) is the latest program product in the field of VSAM data sets and catalog management; however, it is available for MVS environments only. DF/EF provides more control over shared data, along with some improved features of data set processing. For the MVS/XA environment, IBM has bundled several program products into one package, which it named the Data Facility Product (DFP).

If you are working in an MVS/XA environment, you have no choice but to have DFP, of which DF/EF is a component. If you are in a non-MVS/XA environment, you may have either VSAM or DF/EF. The chances are that you will have DF/EF. In OS/VS1 you can have only VSAM and not DF/EF. In DOS/VSE, although DF/EF is not supported, VSAM has some comparable features that provide the same capabilities as DF/EF. The DFP (or DF/EF) program product *must* be installed if you want to use ICF catalogs.

1.7.2 VSAM Catalogs and ICF Catalogs

All VSAM data sets must be cataloged in either VSAM or an ICF catalog. Non-DF/EF VSAM software supports VSAM catalogs only. DFP (or DF/EF) supports VSAM as well as ICF catalogs. ICF catalogs have an advantage over VSAM catalogs in performance, space utilization, the volume ownership concept, and catalog recovery. ICF catalogs can replace both VSAM catalogs and OS control volumes (CVOLs). Both VSAM and non-VSAM data sets can be cataloged in an ICF catalog.

An ICF catalog can have ownership of more than one volume. While each volume can be owned by up to 36 catalogs, a specific data set on a volume can belong to only one catalog. *All VSAM data sets cataloged in an ICF catalog have their own unique VSAM space. There is no concept of suballocated* VSAM space in an ICF catalog environment. The master catalog may be a VSAM or an ICF catalog, and VSAM and ICF catalogs, whether they are user or master, can coexist in an MVS system in any combination.

chapter 2

VSAM File Architecture and I/O's

2.1 CONTROL INTERVALS AND CONTROL AREAS[1]

The index and data components of a VSAM data set consist of control intervals (CIs) and control areas (CAs). A KSDS (key-sequenced data set) or an alternate index, each of which consist of a data component and an index component, may have an index CI size different from the data CI size. A control interval, whether it belongs to the index or the data component, is the smallest unit of information storage transferred between the buffers and a direct access storage device (DASD).

Control intervals are part of a larger storage structure called a *control area*. A control area may consist of many control intervals. An example of a control area is one cylinder of an IBM 3380 disk pack.

The storage organization of a VSAM data set can be summarized as follows:

- A *data set* consists of a *data component* plus an *index component* for a KSDS or an alternate index cluster.
- Each component consists of one or more *control areas*.
- A control area may consist of many *control intervals*.

[1]Refer to Ranade and Ranade, *VSAM: Concepts, Programming, and Design* (Macmillan 1986), Chap. 2.

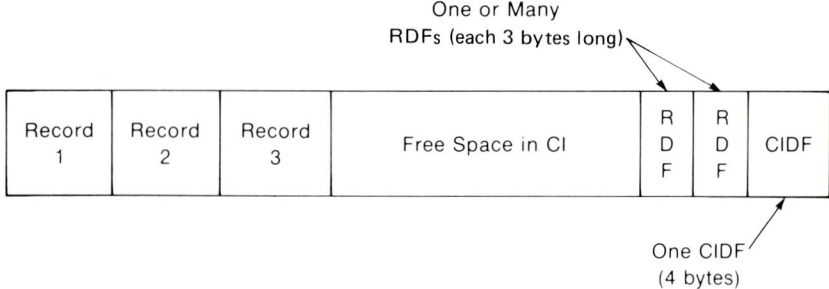

Figure 2.1 Records, free space, RDFs, and a CIDF within a data component control interval.

- A control interval may have one or more *records*.
- For a data component, a record may span *many* control intervals.

2.1.1 Data CIs and CAs

A data CI must be a multiple of 512 bytes if its size falls between 512 and 8192 bytes. However, if its size falls between 8192 and 32,768 bytes, it must be a multiple of 2048.

There are four components within the physical space owned by a CI (Fig. 2.1). The first component consists of the records that your program is interested in processing. The second is called a *control interval description field* (CIDF). It is 4 bytes long, occupies the last 4 bytes of the CI, and contains information about the free space available within the CI. The third component is called the *record description field* (RDF). It is 3 bytes long. A data component CI may have one or more RDFs depending on whether it contains fixed-length, variable-length, or spanned records. RDFs are contained in a space just before the CIDF. The fourth component is free space. Free space within a CI is used for in-place reorganization of KSDSs for additions, updates, or deletions of records within that CI. From an application logic point of view, the program is aware of the existence of only data records and not of the other three components.

A data component control area consists of a minimum of two control intervals. The minimum size of a control area is one track, while the maximum size is one cylinder or a DASD. Figure 2.2 illustrates the data component of a typical KSDS with fixed-length records. It consists of three CAs, each containing three CIs. The free CI within the first CA will be used if there is a CI split in that CA. A completely free control area at the end of the data set will be used if an update activity causes a CA split. The numbers within the records of the illustration identify the prime key value of those records. Note that each CI has control information at its end. Since there are only fixed-length records, the control fields will con-

2.1 CONTROL INTERVALS AND CONTROL AREAS

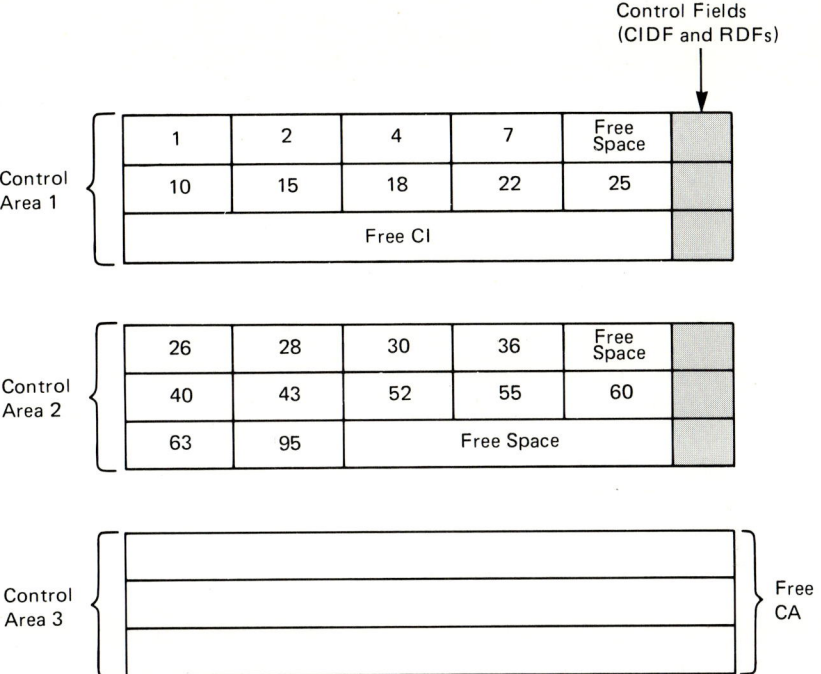

Figure 2.2 A data component of a typical KSDS consisting of three CAs. Each CA in this example has three CIs. Each CI is capable of having a maximum of five fixed-length records.

sist of two RDFs and one CIDF, for a total of 10 bytes. Please note that this example is for a KSDS and not for an ESDS or RRDS.

2.1.2 Index CIs and CAs

The data and index component of a KSDS or an alternate index are jointly referred to as "the cluster." Although the index component is a different data set and has a separate name, in most applications you refer to the cluster name, not to the individual data or index component names.

The control intervals of the index component contain key-pointer pairs that point to the highest record key in the data component CI. A typical index component CI is shown in Fig. 2.3. The CI size of an index component may be different from that of a data component. An application is not concerned with the existence of the index component and does not refer to its contents directly. Only the access method (VSAM) has to decode the key-pointer pairs stored in the index component. It is because of the key-pointer pair storage structure that a KSDS or an alternate index cluster appears to be sequenced on a key. The pointers in this case are the 4-byte relative byte addresses of the start of a data component CI.

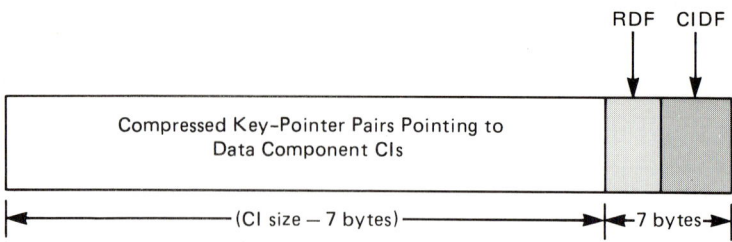

Figure 2.3 Example of an index component CI.

VSAM uses a very efficient and complex algorithm to do front and rear key compression for the storage of key-pointer pairs in the index component. Since the prime or alternate key can be up to 255 bytes long, it would be very inefficient for VSAM to store it without compression in the index component.

In OS/VS1, MVS/SP, and MVS/XA environments, the CI sizes for an index component can be only 512, 1024, 2048, or 4096 bytes. As we will see in Chap. 9, this sometimes causes problems. A 4096-byte index component may not store enough key-pointer pairs to point to all the CIs of a data component CA. In a DOS/VSE environment, the index component CI can also be 8192 bytes in size. Therefore, in DOS/VSE this problem is not so acute.

An index component CI has one CIDF and one RDF, for a total of 7 bytes for the control fields. An index CI is also commonly referred to as an *index record*. Again, only VSAM manipulates, controls, and deciphers the contents of the index CI, and not an application program.

Typically, the CA size of the index component is determined by Access Method Services; it is usually one track long. Every time a CA split takes place in the data component, it results in a CI split in the index component. This is due to the fact that a new index CI has to point to the data CIs that have been moved to the new CA. CI splits in the index component should not be a major performance concern because of their lower I/O overhead.

2.2 KEY-SEQUENCED DATA SET (KSDS)

Now that we are familiar with the data and index components of a KSDS, let us see how they fit into the overall structure of the base cluster. Figure 2.4 shows a typical KSDS with three levels of index.

At the highest level of the index, there is always one and only one record. It points to the next lower level of index component records in the hierarchy. These then point to index records still lower in the hierarchy. Eventually, after one to three levels, the pointers point to the CIs of the data component. It is through this chain of pointers in the index component that a KSDS appears to be sequenced on the prime key. This also

2.2 KEY-SEQUENCED DATA SET (KSDS)

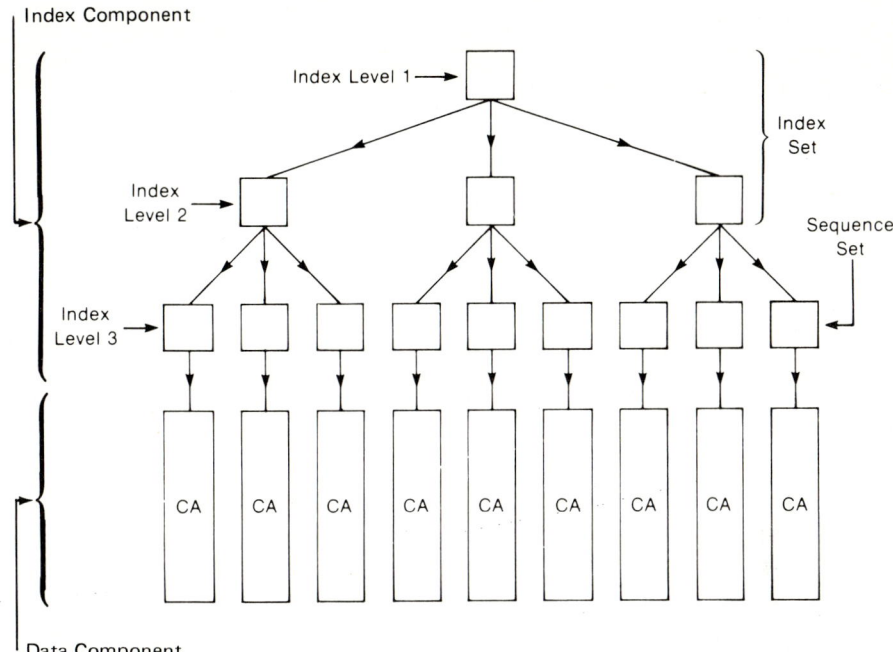

Figure 2.4 The index and the data components of a typical KSDS. In this case, the index has three levels.

applies to an alternate index cluster, because an alternate index is, in fact, a KSDS whether it belongs to an ESDS or a KSDS base cluster.

Before we proceed, let us be clear about a very simple fact of computing. A CPU cannot process data while it is residing on a DASD. The data has to be read into memory (buffers, in the case of VSAM CI) before any logic can be applied to its contents. Therefore, every time we speak of following the pointers from an index CI, that CI will have to be read in through an I/O operation unless it has already been read into buffers by some previously executed I/O. Another fact we must keep in mind is that VSAM cannot just read a logical record alone. It has to read the whole CI in which that logical record resides. In a nutshell: *A CI is the smallest unit of information storage that gets transferred between the file buffers and DASD.*

Let us assume that we have a KSDS like that in Fig. 2.4. A read file request is issued, and, after some time, addressability to the record that has been read into the buffers is established. All the processing that occurs between the issuance of the file request and the movement of the data CI to the buffers is performed by the access method, which in this case is VSAM. Let us also assume that we are using all system defaults, which means that only one index buffer and two data buffers are allocated for this data set. VSAM will perform the following operations, in sequence, to read the data CI:

1. Read the highest level of the index (level 1) into core. This is the first I/O. The address of the highest level index is in the catalog. This retrieves the pointers to the second level of the index.
2. Read the second level of the index into core, overlaying the contents of the buffer containing the previous CI. This is the second I/O. This establishes the pointers to the third level.
3. Read the third level of the index into core, thereby replacing the second level in the buffers. This is the third I/O. This establishes the pointers to the data component CI.
4. Read the data component CI into the data buffers and give the addressability of the logical record to the program. This is the fourth I/O.

We can see that in this particular case, a simple read operation has performed four I/O's. Remember that this analysis applies to a KSDS with three levels of index and the buffer allocation has been done from the default parameters.

2.2.1 Levels of Index

In the previous example, we assumed that the KSDS has three levels of index. This may not always be true. Depending on the size of the data set, a KSDS may have anywhere from one to three levels of index. The following rules apply.

- If the data component has *one and only one CA,* then the index component will have *only one level of index.*
- If the data component has more than one CA, the index component will have either two or three levels of index. A small data set will have two levels, while a relatively large one will have three levels.
- Although theoretically it is possible to have four levels of index, it does not usually happen in real life due to VSAM's use of a highly efficient key compression algorithm.

The simplest technique to determine the number of index levels is to execute the LISTCAT command of AMS on the data set. The index component statistics will show the number of index levels. In the previous example, if the index component had one or two levels, it would have incurred two or three I/O's, respectively, on a read request.

2.2.2 Index Set and Sequence Set

In a multilevel index component, the lowermost level of index is called the *sequence set.* Any levels above the sequence set are called the *index*

2.2 KEY-SEQUENCED DATA SET (KSDS)

set. In Fig. 2.4, the third level is the sequence set, while the first and second levels jointly are the index set. Both sets are referred to as a unit called the *index component*. The CI size of both sets is *always* the same, although it may not be the same as the CI size of the data component. The index set and sequence set have different characteristics when it comes to file buffers:

1. If enough index buffers are allocated to enable the system to put the whole index set in core, VSAM will not perform any I/O's on the index set levels. For example, in Fig. 2.4, a file request will not cause I/O's for levels 1 and 2. VSAM always does a *look-aside* for the index set buffers and requests an I/O *only* if it does not find them in core. This feature is used to reduce I/O's on a data set. If you are dealing with a KSDS that has three levels of index, placing the first and second levels in core already cuts I/O's by 50%!
2. VSAM *does not usually look aside for the sequence set buffers* unless the file request is being made within the *same* task. So in a CICS environment it is possible to have 10 different tasks running concurrently, with 10 copies of the same sequence set CI in 10 different buffers. Even if the sequence set CI is in the index buffers, VSAM will perform an I/O to refresh it. So remember, *you can save index set I/O's by keeping the index set in core, but you cannot save sequence set I/O's even if the sequence set is already in core*. However, you will learn in Chap. 17 that by using the Local Shared Resource (LSR) pool in CICS/VS, you *can* also put the sequence set in core and use the look-aside feature to reduce I/O's.
3. While the IMBED option of the AMS DEFINE commands applies to the sequence set, REPLICATE applies to the index set.[2]
4. If a data set has only one level of index, it is considered an index set.

2.2.3 File Requests and I/O's

Default Index Buffer Allocation In the previous example, we assumed three levels of index, default index buffer allocation, and execution of a read request. We also learned that we can have one to three levels of index. The types of requests that can be executed include

1. READ
2. WRITE
3. REWRITE
4. DELETE
5. START
6. READ NEXT

---

[2]IMBED and REPLICATE are discussed in Chap. 11.

| | Index level | | |
File request	One	Two	Three
READ	1	3	4
WRITE	2	4	5
REWRITE	2	4	5
DELETE	2	4	5
START	1	3	4
READ NEXT	0 or 1 or 2	0 or 1 or 2	0 or 1 or 2

Figure 2.5 I/O's incurred on file requests on a KSDS with one, two, or three levels of index. It is assumed that no CI/CA splits have taken place. The index buffer allocation is through the default value.

Let us analyze the I/O's for each of the file requests, using different index levels and default index buffer allocations. Figure 2.5 presents the I/O's for the file request executions on a one-, two-, or three-level index data set. We are assuming that the REWRITE and DELETE requests include reading the record prior to its replacement or deletion. Also, *no* additional buffer allocation has been made to put the index set in core. Note that a read request on a one-level index (the data set being one CA in size) does only one I/O, which is on the data component CI. It does not perform I/O on the index CI because the CI is treated as the index set, and once read into core it does not have to be reread.

The browse request (READ NEXT) requires some clarification. A sequential search may find the next record in the same CI. If so, there is no I/O. If it is not in the same CI, VSAM has to access only the sequence set of the index component (and not the index set) to get the pointers for the next logical data CI. Since the sequence set for the same task will probably already be in core, only one I/O is incurred to retrieve the data CI. If the next logical data CI is in the next CA, two I/O's have to be performed—one for the retrieval of the next sequence set CI and the other for the data CI. So, for a browse operation, I/O's depend on the probability of finding a sequence set or a data CI already in core.

Ideal Index Buffer Allocation Let us see what the effect on I/O's will be if the index set CIs are put into core at the time the data set is opened. If the index has only one level, it will always be in core. If it has two levels, only the first level will have to be in core. Since there is always one index CI at the first level, only one additional buffer will have to be allocated. If the index has three levels, the first two will have to be kept in core. Depending on the data CI size, the index CI size, key compression, and key length, there can be anywhere from 3 to 20 (sometimes more) *index set CIs* in a three-level index. As far as the sequence set is concerned, *there is one sequence set CI per data component CA*. Figure 2.6 gives the

2.3 ENTRY-SEQUENCED DATA SET (ESDS)

	Index level		
File request	One	Two	Three
READ	1	2	2
WRITE	2	3	3
REWRITE	2	3	3
DELETE	2	3	3
START	1	2	2
READ NEXT	0 or 1 or 2	0 or 1 or 2	0 or 1 or 2

Figure 2.6 I/O's incurred on file requests on a KSDS with one, two, or three levels of index provided that the index set CIs of the index component are kept in core. Again, it is assumed that no CI/CA splits have taken place.

I/O's for the same operation as in Fig. 2.5 except that the index set CIs are in core.

Comparing the data in Figs. 2.5 and 2.6, we can draw the following conclusions:

- If the index has only one level, by default the index CI is kept in buffers and no I/O is incurred on it.
- If the index has two levels, keeping the highest level in core will save one I/O on each file request.
- If the index has three levels, keeping the two highest levels in core will save two I/O's on each file request.
- Sequential browse (READ NEXT) is *not affected* by index buffers because it refers only to the sequence set CIs.

You may be wondering why we have discussed putting index set CIs in core but not the methodology to do it. The procedures are very simple and will be discussed in Chap. 15 for batch jobs and Chaps. 16 and 17 for CICS/VS.

2.3 ENTRY-SEQUENCED DATA SET (ESDS)

An ESDS does not have an index component, so the analysis of the file requests and associated I/O's is very simple. Figure 2.7 gives a table of file requests and corresponding I/O's.

For the write request, the number of I/O's can be one or two, depending on whether the CI is already in the buffers. Since record adds to an ESDS are always done sequentially, the chances of finding the CI in the buffers are high. A sequential browse (READ NEXT) will have one or two I/O's depending on whether the next record is in the previously retrieved CI. A widely misunderstood notion about ESDS files in a CICS environment is that a CI gets written to the DASD only after its buffers

File request	I/O
READ	1
WRITE	1 or 2
REWRITE	2
READ NEXT	0 or 1
START	1

Figure 2.7 File requests and I/O's for an ESDS.

File request	I/O
READ	1
WRITE	2
REWRITE	2
DELETE	2
READ NEXT	0 or 1
START	1

Figure 2.8 File requests and I/O's in an RRDS.

are full and it cannot contain another logical record. In fact, a CI gets written as soon as an EXEC CICS WRITE command is issued by the program. If a CI can contain 10 logical records, each write request issued by a program will write the CI to the DASD, adding up to 10 I/O's before moving on to the next CI. Also, note that record deletion is not included in Fig. 2.7, since you cannot delete a record from an ESDS file.

2.4 RELATIVE RECORD DATA SET (RRDS)

An RRDS does not have an index component. So, like an ESDS, the analysis of the different file requests and associated I/O's is very simple. Figure 2.8 lists the file requests and their associated I/O's.

2.5 ALTERNATE INDEXES

There can be up to 253 alternate indexes over an ESDS or a KSDS file. RRDS does not support them. However, the architecture of an alternate index is the same as that of a KSDS. An alternate index is, in fact, a KSDS whose alternate key-pointer pair records are logically related to an ESDS or a KSDS base cluster. Most of the rules that apply to the fine tuning of a KSDS, therefore, also apply to alternate indexes.

2.5 ALTERNATE INDEXES

2.5.1 Levels of Index

Alternate index clusters usually are a small subset of the base clusters. They are small in size and have one or two levels of index. For efficient performance, their index set CIs must also be kept in core by allocating the appropriate number of buffers.

2.5.2 Upgrade Set

An alternate index associated with a base cluster may be defined with either the UPGRADE option or the NOUPGRADE option. Those defined with the UPGRADE option become members of the "upgrade set" of the base cluster. Whenever such a base cluster is opened for output processing, its associated upgrade set is automatically opened also. Any changes made to the base cluster will automatically be reflected in the alternate index clusters of the upgrade set. *Alternate indexes that are not members of the upgrade set will not contain those updates.*

To fully understand the impact of the upgrade set on I/O's, consider the following points:

- A record added to the base cluster will cause an add of a record to each of the unique key alternate indexes and add or modify a record in each of the nonunique key alternate indexes.
- A record delete to the base cluster will delete a record in each of the unique key alternate indexes and delete or modify a record in each of the nonunique key alternate indexes.
- A base cluster record change that alters the alternate keys will cause a record add plus a delete in each of the unique key indexes, and a record add plus a delete or modification in each of the non-unique key alternate indexes.

In other words, when you issue an update file request on a base cluster, do not forget that a corresponding file request is automatically being issued on all members of the upgrade set. Since these additional I/O's could cause a potential performance problem, you must weigh the pros and cons of *need* versus *speed* when dealing with an upgrade set.

Reading the base cluster records via an alternate index path returns the base cluster records in the alternate key sequence. But this does not come without a price. Retrieving records via a path first incurs I/O's on an alternate index cluster to find the base cluster key or RBA. Subsequently, it issues I/O's to the base cluster to retrieve the data record. Keep in mind that *read requests via an alternate index path almost double the number of I/O's.*

chapter 3

Control Interval and Control Area Splits

3.1 THE PROBLEM OF CI AND CA SPLITS

CI and CA splits are a major cause of poor performance in many IBM installations. While both increase I/O's at the time of the split, CA splits have a more pronounced effect. CI and CA splits occur in a KSDS only, not in an ESDS or an RRDS. Alternate indexes, whether on a KSDS or an ESDS, are also subject to CI and CA splits.

A split occurs when an update activity within a CI or CA needs more space than the particular CI or CA is able to provide. The update activity may be a record add or a record update with a change in record length, random or sequential, batch or on-line. A read-only activity will not cause a split.

You can determine the total number of CI or CA splits by using the LISTCAT command of Access Method Services. This will list the splits for the data and index components separately. You can determine how many CI and CA splits were caused by a particular job by running LISTCAT on the data set before and after execution of the job. The job could be CICS/VS, IMS/DC, a batch job, etc. Figure 3.1 shows part of a LISTCAT-generated listing that highlights the CI and CA splits for the data and index components of a KSDS.

A CI split in the data component *does not* trigger any splits in the index component. A CA split in the data component, however, will always cause at least one CI split in the index component.

3.2 CONTROL INTERVAL SPLIT

CI and CA splits are a cause for concern for the following reasons:

1. They cause excessive I/O's *while the split is taking place*. A CA split generates far more I/O's than a CI split, increasing run time and CPU time for a batch job and increasing response time for an on-line (e.g., CICS/VS) transaction.
2. CA splits disperse logically adjacent data to different physical locations on the DASD. This may not affect random retrievals, but sequential processing is slowed because seek time is increased.
3. There are certain points in time during a CI and CA split when abnormal termination of the system (say, CICS/VS) will render the file unusable. This will be discussed in section 3.3.3.
4. In an on-line system (e.g., CICS/VS), all tasks needing access to the data residing in a *splitting* CI will wait until the split is finished. Similarly, during a CA split, all tasks needing access to any record in the whole data set will wait until the CA split is completed successfully. This may build up queues for tasks requiring access to the file and thus increase storage (Dynamic Storage Area) requirements in CICS/VS (as well as response time problems, of course).

3.2 CONTROL INTERVAL SPLIT

Section 3.2.1 has been excerpted from Ranade and Ranade (1986), *VSAM: Concepts, Programming, and Design*. If you are already familiar with the internal mechanism of a CI split, you may skip it and go directly to the Section 3.2.2.

3.2.1 How Does a CI Split Take Place?

Let's assume that our KSDS has the structure outlined in Fig. 3.2 to begin with. For simplicity, let us also suppose that it consists of only fixed-length records. In our example, we represent a record by its key value. As you can see, there are many records scattered over different control intervals in the data set.

All the horizontal boxes in Fig. 3.2 represent control intervals of the index component, while the vertical boxes represent control intervals within their respective control areas of the data component. The index component is further subdivided into two parts called the *index set* and the *sequence set*. As explained in Chap. 2, these are the two hierarchical levels of the index component. The sequence set is always at the lowermost level of the index and points to control intervals in the data component. The index set may consist of one to two levels, each pointing to the next lower level until the sequence set is reached. The number of index set levels depends on the size of the file and other factors such as CI size, CA size, and free space allocation.

```
CLUSTER ------- TEST.KSDS3.CLUSTER
    IN-CAT --- SYS1.ICFUCAT.UCAT1
    HISTORY
        OWNER-IDENT------(NULL)         CREATION--------87.079
        RELEASE----------2              EXPIRATION------00.000
    PROTECTION-PSWD-----(NULL)          RACF------------(NO)
    ASSOCIATIONS
        DATA-----TEST.KSDS3.DATA
        INDEX----TEST.KSDS3.INDEX

DATA  ------- TEST.KSDS3.DATA
    IN-CAT --- SYS1.ICFUCAT.UCAT1
    HISTORY
        OWNER-IDENT------(NULL)         CREATION--------87.079
        RELEASE----------2              EXPIRATION------00.000
    PROTECTION-PSWD-----(NULL)          RACF------------(NO)
    ASSOCIATIONS
        CLUSTER--TEST.KSDS3.CLUSTER
    ATTRIBUTES
        KEYLEN-----------15             AVGLRECL--------4000     BUFSPACE--------12288    CISIZE----------4096
        RKP--------------0              MAXLRECL--------4000     EXCPEXIT--------(NULL)   CI/CA-------------140
        SHROPTNS(2,3)   SPEED           UNIQUE      NOERASE      INDEXED     NOWRITECHK   IMBED      NOREPLICAT
        UNORDERED       NOREUSE         NONSPANNED
    STATISTICS
        REC-TOTAL--------1824           SPLITS-CI-------0         EXCPS----------77691
        REC-DELETED------17853          SPLITS-CA-------12        EXTENTS---------1
        REC-INSERTED-----19553          FREESPACE-%CI---0         SYSTEM-TIMESTAMP:
        REC-UPDATED------17440          FREESPACE-%CA---0         X'9C763C8817C6A801'
        REC-RETRIEVED----43550          FREESPC-BYTES---50479104
    ALLOCATION
```

```
SPACE-TYPE-------CYLINDER
SPACE-PRI--------------100
SPACE-SEC--------------10
VOLUME
  VOLSER------------X'301C00C2'      HI-ALLOC-RBA-----5734000      EXTENT-NUMBER------1
  DEVTYPE-----------X'301C00C2'      HI-USED-RBA-----10321920      EXTENT-TYPE-----X'00'
  VOLFLAG-----------PRIME
  EXTENTS:
    PHYREC-SIZE----------4096
    PHYRECS/TRK-----------10
    TRACKS/CA-------------15
  LOW-CCHH--------X'0001000E'        LOW-RBA--------------0
  HIGH-CCHH-------X'0006400E'        HIGH-RBA--------57343999      TRACKS-------------1500

INDEX ------- TEST.KSDS1.INDEX
  HISTORY
    OWNER-IDENT-------(NULL)         CREATION----------87.079
    RELEASE2-PSWD-----(NULL)         EXPIRATION--------00.000
  PROTECTION-PSWD----(NULL)          RACF-------------(NO)
  ASSOCIATIONS
    CLUSTER--TEST.KSDS1.CLUSTER
  ATTRIBUTES
    KEYLEN----------------15         AVGLRECL-----------0          BUFSPACE-----------(NULL)   CISIZE------------4096
    RKP---------------------0        MAXLRECL--------4089          EXCPEXIT----------(NULL)    CI/CA--------------10
    SHROPTNS(2,3)     RECOVERY       UNIQUE          NOERASE       NOWRITECHK        IMBED     NOREPLICAT   UNORDERED
  STATISTICS
    REC-TOTAL-------------19         SPLITS-CI-----------17                                    INDEX:
    REC-DELETED-----------10         SPLITS-CA------------0        EXCPS---------------5802    LEVELS--------------2
    REC-INSERTED-----------0         FREESPACE-%CI--------0        EXTENT-TIMESTAMP:           ENTRIES/SECT--------11
    REC-UPDATED------------0         FREESPACE-%CA--------0        SYSTEM  X'9C763C8817C6A801' SEQ-SET-RBA-----40960
    REC-RETRIEVED-----37200          FREESPC-BYTES----372736                                   HI-LEVEL-RBA--------0
  ALLOCATION
    SPACE-TYPE--------TRACK          HI-ALLOC-RBA-----450560
    SPACE-PRI-------------1          HI-USED-RBA------114688
    SPACE-SEC-------------1
  VOLUME
    VOLSER------------X'301C00C2'    PHYREC-SIZE--------4096       HI-ALLOC-RBA------40960     EXTENT-NUMBER------1
    DEVTYPE-----------X'301C00C2'    PHYRECS/TRK----------1        HI-USED-RBA-------4096      EXTENT-TYPE-----X'00'
    VOLFLAG-----------PRIME          TRACKS/CA------------11
    EXTENTS:
    LOW-CCHH--------X'0006500D'      LOW-RBA-------------0
    HIGH-CCHH-------X'0006500D'      HIGH-RBA--------40959         TRACKS---------------1

  VOLUME
    VOLSER------------X'301C00C2'    PHYREC-SIZE--------4096       HI-ALLOC-RBA-----450560     EXTENT-NUMBER------1
    DEVTYPE-----------X'301C00C2'    PHYRECS/TRK---------10        HI-USED-RBA------114688     EXTENT-TYPE-----X'80'
    VOLFLAG-----------PRIME          TRACKS/CA-----------15
    EXTENTS:
    LOW-CCHH--------X'0001000C'      LOW-RBA----------40960
    HIGH-CCHH-------X'0006400C'      HIGH-RBA--------450559        TRACKS-------------1500
```

Figure 3.1 An example of the LISTCAT-generated printout to highlight CI and CA splits for KSDS.

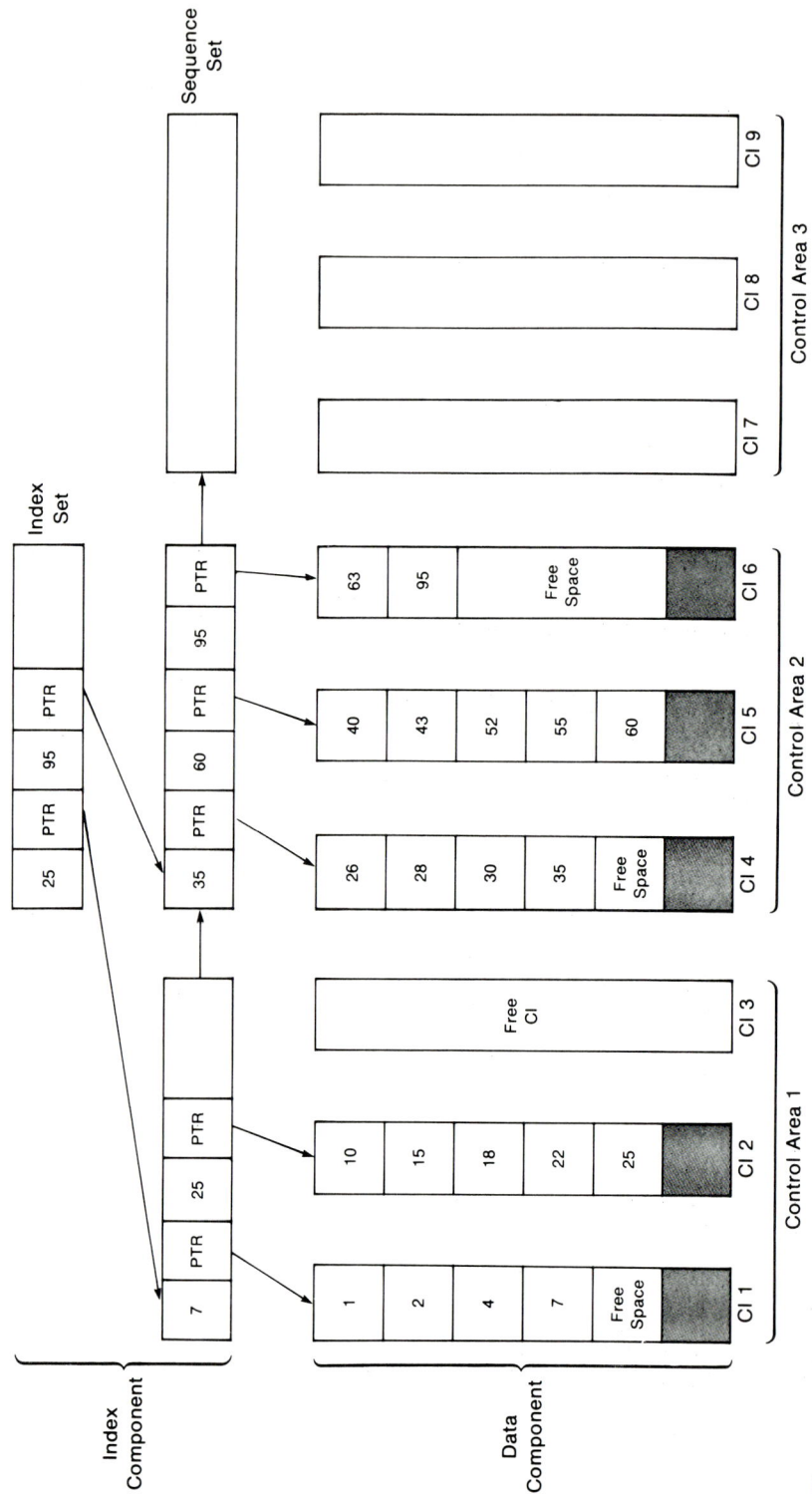

Figure 3.2 Composition of a typical key-sequenced data set.

3.2 CONTROL INTERVAL SPLIT

In our example, the data component consists of three control areas. Each CA contains three CIs, each of which can contain five fixed-length records. The shaded portions within the CI contain CIDFs and RDFs. *There is always one and only one sequence set record (called sequence set CI) for each data CA.* As shown in Fig. 3.2, three sequence set records point to their respective CAs. Each entry in a sequence set record points to the highest key record in the corresponding data component control interval. Further up in the index hierarchy, each entry in the index set record points to the highest key record in the corresponding sequence set control interval.

Free space within the CIs may be used for the addition or update of records. There is also a free CI in control area 1, which will be used if a CI split takes place in that CA. The last control area (CA 3) is completely empty. It will be used if any other CAs are split.

Update Without CI Split Now, let's say that we want to add a record whose key value is 5. VSAM will try to find the appropriate data component CI where this record should be placed. Traversing the hierarchical chain, we find that a record with a key value of 5 logically belongs to the first control interval of the first control area. VSAM will determine that there is enough free space to insert another record. Record 5 logically fits between records 4 and 7, so VSAM will push record 7 down to free space and place record 5 in the location previously occupied by record 7. It will then update the RDF and CIDF information to indicate that there is no free space left in that CI. *No* CI split has taken place. A CI of the data component has been updated, but none of the CIs of the index component, whether index set or sequence set, have been modified.

Now let's see the number of I/O's generated by a single update. We will assume that the index component has three levels (although Fig. 3.2 shows only two). The top two levels will belong to the index set, and the third level will be the sequence set. I/O's will be as follows:

1. Since a random search always starts from the first level, one I/O will take place to read the CI at the top of the index component. If sufficient index buffers are allocated, the index CI may already be in core and no physical I/O to the DASD will take place. The BUFNI parameter of the CICS File Control Table and batch JCL (AMP) controls the buffer allocation; this is discussed in Chaps. 15, 16, and 17.
2. An I/O will be done to retrieve the index CI at the second level. Again, a properly coded BUFNI may make it possible to keep the second level in core so that no physical I/O need take place.
3. An I/O will almost always be done to retrieve the index CI at the lowermost level, i.e., the sequence set. Under most circumstances, VSAM architecture dictates a sequence set record retrieval *even if the sequence set CI is already in core.*
4. An I/O will be done to retrieve the data component CI.

5. An I/O will be done to rewrite the data component CI after the record add (or update or delete).

We can see that three I/O's (discussed at points 3–5 above) are unavoidable. *Depending upon the buffer allocation, a CI update may require anywhere from three to five I/O's even without a CI split.* In Chap. 17, when we discuss the buffer pool allocation using the Local Shared Resource (LSR) pool, the I/O's *may* even be less than three for an update. An LSR pool is normally used in a CICS environment.

Control Interval Split Now let's find out how a CI split occurs. Let's say after adding the record with key value 5, we would like to insert another record whose key value is 20. VSAM determines that this record belongs to CI 2 between records 18 and 22. It also determines that there is not enough free space in that CI in which to place the record. So VSAM locates a free CI (CI 3) within *that* control area. It then moves approximately half the records from CI 2 to the newly acquired free CI. *This process is called a CI split.* VSAM also updates the information in sequence set 1 to reflect the new key-pointer pairs that point to the highest key in each control interval. After records 5 and 20 are added, the KSDS looks like Fig. 3.3. Note that sequence set 1 has been updated so that it points to the highest key records in the control intervals after the split.

CIDF Busy Bit In a multitasking system like CICS/VS, it is quite possible that two or more tasks originating from different terminals intend to update the records of the same CI. Concurrent update of a CI while the split is in progress could result in loss of data integrity. VSAM resolves this problem by writing the splitting CI with its CIDF (control interval description field) *busy bit* on before the split can take place. CIDF is a 4-byte field that controls the information on free space within a CI and its offset from the beginning of the CI. It is always the last 4 bytes of *every* CI. The CIDF busy bit is one bit of information in the 32-bit (4-byte) CIDF in a CI. When the value of the bit is 1, the CI split is in progress. It is turned off to 0 when the split has successfully occurred.

3.2.2 I/O's in a CI Split

Let's look at a specific example so that we can explore the effect a CI split has on I/O's. We will assume that the index component has three levels (although Figs. 3.2 and 3.3 show only two). The top two levels will belong to the index set, and the third level will be the sequence set. I/O's will be as follows:

1. If buffer allocation is insufficient, the top level of the index will not be in core. An I/O will take place to read that index CI and to follow the pointers to the next level down.

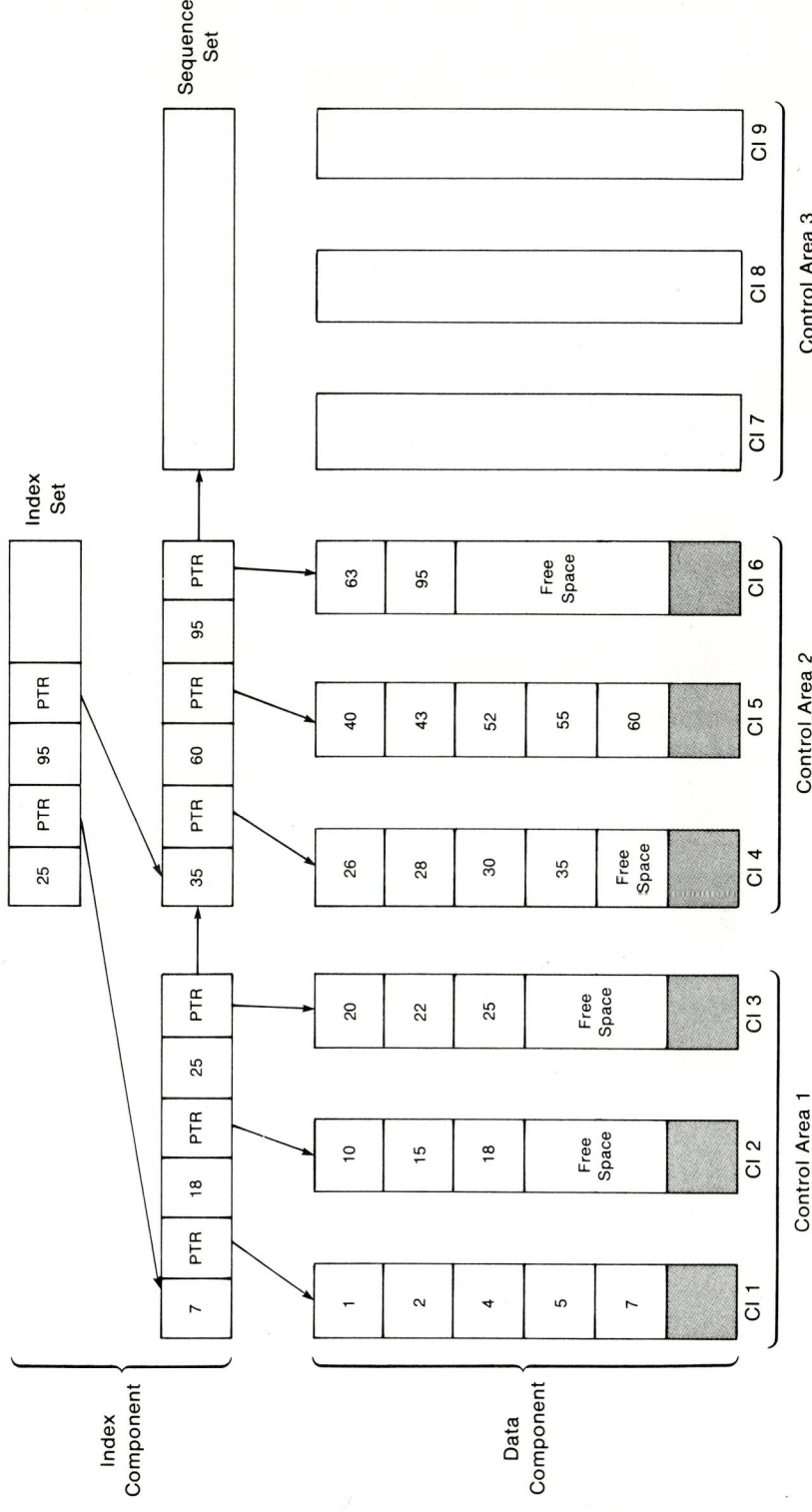

Figure 3.3 Records with keys 5 and 20 were added to the data set illustrated in Fig. 3.2. This diagram illustrates what the data set looks like after a CI split.

I/O's on a KSDS update*	Without CI split	With CI split
Best case (index set in core)	3	6
Worst case (default buffers)	5	8

*Update includes record add, delete, and change.

Figure 3.4 I/O's incurred in a KSDS update without and with a CI split.

2. If index buffers are insufficient, an I/O may take place at the second level of the index component.
3. Under most circumstances, an I/O will take place at the lowermost level of the index component, i.e., the sequence set.
4. An I/O will be performed to retrieve the data component CI.
5. At this point, VSAM will determine that the current CI is unable to accommodate the record insertion. It will write the CI back to the DASD with the CIDF busy bit on. All other tasks trying to access that CI will wait until the busy bit is turned off.
6. VSAM will acquire a free buffer and move approximately half the records into the new buffer, providing new free space in the original buffer. Then it will insert the new record into the buffers of the CI that previously could not accommodate it. VSAM then writes the *new buffer* to the DASD.
7. VSAM updates the sequence set buffers to provide the key-pointer pair needed by the new CI. It will overlay the old sequence set CI with this updated buffer.
8. VSAM will write the old data buffer with the newly inserted record and the CIDF busy bit off.

Thus, in the worst possible case, a CI split can incur eight I/O's. Under ideal circumstances, there will be no I/O's at steps 1 and 2, reducing the number of I/O's to six. Figure 3.4 summarizes the I/O's in an update without and with a CI split.

Note that a CI split under ideal index buffer allocation incurs only one I/O more than a simple record insertion without the proper index buffer allocation (six vs five). Even under ideal conditions, a CI split causes *only* twice as many I/O's as an ordinary update (six vs three). Three extra I/O's due to *an occasional CI split is not as bad as many performance analysts believe it to be.*

Although we will talk about ideal (and not so ideal) index buffer allocations in a later chapter, it is worthwhile to state that the default index buffer allocation will give you the worst-case I/O's. You get the default index buffers if you do not explicitly code a BUFNI value in the AMP parameter of a batch job or the File Control Table of CICS/VS.

Also, remember that *a record update (read and rewrite) and a delete go through the same I/O process as a record add.* The I/O's for all three processes will be the same, except that a record delete will not cause a CI split.

3.3 CONTROL AREA SPLIT

Section 3.3.1 has been excerpted from Ranade and Ranade (1986), *VSAM: Concepts, Programming, and Design.* If you are already familiar with the internal mechanism of a CA split, you may skip it and go directly to Section 3.3.2.

3.3.1 How Does a CA Split Take Place?

We will start with the data set configuration of Fig. 3.3. Suppose you want to add a record with key 45. It should logically be inserted between record keys 43 and 52 in CI 5. However, there is not enough free space in that CI. VSAM tries to find a free CI within CA 2. Since there is no free CI in that CA, VSAM performs a CA split. First it acquires a free CA within the data set. If there is no free CA available, VSAM makes a secondary space allocation of the data set, if possible, and acquires a CA from the secondary allocation. (It is assumed that you did provide for secondary space allocation when allocating the cluster.) In our example, CA 3 is free and will be used by VSAM for this purpose.

VSAM will move approximately half the records from the splitting CA to the newly acquired CA, spreading them over the new CIs. It also updates information at the various levels of the index component so that each key-pointer again points to the highest key element at the next level in the hierarchy. *The process just completed is called a CA split.* Figure 3.5 illustrates the data set after a CA split caused by the addition of a record with key 45.

3.3.2 I/O's in a CA Split

A CA split requires a large number of I/O's. The number of I/O's depends upon the CI size, the CA size, and the number of free buffers available at the time of the split. In the following example, we will assume that the DASD is an IBM 3380 and that the CA size for the data set is one cylinder. Let's also assume that the CI size for the data component is 4096 bytes. Using the NOIMBED option at the time of the DEFINE CLUSTER results in 150 CIs in each CA. The splitting CA and the newly acquired empty CA will each have 150 CIs. The I/O's will be as follows:

1. Depending upon the index buffer allocation, as many as two I/O's could be performed to retrieve the top two levels of the index component.

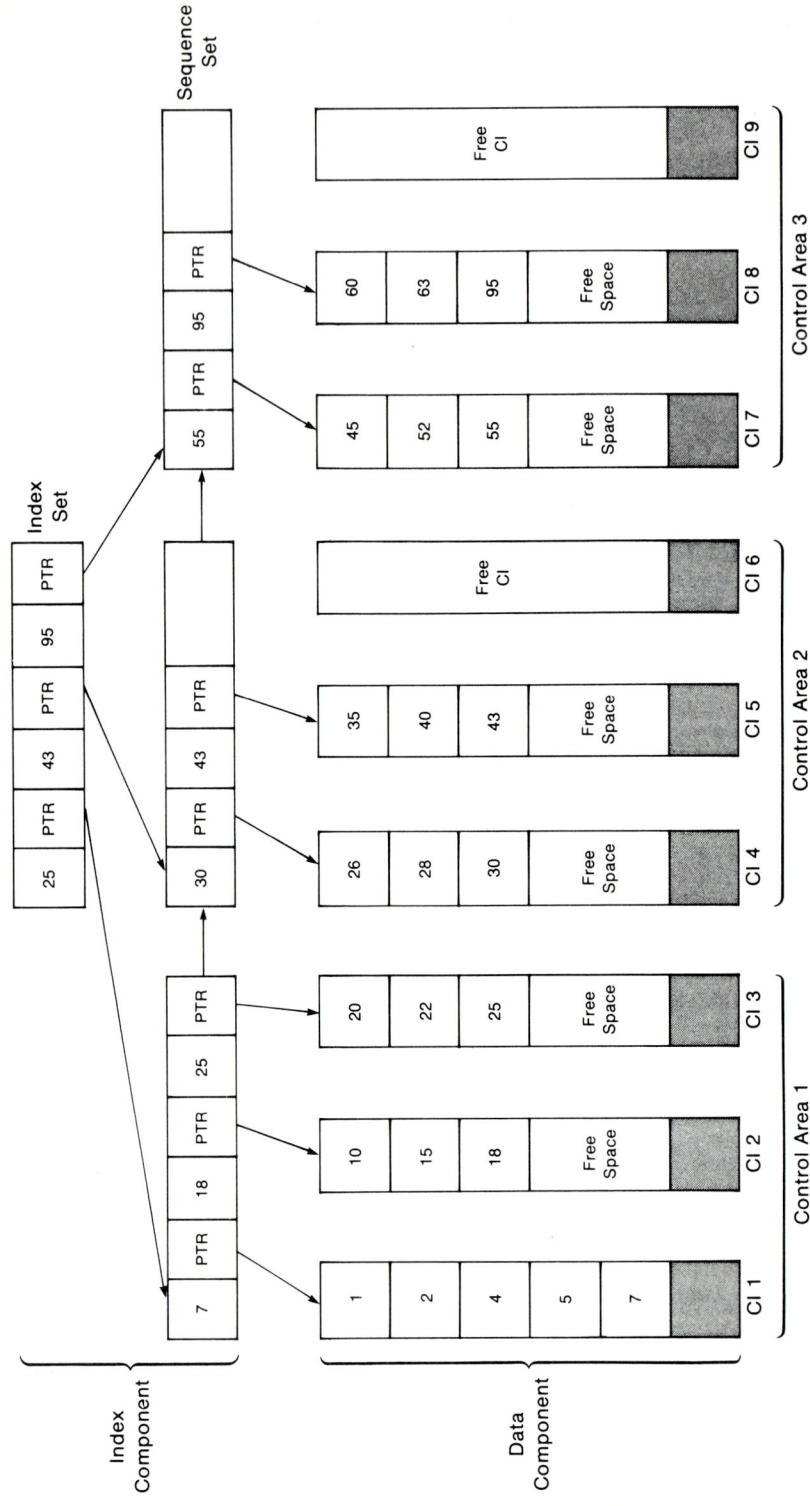

Figure 3.5 A record with key 45 was added to the data set illustrated in Fig. 3.3. This diagram shows the data set after a CA split.

3.3 CONTROL AREA SPLIT

2. One I/O will be needed to read the sequence set record.
3. One I/O will be used to read the data component CI. At this time, VSAM will determine that the data CI does not have enough free space in it and also that there is no free CI within that CA.
4. VSAM will *preformat* all 150 CIs of the *new* CA. Under normal circumstances, writing data to 150 CIs should be counted as 150 I/O's. However, preformatting is done in full track units. Since there are 15 tracks in one cylinder of the IBM 3380 DASD, preformatting will be roughly equivalent to 15 I/O's worth of time.
5. VSAM acquires as many data buffers as possible to allow the CA split process to proceed with a minimum number of I/O's. We will assume that the system in this example is CICS/VS, that all the additional buffers have already been acquired by other tasks in the system, and that therefore there is only one buffer available for the split process. Starting at the midpoint of the old CA, VSAM will move CIs to the acquired buffer one at a time and then write them to the new CA that has just been formatted. So there will be approximately 75 I/O's to read the CI's from the old CA and 75 I/O's to write these CI's to the new CA, for a total of 150 I/O's.
6. VSAM builds a new sequence set CI for the new CA and writes it to the DASD in one I/O.
7. VSAM obtains an empty buffer and builds a free space CI in it. All the CI's in the old CA that have been moved to the new CA (about 75 of them) are replaced, one at a time, by the free space CI. This process deletes the records that have been transferred to the new CA and requires about 75 I/O's.
8. VSAM updates the old sequence set CI buffer to reflect the key-pointers deleted when 75 data CI's were moved to the new CA and writes it back in one I/O.
9. VSAM updates the higher-level indexes to reflect the changes in the sequence set records. This could be one or two I/O's, depending on the number of index set levels affected.

The I/O's in the above steps add up to a total of 248. This is a relatively high number compared to the 6 to 8 I/O's incurred on a CI split. At the rate of 12 I/O's per second,[1] 248 I/O's will take about 20.6 seconds to execute. This is a considerable time to wait in an on-line system! The situation could be worse if the I/O service time is higher or the DASD is also executing I/O's for other data sets at the time of CA split.

The I/O count of 248 is based on a CA size of one cylinder, a CI size of 4096 bytes, a NOIMBEDed sequence set, and the device being an IBM 3380. The number of I/O's will vary if the CI size is not 4096 bytes. This will depend upon how many control intervals can fit into one control area.

---

[1]Normally, if our I/O service time is approximately 25 milliseconds (ms) and the DASD is kept about 30% busy, there will be 12 random I/O's executed each second.

Data CI size	Number of data CIs per CA	Approximate number of I/O's on a CA split
512	690	1058
1,024	465	720
2,048	270	428
4,096	150	248
6,144	90	158
8,192	75	135
12,288	45	90
16,348	37	78
32,768	18	50

Figure 3.6 Number of CIs per CA and approximate number of I/O's executed on a CA split for selected data CI sizes. It is assumed that the device is an IBM 3380, the CA size is one cylinder, and NOIMBED was specified in DEFINE CLUSTER.

Figure 3.6 gives the number of I/O's on a CA split for various CI sizes, all other factors remaining the same.

Don't be tempted to increase the CI size just because a larger CI incurs fewer I/O's on a CA split (Fig. 3.6). The selection of the proper CI size is an entirely different issue (see Chap. 9).

CA splits are a major performance concern *only* at the time of their occurrence. Once completed, random access to the data in the split CAs and the new CAs is *not* affected at all. I/O performance for random access remains the same, although sequential access is somewhat slow because the physical dispersion of the data increases the seek time.

3.3.3 Points of Failure in a CA Split

CA splits can also become a major cause for concern from the point of view of data integrity and system maintenance. You may have noticed in the previous section that at some points in time, the splitting CA and the new CA both have copies of the same records. A system failure (e.g., CICS abnormal termination) at that point will leave duplicate records in the data set, and subsequent opening of the file will not correct the situation. You may be left with only one option: restoring the data set from a previous backup and performing forward recovery by reapplying the updates. Therefore, it is important that you use all possible techniques to minimize or eliminate CA splits. Some of the techniques are discussed in section 3.4.

3.4.4 Shareoption 4 and CA Split

A data set may be defined with a cross-region or cross-system shareoption of 4 as follows.

SHAREOPTIONS(4,4)

ALTER command can also be used to change this value later.

In a non-DF/EF or non-DFP environment, if a KSDS is defined with a shareoption of 4, the high used relative byte address (HURBA) of the data set cannot change. *This means that the data set cannot have a CA split.* This prevents the data set from growing in size. While updating such a file, you should expect to receive a file status of 24 in batch Cobol or a NOSPACE condition in CICS/VS.

In general, shareoption 4 also has an adverse effect on the performance of a system. The index buffers of such a data set are refreshed on each file request. Therefore, the allocation of additional index buffers to keep the index in core has no positive performance impact on such a KSDS. One I/O will be performed for each level of index, *even if* the corresponding index CI may already be in the buffers.

3.4 TECHNIQUES TO MINIMIZE CI AND CA SPLITS

As we have discussed, CI splits are not so much a cause for concern as CA splits. Applying various techniques through the use of the FREE-SPACE parameter can dramatically reduce or even eliminate CA splits. Although these techniques are discussed in detail in Chap. 12, a quick review of them is provided here to make you aware of the various alternatives.

3.4.1 Fixed Free Space Allocation

CI splits occur when a particular CI does not have enough free space left to accommodate a new record or an updated record. A CA split occurs when there is no free CI in that CA to accommodate a CI split. Providing enough CI and CA free space at the time of initial load can minimize the possibility of their occurrence.

3.4.2 Variable Free Space Allocation

Fixed free space allocation works fine if there is uniform update activity throughout the data set. This may not be true for many applications. If you determine that most of the splits are occurring within a particular key range, you may leave more free space in that key range and less in the rest of the data set. The ALTER command comes in handy for altering the free space within a data set.

3.4.3 Internal Formatting

Internal formatting of a data set is an excellent technique for controlling CA splits in on-line data collection files. More on this in Chap. 12.

3.4.4 Premature CA Splits

We already know that a sequence set CI (lowermost level of the index component) has compressed keys and pointer records to all the data CIs of one data CA. If the sequence set CI is too small to contain all possible key-pointer pairs, the effective utilization of the data CA may be less than ideal. This will render some data CIs unusable because they are unaddressable and cause premature CA splits. The cause and solution for this problem are discussed in greater detail in Chap. 9.

3.4.5 KSDS vs ESDS with Alternate Index

Since a KSDS is the only data set organization of VSAM that encounters CI and CA splits, you may wish to use an ESDS file instead of a KSDS file. An ESDS does not have any CI or CA splits. In order to emulate the functions of random key access in an ESDS, you may allocate a unique key alternate index over it. The alternate key over the ESDS might be the same as what would have been the prime key of the KSDS. Define the alternate index on the ESDS with the UPGRADE option. Since an alternate index is in fact a KSDS, it may have its own CI and/or CA splits, but there will be fewer splits because the alternate index records are a subset of the base record.

You can access an ESDS through an alternate index in a CICS/VS system. However, keep in mind that COBOL compilers in a batch environment *do not* support alternate indexes over an ESDS.

3.5 CI AND CA SPLITS AND FILE SHARING

A file is said to be shared if it can be accessed by more than one job at a time. The job can be a CICS/VS region, a batch program, and/or any separate address space. In cross-region sharing (jobs running in the same CPU), write integrity is ensured with shareoptions 1 and 2. With shareoptions 3 and 4, whether it is cross-region or cross-system sharing, write

3.5 CI AND CA SPLITS AND FILE SHARING

integrity becomes a primary issue. Most write integrity problems are caused by CI and CA splits. The scenario is illustrated in Figs. 3.7 through 3.9.

In *stage 1* (Fig. 3.7), the data set is opened by programs A and B, both of which have the intention of performing updates. The control blocks in jobs A and B have the HURBA of the data set as 1,228,800 bytes, which means that the first two data CAs have records. We assume that the DASD is an IBM 3380, CA size is one cylinder, and CI size is 4096 bytes.

In *stage 2* (Fig. 3.8), program A adds a record with key value 6, causing a CA split in the first CA. VSAM moves half the records from CA 1 to CA 3. VSAM also updates the HURBA in the control blocks of job A to 1,843,200 bytes. However, it *does not* update the control blocks of job B. Job B has a HURBA of 1,228,800 bytes and thus is not aware that records have been moved to CA 3. Since program B does not have access to the records of CA 3, it is faced with a read integrity problem.

In *stage 3* (Fig. 3.9), program B adds a record with key value 41, thus causing a CA split in CA 2. Since the HURBA in the control block of job B is 1,228,800 bytes, it assumes that CA 3 is free to receive the records of the CA split. Therefore, it moves approximately half the records from CA 2 to CA 3 and overlays the existing records. Thus records 10, 15, 18, 20, 22, and 25 have permanently disappeared from the data set. The file has lost its data integrity!

Be aware that shareoptions 3 and 4 can cause data integrity problems because they make the file eligible for concurrent updates from multiple jobs. In a non-DF/EF environment, since shareoption 4 does not permit CA splits, it provides some protection. However, CI splits can cause similar problems, though to a lesser extent.

To ensure data integrity, you must issue ENQ and DEQ macros to serialize updates to a data set in a cross-region sharing environment. In cross-system sharing (across CPUs), the use of RESERVE and RELEASE macros is recommended. However, high-level languages like Cobol do not provide for the use of these macros, and you have to use Assembler routines to take care of that. Use of these macros, especially RESERVE, can cause severe performance problems, which should also be a major consideration.

3.5.1 The CICS Environment

If you intend to update a VSAM file from multiple CICS/VS regions, you should give one CICS region the ownership for updates. Other tasks from other CICS regions can use function shipping requests to the CICS region that owns the data set. These requests can use MultiRegion Operation (MRO) for cross-region (within the same CPU) requests and InterSystems

- HURBA* in the catalog is 1,228,800 bytes
- Program A opens the file for update;
  HURBA in the Control Blocks of program A is 1,228,800 bytes
- Program B opens the file for update;
  HURBA in the Control Blocks of program B is 1,228,800 bytes

*HURBA = High Used Relative Byte Address. For an IBM 3380, if the Control Area is one cylinder and the Control Interval is 4096 bytes, HURBA of 1,228,800 means that the first two CAs contain data (each CA being 614,400 bytes).

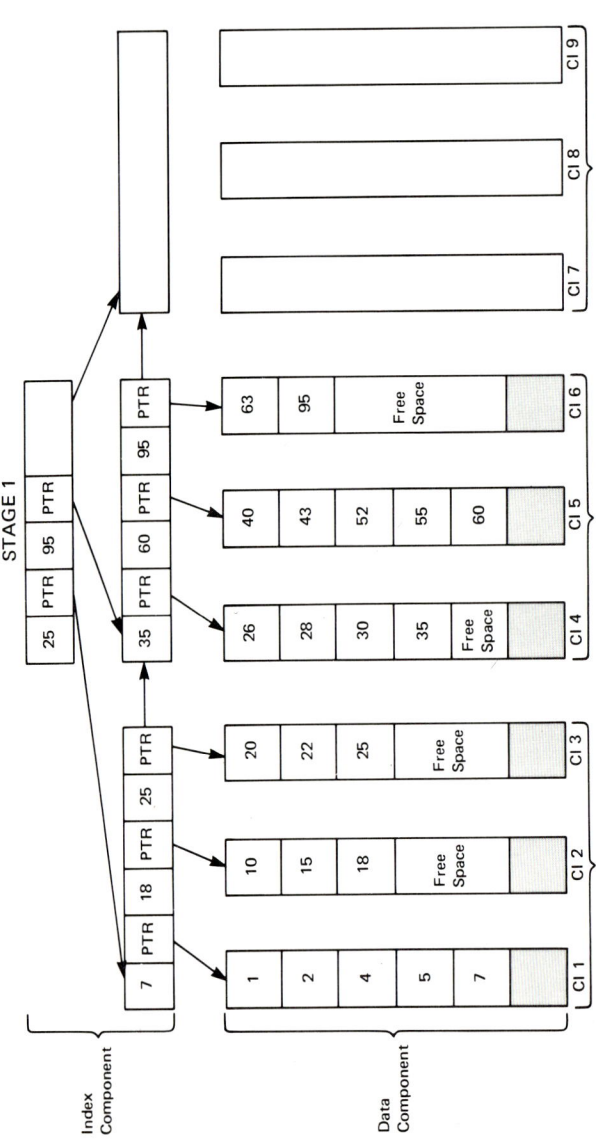

Figure 3.7 First stage in sharing of a KSDS for concurrent updates by programs A and B. It is bound for disaster, as you will see in Figs. 3.8 and 3.9, which illustrate the second and third stages.

- HURBA in the catalog is 1,228,800 bytes
- Program A adds a record with a key value of 6 to data, as in Fig. 3.7, and thus causes a CA split. Half of the records from CA 1 are moved to CA 3, and index records are updated accordingly
- Now, HURBA in the control blocks of program A is 1,843,200 bytes
- *Warning*: HURBA in the control blocks of program B is still 1,228,800 bytes. Program B is unaware of the CA split caused by program A. Program B can't access records of the third CA; it has access to fewer records in the first CA.

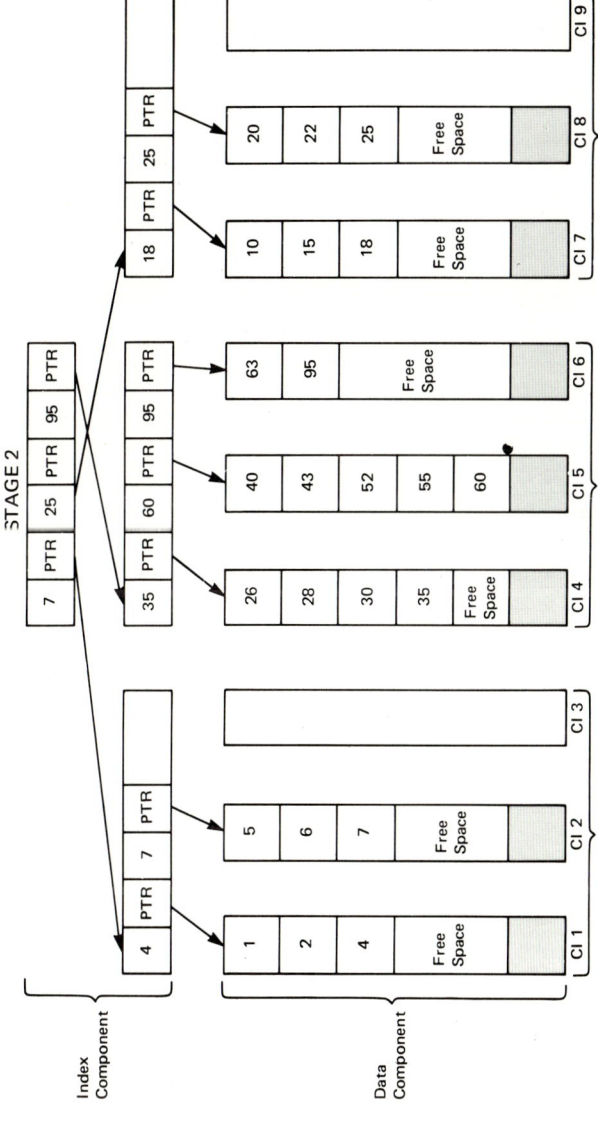

Figure 3.8 Second stage of KSDS sharing. Program A causes a CA split but program B is not aware of record movement. So far, program B has only read-integrity problem.

- HURBA in the catalog is 1,228,800 bytes
- *Disaster:* Program B adds a record with a key value of 41 to data, as in Fig. 3.8, and causes a CA split in the second CA. Because it is unaware of the existence of records in the third CA (since its control blocks have a HURBA of 1,228,800 bytes), it overlays those records with the split

  HURBA in the control blocks of program B is 1,843,200 bytes
- HURBA in the control blocks of program A is also 1,843,200 bytes, but its sequence set record points to erroneous data

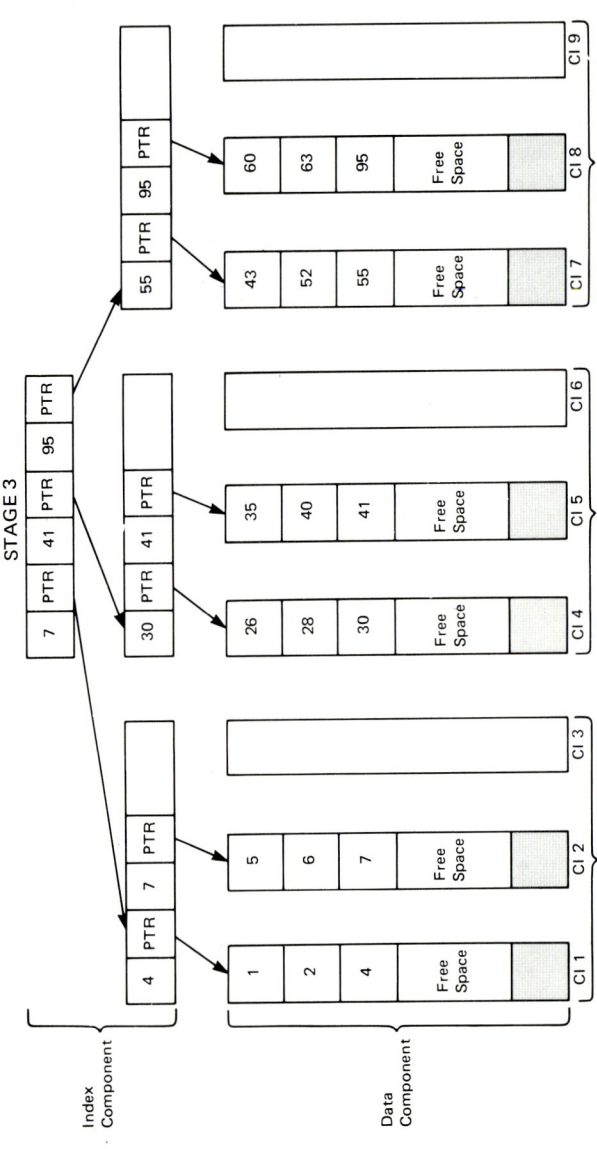

Figure 3.9 Third stage of KSDS sharing. Program B causes a CA split, thus overlaying the records in CA 3. Records 10, 15, 18, 20, 22, and 25 have permanently disappeared from the data set. This disaster has been caused by sharing!

42

3.5 CI AND CA SPLITS AND FILE SHARING

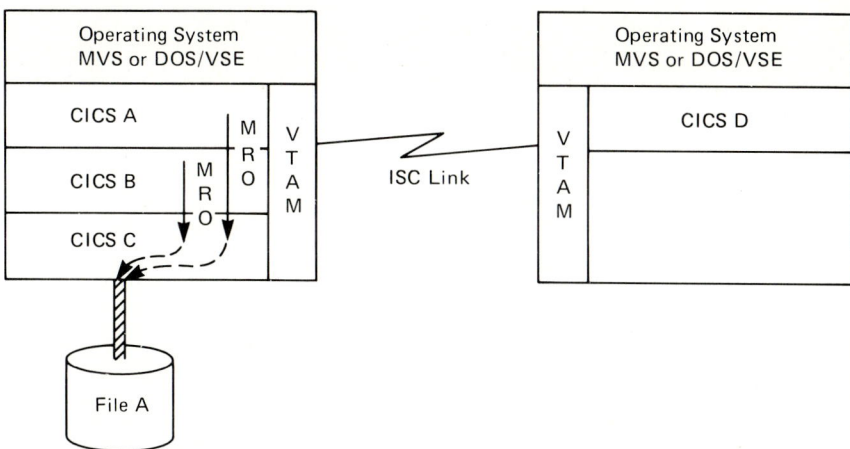

Figure 3.10 CICS C owns file A. CICS A and CICS B send function shipping requests to CICS C using MRO facilities. CICS D, which runs in a different CPU, sends function shipping requests to CICS C using ISC facilities. This configuration ensures complete read and update integrity.

Communications (ISC) for cross-region and cross-system (different CPUs) requests. Although it may sound like a complex task, it only requires making a minor change to the File Control Table (FCT) entry, and the rest is transparent to application programs. Figure 3.10 shows such a configuration. The physical connection to establish an ISC link can be a channel-to-channel (CTC) link or a twin tail IBM 37×5 link or IBM 37×5s linked over communication lines.

chapter 4

Glossary and Features of Fine Tuning

4.1 DEFINITIONS

Some performance-related VSAM buzzwords are used throughout this text. Knowledge of their meaning is essential to a proper understanding of the concepts and theory of VSAM fine tuning. Although their definitions are documented in the appropriate chapters, they are consolidated here for ease of reference.

4.1.1 Strings

Physically, a string consists of some VSAM control blocks, at least one index buffer (for KSDS), and at least one data buffer. Increasing the number of strings also increases the index and data buffer requirements, and hence there is more virtual storage demand on the system.

Figure 4.1 shows the relationship between strings and the data and index buffers used to execute the file requests. This example has four strings for the data set.

When a program issues a file request to VSAM file, VSAM needs a string to process that file request. Usually, a batch job requires only one string for each VSAM data set it processes. In an on-line environment (e.g., CICS/VS) there may be multiple terminal users initiating many con-

4.1 DEFINITIONS

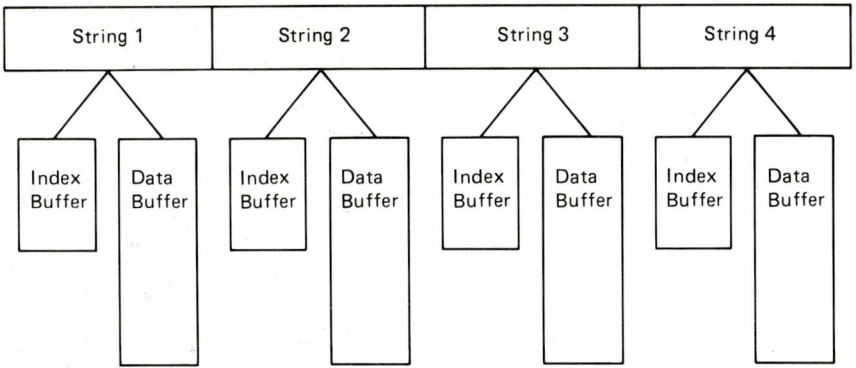

Figure 4.1 Four strings allocated for a KSDS file. Each string requires a minimum of one index buffer and one data buffer.

currently executing tasks. If there were only one VSAM string per data set in such an environment, tasks would have to serialize the I/O requests and wait for the string to become available. This could cause long delays. So for an on-line system you can allocate more strings for a VSAM data set to reduce the string waits. *The number of strings determines the number of concurrent file requests (read, write, rewrite, delete, etc.) that can be issued against a data set at one time.*

In CICS/VS, you can always determine whether or not enough strings have been allocated for a data set. CICS/VS shutdown statistics report total string waits for each data set. The total number of strings allocated depends upon what value you specify in the STRNO parameter of AMP in the batch MVS JCL. In CICS/VS, you may specify the value in the STRNO operand of the DFHFCT TYPE=DATASET macro of the File Control Table.

4.1.2 Index Buffers and Data Buffers

VSAM cannot process the contents of a control interval while it is residing on the DASD. The CI must first be transferred to virtual storage. The portion of virtual storage used for this purpose is called a buffer. Index component CIs use index buffers, and data component CIs use data buffers. The size of each index buffer is equal to the index CI size, which may be ½K, 1K, 2K, or 4K. The size of each data buffer is equal to the data CI size, which may vary from ½K to 32K.

The more strings you allocate, the more index and data buffers you need to process I/O requests associated with those strings. The minimum number of index buffers is one for each string, and the minimum number of data buffers for a KSDS is one for each string plus one reserved for

CI/CA splits. Therefore, for a KSDS the *minimum* buffer requirements are

$$\text{Index buffers} = \text{number of strings}$$
$$\text{Data buffers} = \text{number of strings} + 1$$

You cannot allocate index and data buffers indiscriminately. Each buffer requires virtual storage. In a non-MVS/XA environment, users usually face virtual storage constraints because of the 24-bit addressability limitation.

The performance effect of the allocation of index and data buffers in excess of the minimum requirement will be discussed in Chaps. 15, 16 and 17.

In a batch MVS environment, the value of BUFNI and BUFND in the AMP parameter of JCL determine the number of index and data buffers, respectively. The following is an example of the use of the AMP parameter:

```
//ABC      DD   DSN=VSAM.FILE,DISP=SHR,
//              AMP=('BUFNI=2','BUFND=11')
```

This will allocate two index buffers and 11 data buffers for a data set named VSAM.FILE.

In CICS/VS, the value of the BUFNI and BUFND operands of the DFHFCT TYPE=DATASET macro determine the number of index and data buffers, respectively. In a batch DOS/VSE environment, since there is no equivalent of the AMP parameter in the DLBL statement, the allocation of buffers is controlled through the value of the BUFSP parameter on the DLBL card.

4.1.3 Buffer Space

The amount of virtual storage required to allocate the index and data buffers is called the buffer space requirement for that particular data set. The following formula will help you to calculate the buffer space value:

Buffer space = (index CI size × BUFNI) + (data CI size × BUFND)

where BUFNI = number of index buffers and BUFND = number of data buffers. The buffer space can be specified in the BUFFERSPACE parameter of

- The DEFINE CLUSTER or DEFINE AIX commands of AMS
- The BUFSP parameter of AMP in the MVS JCL
- The BUFSP parameter of DLBL statements in DOS/VSE
- The BUFSP operand of "DFHFCT TYPE=DATASET" macro of the File Control Table in CICS/VS (up to release 1.6.1 only)

4.1 DEFINITIONS

Since VSAM can calculate the value of the buffer space requirement from the BUFNI and BUFND values (except in DOS/VSE batch jobs), the use of BUFFERSPACE is usually not recommended. The only exceptions are the dynamically opened VSAM files, which will be discussed in Chap. 15.

4.1.4 Buffer Look-Aside

The capability of VSAM to save an I/O to a DASD by verifying the existence of the same CI in its buffers is called the buffer look-aside. While the look-aside feature may execute a few machine instructions and use CPU cycles, it is always faster than a physical I/O. The buffer look-aside feature is applicable to both index and data buffers.

If you allocate enough index buffers to put some or all of the CIs of the *index set* of the index component in core, VSAM will always do a look-aside to those buffers before doing a physical I/O. In a sequential browse operation, too, VSAM always looks at the data component buffers in core first. In a Local Shared Resource (LSR) environment, VSAM will *always* look at its buffer pool before attempting a DASD I/O. In a NonShared Resource (NSR) environment, VSAM does not usually do a look-aside for the sequence set and data buffers for a random file request.

4.1.5 Buffer Refresh

In a multiprogramming environment, one region may be performing updates to a portion of a VSAM file that is also being accessed by another region. If one region can be notified that its buffers may not be up to date because of update activity elsewhere, VSAM will attempt to reread those CIs from the DASD. This operation is called a *buffer refresh*. As an example, if a VSAM/KSDS is defined with a shareoption of 4, its index buffers are refreshed on each file request. While the occurrence of a buffer refresh increases the physical I/O activity, its purpose is to preserve data integrity.

4.1.6 NSR Buffers

A VSAM file may have a set of index and data buffers reserved exclusively for its use. No other VSAM file may have access to those buffers for I/O. When the buffer resources of a VSAM file will not be shared with any other VSAM file, they are called NonShared Resource buffers or NSR buffers. Figure 4.2 is a graphic representation of NSR buffers. In this example, if file A does not have any I/O activity at a particular point in time, file B I/O's may not use file A's buffers even though file B has string waits because of heavy I/O activity. NSR buffers are usually rec-

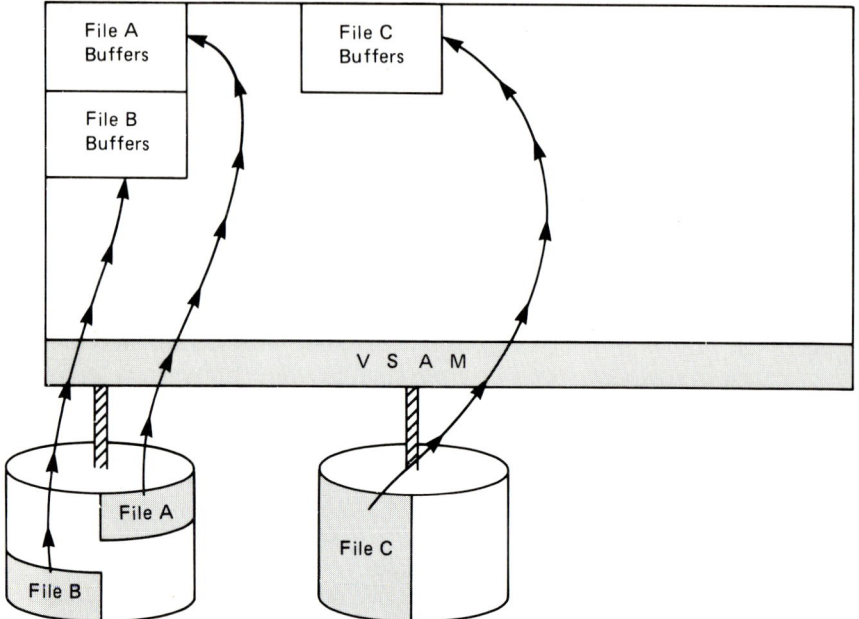

Figure 4.2 An example of NSR buffers. Each file has a buffer pool reserved for its exclusive use.

ommended if a file has consistently heavy I/O activity throughout the execution of a job.

Accessing of VSAM files through Cobol programs always uses NSR buffers. Using Assembler programs, you have the choice of NSR or LSR buffers (LSR buffers are discussed in Section 4.1.7). In CICS/VS also, you have a choice of NSR or LSR buffers. Up to release 1.6.1 of CICS/VS, the default buffer pool allocation was NSR buffers, but beginning with release 1.7 the default is the LSR buffer pool.

4.1.7 LSR Buffers

In Local Shared Resource (LSR) buffer pools, VSAM files share the use of common buffers. There could be many LSR buffer pools varying in size from ½K to 32K. Each pool may have multiple buffers allocated to it. Which buffer pool will be used for a particular VSAM file depends upon its index and data CI size. If the file has different CI sizes for its index and data components, it will use *different* LSR buffer pools for each component. Figure 4.3 gives a graphic representation of an LSR pool. Note that LSR does not distinguish between the index and data components. If the index component of one file (e.g., file B) has the same size as the data component (e.g., file A) of another file, they will both use the same buffer pool.

4.1 DEFINITIONS

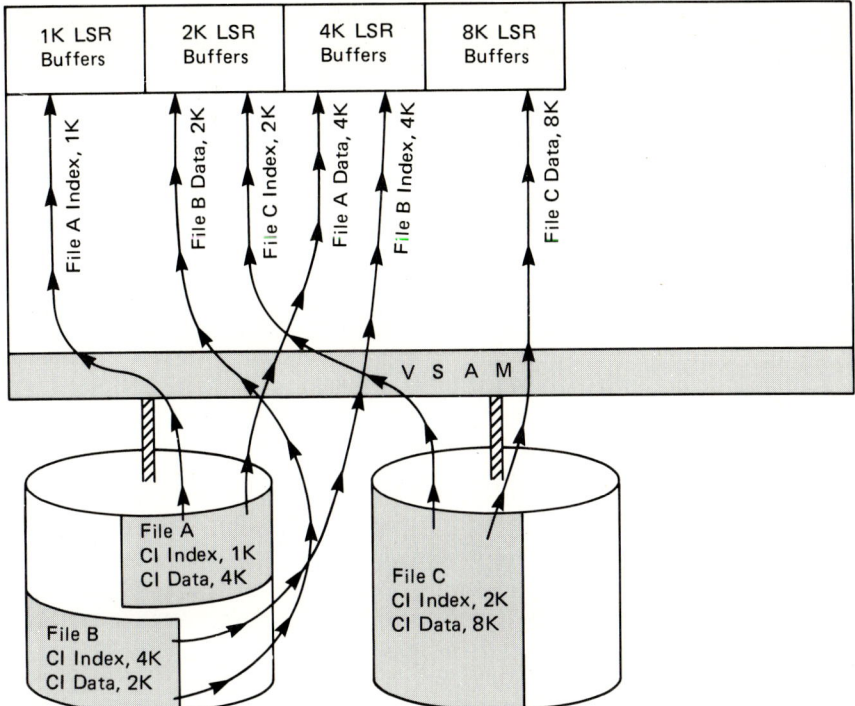

Figure 4.3 An example of LSR buffer pools. Four buffer pools of 1K, 2K, 4K, and 8K size are shared by the index and data components of files A, B, and C.

VSAM *always* does a look-aside at the in-core LSR buffers (data and index) before attempting an I/O to the DASD. Use of LSR and NSR can coexist within the same program, i.e., some VSAM files can have exclusive use of NSR buffers while others may be part of an LSR buffer pool. Beginning with release 1.7 of CICS/VS, LSR is the default for VSAM files, although you can override this and have a VSAM file use NSR buffers.

4.1.8 Read-Ahead

Read-ahead pertains to the reading of multiple data component CIs ahead of time in a sequential browse operation. Because the seek and the rotational delay have already occurred for one data CI, the rest of the CIs are transferred by incurring only the data transfer delay, which is minimal. Since the data component CIs may then already be in core, a file request will fetch the logical record without performing a physical I/O. A read-ahead is performed *only* if there are surplus data buffers left after one is allocated to each string in an NSR environment. If a file is in the LSR pool, read-ahead is *never* done by VSAM. The following are examples of sequential browse operations:

1. Execution of READ in batch Cobol if the ACCESS MODE IS SEQUENTIAL
2. Execution of START and READ NEXT in batch Cobol if the ACCESS MODE IS DYNAMIC
3. Execution of START BROWSE and READ NEXT in CICS/VS

Since a read-ahead will read multiple CIs in a single seek operation, it is a performance-related feature. Read-ahead will be discussed in more detail in Chap. 15.

4.1.9 Control Blocks

VSAM creates various control blocks to keep track of the different pieces of information it needs. Most of the control blocks—for example, Access Method Data Statistics Block (AMDSB) and Extend Data Block (EDB)—are of no special interest to an application program. The control block that is most important to an application program is the Access Method Control Block (ACB).

When a VSAM file is closed, any changed information regarding the data set is transferred from the in-core control blocks to the catalog entry. Since control blocks are volatile, an abnormal termination of a program before a file close will not transfer the information. At times, then, you may notice incorrect statistics in a listing produced by the LISTCAT command. The statistics may include the number of records in the file, the number of CI/CA splits, EXCP (I/O) count, etc. If some of the critical information, such as the HURBA, is not transferred from the control blocks, it can be corrected by issuing the VERIFY command of Access Method Services. However, this command does not correct the statistical information. Also there is no indicator in the catalog to specify if the statistics might be incorrect due to an abnormal termination.

4.2 SOME IMPORTANT FEATURES OF VSAM

Some features of VSAM architecture help in understanding and manipulating the performance aspects of data set and program design. Although these features have also been discussed at various other places in the text, they are consolidated here to facilitate reference and review.

Index CI and Index Record Index CI and index record are synonymous terms. Since one index CI has *one and only one* index record in it, these terms are used interchangeably. For analysis purposes,

$$\text{Index record size} = \text{index CI size} - 7$$

4.2 SOME IMPORTANT FEATURES OF VSAM

The 7 bytes contain the CIDF and one RDF. Maintenance of the index record is, of course, the responsibility of VSAM.

One Sequence Set Record for Each Data CA The lowermost level of the index component is called the sequence set. There is always *one and only one* sequence set record (or CI) containing pointers to the CIs of an entire data CA. Thus, the sequence set record has the key-pointer information that points to the highest record in each CI within that data CA. A data set will have as many sequence set records as there are data CAs.

Key Compression The index component records store the keys of the data component in a compressed format. With the use of a technique for front key compression and rear key compression, the size of the key can be shrunk considerably (remember the key can be up to 255 bytes long). Without key compression, very large index CIs would be required to store large key-pointer records. Because of key compression, a dump of the index component does not produce easily decipherable information.

Data and Index Components are Separate Entities In a KSDS or an alternate index, the index component and the data component are two separately addressable data sets. If the cluster is defined with the UNIQUE option, you will notice two data set names in the VTOC listing. Either data set may be printed or dumped separately. For all practical purposes, however, reference is made to the cluster names, which encompasses both components.

ESDS and RRDS Files Have No Index Component ESDS and RRDS files consist of a data component only. There is no I/O for searching index levels, and BUFNI (index buffers) has no meaning.

Alternate Index Is a KSDS Whether it belongs to an ESDS or a KSDS, an alternate index is itself a KSDS in organization. It has its own index and data components. Most of the KSDS performance-related issues also apply to an alternate index.

IMBED and REPLICATE The IMBED option of DEFINE CLUSTER applies to the *sequence set* of the index component only. The REPLICATE option applies only to the *index set* of the index component. These options are the subject matter of Chap. 11.

FREESPACE Has No Meaning for ESDS and RRDS Since ESDS and RRDS files are not subject to CI/CA splits, the FREESPACE parameter of DEFINE CLUSTER does not apply to them.

FREESPACE Parameter Has No Meaning for Random Updates The FREESPACE parameter is significant only during sequential loading and resume loading of a file. In batch Cobol, a sequential load is performed when the file is opened as OUTPUT. Resume load occurs when the file is opened as EXTEND. Once the file has been loaded and random updates or adds take place, the parameter loses its significance. It is the free space left in the file that is used for random updates and adds. CI and CA splits are reduced because of the free space physically remaining after sequential or resume load operations, not because of the value of the FREESPACE parameter during random adds or updates.

FREESPACE is a highly misunderstood parameter. In many installations the file is loaded sequentially with a low FREESPACE value. After the load is completed successfully, the FREESPACE value is changed to a higher number with the ALTER command, and all subsequent updates are random. The alteration in the value of FREESPACE will have *absolutely no effect* in reducing CI/CA splits during random adds and/or updates.

FREESPACE Applies Only to the Data Component FREESPACE applies to the data component of a KSDS or an alternate index. It does not affect the index component at all.

CI/CA Splits and Performance Since CI and CA splits increase I/O activity, they cause performance problems at the time of the split activity. Later random access of records from the same data set does not cause any performance degradation. However, a long sequential browse on that data set may be slightly slower.

Sequence Set I/O You should attempt to put the index set records in core through the proper allocation of buffers. However, it does not pay to put the sequence set records in core. Due to the large number of sequence set records, the probability of a sequence set record being accessed by two different tasks at the same time (e.g., CICS tasks) is very low. For all practical purposes, then, VSAM almost always does an I/O to the sequence set CI to locate the pointers to the data component CI.

Free CAs and CIs VSAM grabs a free CA during the CA split process so that about half the records can be moved to the newly acquired free CA. Such a CA is always the first one at the end of the HURBA control area. If all the records of a control area are deleted during processing, the CA *does not become eligible to act as a free CA* during CA split activity.

In a DFP or DF/EF environment, a CI whose records have been deleted *does* become eligible to act as a free CI during a CI split process.

Add, Update, and Delete The number of I/O's on an add, update, or delete are *the same*. However, while an add or an update that increases the record length can be the cause of a CI/CA split, a delete never is.

4.2 SOME IMPORTANT FEATURES OF VSAM

Default Index Buffers If there is only one index level, the default allocation of index buffers (i.e., one per string) is sufficient. If there are two or three index levels, the default VSAM buffer allocation can give you the worst performance. Use the techniques discussed in Chaps. 15, 16, and 17 for extra buffer allocation to reduce index component I/O's.

two

HARDWARE AND PERFORMANCE

Performance of an I/O is directly affected by the type of DASD where the data is stored. Chapters 5 and 6 discuss the internals of an I/O and the characteristics of physical storage media, respectively. Chapter 7 includes detailed discussions on the cache DASD storage, which is becoming more popular due to its high-performance characteristics. Expanded memory, which has been introduced by IBM for its 3090 series of mainframes, is the subject matter of Chap. 8. Chapter 8 also includes a discussion on solid state devices, which are high-performance DASDs without any electromechanical moving parts. Mass storage systems, which can adversely affect performance, are also discussed in Chap. 8. With current changes in technology, new hardware equipment will be introduced by vendors in the future, and its performance and storage characteristics will also be different than what they are today. Although the most up-to-date announcements are reflected in this text, readers are advised to refer to vendor documents when new products are released.

chapter 5

Internals of an Input/Output

5.1 A DASD CONFIGURATION

DASDs are not directly attached to a CPU. A string of DASDs (discussed in Section 5.1.1) is attached to a *DASD controller* (also called a DASD control unit). A series of DASD controllers are further attached to a *channel*. Figure 5.1 shows such a configuration.

5.1.1 Disk Drives

Disk drives are the devices that house DASDs. In the IBM 3380 world, a boxlike device called a *unit* contains two drives, and each drive has two actuators. Each actuator (loosely defined, the set of read-write arms that have access to the data on the DASD) has access to data that is referred to by a volume serial *(volser)* number. Therefore each unit has access to four volser numbers. A group of four such units (16 volsers) is called a *string*. One string of a *single-density* IBM 3380 has 10,080 megabytes (10.08 gigabytes) of storage capacity, while one string of *double-density* IBM 3380 has twice the storage capacity (20.16 gigabytes). Single-density IBM 3380 models are models A4, B4, AA4, AD4, and BD4. Double-density models are the AE4 and BE4. Figure 5.2 gives the characteristics of some commonly used disk drives.

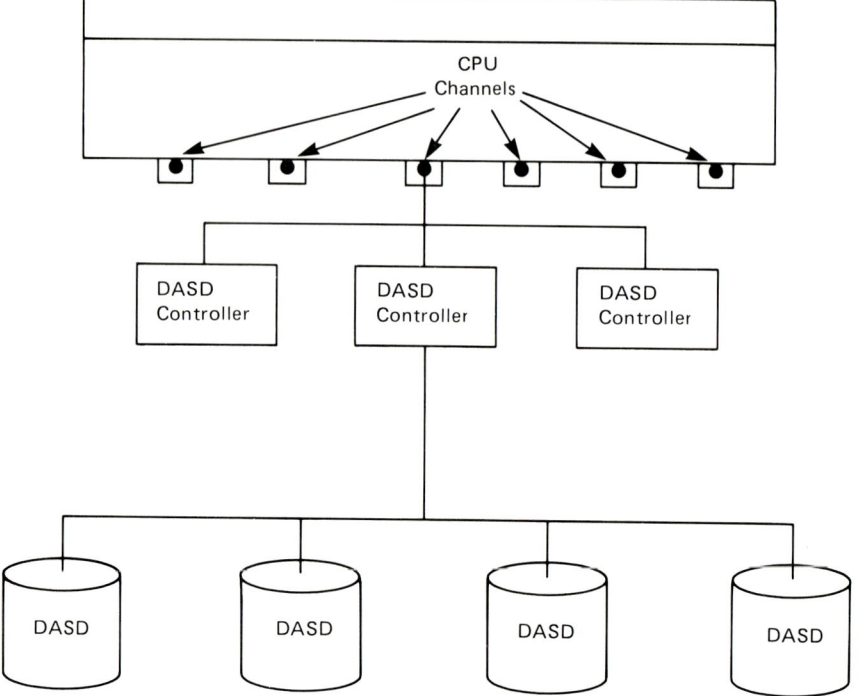

Figure 5.1 A symbolic configuration showing a CPU, channels, DASD controllers, and a string of DASDs.

Some non-IBM disk drive vendors (e.g., Memorex, CDC, STC) make IBM-compatible DASDs with similar performance and storage characteristics.

5.1.2 DASD Control Unit

A DASD control unit (or DASD controller) sits between the channel and a string of DASDs. IBM 3880 Models 2 and 3 are examples of DASD control units. (Note that these models are not the same as an IBM 3380, which is a DASD, not a DASD controller.) An IBM 3880 Model 3 controls only IBM 3380 DASDs, while the Model 2 can control 3330s, 3340s, 3350s, 3370s, 3375s, and 3380s.

A DASD control unit receives a command from the channel and executes it on the DASD. The commands include SEEK, SEARCH, READ, and WRITE. The SEEK command positions the read-write access mechanism at the desired cylinder. The SEARCH command compares data on the DASD and in main storage. The READ and WRITE commands are self-explanatory. The DASD control unit sends feedback to the host on the status of the execution of each command. All data

5.1 A DASD CONFIGURATION

IBM DASD*	Model	Cylinders/ volser	Tracks/ cylinder	Bytes/ track	Megabytes/ volser
2305 (fixed head)	Model 2	64	24	14,660	22
3350	A2, A2F, B2, B2F, C2, C2F	555	30	19,254	317
3375	A1, B1	959	12	36,000	410
3380 (SD)	A4, AA4, B4, AD4, BD4	885	15	47,968	630
3380 (DD)	AE4, BE4	1770	15	47,968	1260
3370† (FBA)	A1, B1	750	12	31,744 (62 blocks)	286 (558,000 blocks)

*SD = single-density; DD = double-density.
†Logically, an FBA device has no concept of tracks. Each cylinder is considered to be a tring of contiguous 512-byte blocks.

Figure 5.2 Characteristics of some commonly used DASDs.

transfers between the host and the DASD performed by the DASD control unit are carried through the channel.

Some models of DASD control units have cache memory associated with them. Cache memory, if used properly, can have a significant effect on I/O performance. This feature is discussed in Chap. 7.

5.1.3 Channels

A channel is, in fact, a *processor*. It controls the I/O operations of all the DASDs within its domain. Depending upon the model, an IBM computer may have anywhere from 6 channels (e.g., an IBM 4341) to 128 channels (e.g., an IBM 3090 Model 600E). In the future, we will see new processors that expand the number of channels. A channel controls one or more DASD controllers (DASD control units). I/O instructions to a channel are given by the access method (e.g., VSAM) through channel commands. A channel retrieves these commands from the main storage of the computer, passing each one to the appropriate DASD controller.

The process of transferring data to or from a DASD cannot be faster than the speed of the channel that controls it. Since a channel may control a number of DASD controllers, each one of which may control a number of DASDs, it may become a bottleneck when there is high activity on the DASDs it controls. Channel activity is measured by "channel busy" considerations. Resource Measurement Facility (RMF), Generalized Trace Facility (GTF), Omegamon/MVS, and fast-DASD are some of the tools that can be used to measure the channel busy rate. IBM recommends that a channel should not be more than 35% busy. Anything higher requires load balancing by moving high I/O activity data sets to DASDs whose controlling channel is less busy. In an MVS/XA environment, the *dynamic path reconnect* feature makes it possible to have two different channels used for an I/O. With this feature, a channel can free itself from the unnecessary wait period required between the forwarding of a channel instruction to the DASD controller, completion of the seek and the rotation, and transfer of data to or from the DASD. Therefore, in an MVS/XA environment, with the proper configuration it is possible to have up to 70% channel busy without adversely affecting performance.

5.2 PATH OF AN "IDEAL WORLD" I/O

An I/O can involve a read or a write operation. Our "ideal world" I/O will take place if all the computing resources are exclusively at the disposal of that I/O and there is no contention with any other I/O request. Let's look at the components of such an I/O.

Access Method Processing Time Upon issuance of an I/O request by an application program, the access method takes over and processes the request. It consumes CPU cycles for the performance of its functions such as analysis of the request and creation of channel command words. Usually, the *access method processing time* is negligible and can be ignored.

Seek Time The channel retrieves channel commands from the main storage of the host. For our example, it issues a seek to the DASD control unit. The execution of the command positions the access mechanism at the desired cylinder. The time it takes to perform the function is called *seek time*. The *maximum seek time* is the time in milliseconds (1 ms = 1/1000 s) the access mechanism takes to traverse from the first cylinder to the last cylinder. The *average seek time* is the time it takes to traverse one-third the total number of cylinders. Figure 5.3 tabulates the maximum and average seek times for commonly used DASDs.

The *minimum seek time* is the time it takes for the access mechanism to move from a particular cylinder to the next *adjacent* cylinder. Note that this time is disproportionately higher for the amount of distance covered. This is due to a relatively high start-up time needed for electromechanical devices to accelerate. Also note that since an IBM 2305 (also known as a drum) is a fixed-head DASD, the seek time is zero.

Read-Write Head Selection Delay An access mechanism has many read-write heads—in our case, one head per surface. Once the seek to a cyl-

5.2 PATH OF AN "IDEAL WORLD" I/O

IBM DASD*	Maximum seek time, ms	Average seek time, ms	Minimum seek time, ms
3310	46	27	9
3330	55	30	10
3340	50	25	10
3350	50	25	10
3370	40	20	5
3375	38	19	4
3380 SD	30	16	3
3380 DD	31	17	3
2305	0	0	0
9335	37	18	4.5
9332	Approx. 50	23–25	3–5

*SD = single-density; DD = double-density.

Figure 5.3 Maximum, average, and minimum seek times for some IBM DASDs.

inder is completed, the proper read-write head must be directed to the proper track. This electronic switching does not involve any electromechanical movement, so the *read-write head selection delay* can be ignored.

Rotational Delay After the read-write head selection has been accomplished, the required starting point on the rotating DASD must come under the read-write head to begin the data transfer to or from the main storage. The data transfer will be from the DASD to the main storage buffers for a read request and from the main storage buffers to the DASD for a write request. This may take anywhere from a minimal distance of one IBG (interblock gap) to the full rotation of the track. For all practical purposes, I/O *rotational delay* is estimated at one-half the full-track rotational delay. Figure 5.4 tabulates maximum (full-track) and average rotational delays for some commonly used DASDs.

Data Transfer Delay After the necessary rotational delay, the correct data beginning is positioned under the read-write head. The time required to transfer the data from the DASD to main storage (or vice versa) is the *data transfer delay*. This delay depends upon the rotational speed of the DASD and the density of the recorded data on the track. For example, an IBM 3380 will transfer 47,968 bytes of data (a full track) in 16.7 ms (full rotational delay). This is approximately 3.0 MBS. For an IBM 3350, the data transfer rate is 19,254 bytes (a full track) in 16.8 ms, which is approximately 1.20 MBS. Figure 5.5 illustrates the data transfer rates for some IBM DASDs and the data transfer delay for a 4K control interval.

IBM DASD*	Maximum rotational delay, ms	Average rotational delay, ms
3330, 3350, 9335 3380 (SD and DD)	16.8	8.4
3340, 3370, 3375	20.2	10.1
3310, 9332	19.1	9.6
2305	10	5

*SD = single-density; DD = double-density.

Figure 5.4 Maximum and average rotational delay for some commonly used DASDs.

IBM DASD	Data transfer rate, MBS	Data transfer delay for a 4K CI, ms
3310	1.03	4.0
3330	0.81	5.0
3340	0.89	4.6
3350	1.20	3.4
3370	1.86	2.2
3375	1.86	2.2
3380 (SD)	3.00	1.3
3380 (DD)	3.00	1.3
2305	1.50	2.7
9335	3.00	1.9
9332	2.60	2.1

Figure 5.5 Data transfer rate for IBM DASDs and data transfer delay for a 4K CI.

Summary We can see that an "ideal world" I/O is affected by seek time, rotational delay, and data transfer delay. Access method processing time and read-write head selection time can be ignored. They occur at tremendous speeds relative to the other three factors, which involve electromechanical movements. Figure 5.6 tabulates "ideal world" I/O time for various DASDs.

From a quick perusal of the table, it appears that an IBM 2305 is the device with the fastest I/O service time. Since it is relatively expensive and has low storage capacity, it is not very widely used.

It should be noted that these timings are for a single random physical I/O for a 4K CI under average conditions. *A random Cobol READ executed on a KSDS can execute two to four such physical I/O's, depending upon the index levels and the buffering techniques used.* The LISTCAT command, when executed on a VSAM data set, gives the physical I/O

5.3 PATH OF A "REAL WORLD" I/O

IBM DASD	Average seek time, ms	Average rotational delay, ms	Data transfer delay for a 4K CI, ms	"Ideal world" I/O time, ms
3310	27	9.6	4.0	40.6
3330	30	8.4	5.0	43.4
3340	25	10.1	4.6	39.7
3350	25	8.4	3.4	36.8
3370	20	10.1	2.2	32.3
3375	19	10.1	2.2	31.3
3380 (SD)	16	8.4	1.3	25.7
3380 (DD)	17	8.4	1.3	26.7
2305	0	5.0	2.7	7.7
9335	18	8.3	1.9	28.2
9332	24	9.6	2.1	35.7

Figure 5.6 "Ideal world" I/O times for commonly used DASDs.

counts for each component under the heading EXCP (EXecute Channel Program).

5.3 PATH OF A "REAL WORLD" I/O

In the real world, there are more than one I/O taking place at any particular point in time. I/O's are single threaded on a DASD because there is only one read-write access mechanism hopping from one cylinder to another. Therefore, a request for an I/O goes through the following cycle.

1. It waits in a queue for the resource to become available. The tasks ahead of yours in the queue will not forgo their turn to give your request preferential treatment. If your I/O request is lucky, there won't be any queue for the utilization of *the resource*. Waiting for a resource delays an I/O.
2. Once each resource is available, the I/O request uses it as described in the "ideal world" I/O.

Excessive queue waits can have a profoundly negative effect on an I/O. In one shop, the author noted a 500-ms queue wait for an IBM 3350. Once the resource became available, the I/O was performed in about 40 ms. The total I/O service time was approximately 540 ms, slightly over ½ second.

The components involved in a real world I/O are the following.

CPU Wait In an excessively busy CPU, access method processing time is preceded by a CPU wait. The CPU is usually not a bottleneck in an

I/O world. If it is, only an upgrade of the hardware to higher MIPS (millions of instructions per second) can eliminate or reduce the CPU wait. For practical purposes, this wait can be ignored.

Access Method Processing Time See Section 5.2.

Channel Busy Wait Since a channel services a number of DASDs, data transfer for another request could already be taking place when a request comes in. An I/O request will be queued until the channel becomes available. In an MVS-XA environment, a channel can be busy up to 70% of the time because of the availability of the *dynamic path reconnect* feature. In a non-XA environment, IBM recommends that a channel busy wait should not occur more than 35% of the time.

DASD Control Unit Busy Since a DASD control unit can service more than one string, each having a number of DASDs in it, an I/O might have to wait for the control unit to become available. Usually the control unit busy wait is negligible.

Device (DASD) Busy Wait A DASD may have several data sets on it. Data on each data set could be requested concurrently from a multiple number of tasks of CICS. There might also be batch jobs requesting I/O's on the same or a different set of files. Since there is only one set of read-write access mechanism, it is likely that I/O's will be queued up while the device is busy. IBM recommends that the *DASD busy wait* should not exceed 30%. Some of the performance measurement tools like RMF, GTF, Omegamon/MVS, Omegamon/CICS, and fast-DASD could be used to get the device busy data.

If a device is excessively busy most of the time, you will have to move some of the data to another DASD for I/O balancing. The KEYRANGES parameter of DEFINE CLUSTER (Chap. 10) might come handy in this situation. The log data set of a heavily used CICS system could virtually monopolize a DASD's access mechanism. Avoid putting other heavily used VSAM data sets on the same volume.

Another major culprit is the device RESERVE macro. This macro is used in association with RELEASE to perform single threading of access to a shared DASD. RESERVE flips a physical switch in the DASD control unit so that other programs cannot access that device until a RELEASE is issued. Even if it is used for only a short duration, this can build up heavy queues for that DASD in an on-line (e.g., CICS/VS) environment. Also, watch out when link editing an object module, because the linkage editor issues a device RESERVE on the volume containing the target load library. RESERVE and RELEASE are discussed in Section 5.4 in more detail.

5.4 SERIALIZING I/O'S   65

Seek Time   See Section 5.2.

RPS Miss   Rotational Position Sensing (RPS) is a standard feature of all the devices discussed so far, with the exception of an IBM 3340, where it is an option. The channel issues a search command to the DASD control unit and then disconnects itself from the control unit so that it can direct the I/O's of other requests. The DASD control unit tries to reconnect to the channel just before the data is due to arrive under the read-write head. If a channel is not available at that moment, the control unit has to try again on the next revolution. This is called an *RPS miss*. This could mean a delay of a full revolution, which is 16.8 ms for an IBM 3380. An excessively busy channel controlling an excessively busy string of DASDs could experience RPS misses.

Rotational Delay   See Section 5.2.

Data Transfer Delay   See Section 5.2.

Summary   I/O service time in the real world may be higher than that illustrated in Fig. 5.6. Strive to keep the overhead as low as possible. Omegamon/MVS and Omegamon/CICS are excellent tools to measure queue depth, I/O service time, queue wait time, etc. The techniques discussed later in this book should be applied to reduce the I/O service time.

5.4 SERIALIZING I/O'S

A VSAM file can be open for update by more than one program (more than one address space) at the same time. VSAM shareoptions 3 and 4 allow this concurrency. However, the update and the read integrity can very easily be lost by concurrent updates. Data can also be lost and the file rendered unusable if more than one address space causes CA splits at the same time.

If the jobs are running in the *same CPU,* data integrity can be ensured by issuing an ENQ macro before the file access. The resource (VSAM file) will be held for a job's exclusive use for the duration of ENQ. After a logical unit of work has been completed, DEQ can be issued to release the resource. The Systems Queue Area (SQA) of MVS keeps track of ENQs and makes sure that no other program uses the resource while the ENQ is in place. This assures data integrity by serializing the resource within the *same CPU* system. Bear in mind that an ENQ is issued on a resource that can also be a VSAM file. In that case, only that particular VSAM file is serialized for use. Other data sets on the same DASD are available for access by the same job or others in the system.

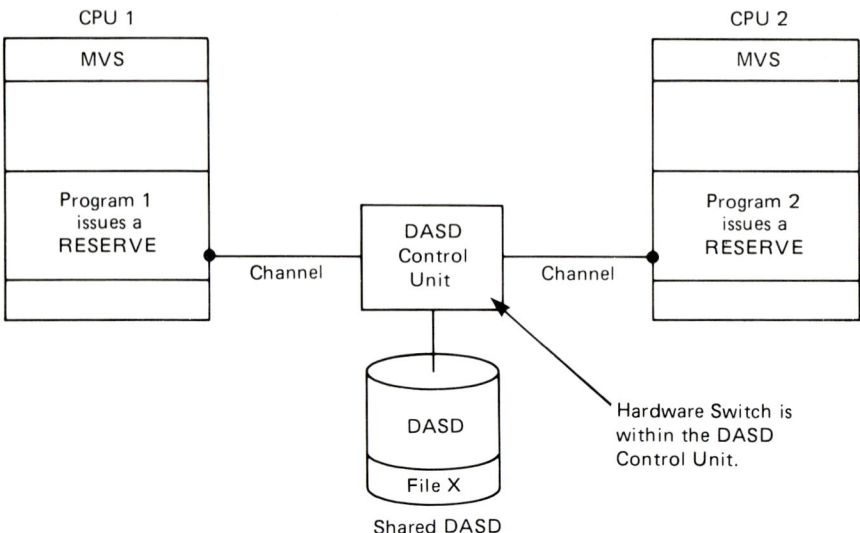

Figure 5.7 Address spaces on multiple CPUs serialize the use of a VSAM file by issuing RESERVE, which flips a hardware switch in the DASD control unit.

5.4.1 RESERVE Macro

If a DASD is shared by more than one CPU, the ENQ macro *will not* serialize the use of the resource. The reason for this is that the ENQ information held in the SQA of one MVS system does not communicate with the ENQ information held in the SQA of another MVS system. In these circumstances, when a file exists on a shared DASD, RESERVE and RELEASE will have to be used to serialize the use of a resource. A RESERVE turns a *hardware switch* on and will not let any other address space access any data on the *same DASD* until a RELEASE is issued (Fig. 5.7).

In Fig. 5.7, program 1, running in CPU 1, issues a RESERVE, causing a hardware switch to flip in the DASD control unit controlling the DASD containing file X. Program 2, running in CPU 2, also issues a RESERVE, but the control unit makes it wait until program 1 has issued a RELEASE. In these cases, *RESERVE serializes the entire DASD*. Other files, unused by program 1 or program 2, also become inaccessible for the duration of the RESERVE. All the I/O requests for the DASD from multiple systems are queued and held while the DASD is in the RESERVE state.

Bear in mind that it is the responsibility of the user of an application program to issue ENQ, DEQ, RESERVE, and RELEASE. These macros *are not* issued automatically. Their only function is to serialize the use of a resource. This ensures data integrity for VSAM files. The side effect is a serious degradation of I/O service time with a buildup of I/O queues.

5.4 SERIALIZING I/O'S

Cobol has no facility to issue such macros. However, Assembler subroutines can be called from a Cobol program to issue them.

The following guidelines can be used to minimize or eliminate the effects of explicit and implicit RESERVEs:

- The Linkage Editor issues a device RESERVE when a link edit step is placing a load module into a load library. Make sure that the test and production load libraries are not on the same volume. In a system development environment, where multiple compiles and link edits are likely, a DASD RESERVE can have a serious impact on the production response time. In a production CICS environment, the loading of programs from the DFHRPL library (CICS application load modules) to the Dynamic Storage Area (DSA) of CICS will be held up when a RESERVE is in place. If the link edit is done through a CLIST under TSO, and the TSO address space for that user is swapped out (for any reason), the RESERVE may be in place for an excessive length of time. So beware of mixing test and production load libraries!
- While a Volume Table of Contents (VTOC) is being updated, MVS issues a RESERVE to prevent other systems from accessing the same DASD. The VTOC update is an I/O bound procedure, and a RESERVE can be in place for a fairly long period of time. In the VSAM world, a VTOC is updated when

    A data set is being defined in an ICF catalog

    An additional extent is being allocated for a data set defined in an ICF catalog

    VSAM space is being extended in a VSAM catalog

    In an on-line environment like CICS/VS and IMS/DC, it is beneficial to prevent the occurrence of data set extensions by allocating sufficient primary space for the VSAM files.
- Use Global Resource Serialization (GRS) to automatically convert a DASD RESERVE to a file ENQ.

5.4.2 Global Resource Serialization (GRS)

A new feature of MVS/SP, called Global Resource Serialization, or GRS, was introduced in release 1.2. GRS is a separate address space in an MVS system. With this new feature, ENQ- and DEQ-related information can be moved from the SQA of MVS to the GRSs own address space. While the SQAs of different MVS systems do not communicate with each other, GRSs have the ability to exchange data with each other through channel-to-channel adapters (CTCs) (Fig. 5.8).

In Fig. 5.8, when program 1 issues a RESERVE, it does not have to reserve the entire DASD for its exclusive use. Instead, it can convert the

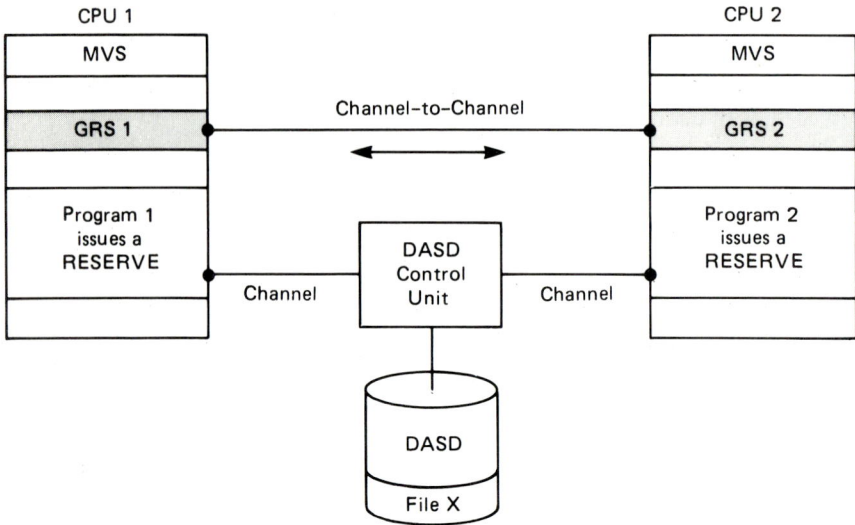

Figure 5.8 Functioning of Global Resource Serialization (GRS) in a multi-CPU environment.

RESERVE to an ENQ on file X. The information on the ENQ for file X will be kept in GRS 1 of CPU 1 and copied to GRS 2 of CPU 2 (over CTC link). Thus, a program intending to access file X from CPU 2 will be prevented by GRS 2 until a RELEASE is issued by program 1. Only file X is serialized for access; other data sets on the same DASD are unaffected. If there were other CPUs sharing the same DASD, their GRS address space would also be modified accordingly. The primary purpose of GRS is to convert a DASD RESERVE/RELEASE to a global ENQ/DEQ. When a RESERVE is converted to a global ENQ for a VSAM data set, all address spaces in the various CPUs appear to be running in the same CPU. Thus, the second SHAREOPTIONS value (cross system) becomes *ineffective* for VSAM files.

5.5 TECHNIQUES FOR FASTER AND FEWER I/O'S

Although we have not yet discussed many of the details of VSAM fine tuning, let's summarize some of the techniques for improving I/O's on a DASD.

How to Perform Faster I/O's

- Reduce seek time by using the IMBED option of VSAM when allocating a KSDS or an alternate index cluster. It reduces seek time and rotational delay by placing the sequence set on the first track of the data component CA and replicating it over the track.

5.5 TECHNIQUES FOR FASTER AND FEWER I/O'S

- Reduce seek time by placing the index component on the fixed-head cylinders of a DASD. Unfortunately, an IBM 3380 does not have fixed-head cylinders.
- Eliminate seek time by placing frequently used but small data sets on a fixed-head DASD such as an IBM 2305. Remember, such DASDs have small capacities and are very expensive.
- Reduce rotational delay for the index set of a KSDS and alternate index clusters by using REPLICATE during allocation. This option is extremely useful for the KSDS component of a HIDAM, HISAM, and secondary index of an IMS data base.
- Use cache memory controllers (see Chap. 7) to keep highly active data in the DASD control units memory. Chapter 7 is devoted to this feature.
- Make use of the Dynamic Path Reconnect feature to reduce channel waits.

How to Perform Fewer I/O's

- Put high-level indexes (index set) in core through the proper use of the BUFNI parameter. This feature is discussed in Chaps. 15 and 16.
- Use those techniques of buffer management that make use of the look-aside feature before performing an I/O. This is done by using the Local Shared Resource (LSR) buffer pool and is discussed in Chap. 17.
- Make use of cache memory in the cache DASD control units (IBM 3880 Models 13 and 23).

chapter 6

Physical Storage Media

6.1 WHAT DOES A DASD LOOK LIKE?

It is essential that you understand the conceptual and physical architecture of a disk pack if you wish to fine tune a VSAM-based system. The conceptual architecture is the one that the programmer visualizes on a disk pack. The physical architecture includes the physical components that constitute the disk pack.

6.1.1 Conceptual Architecture

A disk pack consists of cylinders and tracks. The concentric circles on a stereo record-like surface are called *tracks*. If a number of such surfaces were placed one above the other on a spindle, then each set of tracks positioned one above the other would form a cylinder. In other words, the tracks on a number of stacked records form concentric cylinders.

A disk pack configuration may be summarized as follows:

- A disk pack has many cylinders.
- A cylinder has many tracks.
- A track can store a fixed number of bytes on its surface.

To illustrate, a double-density IBM 3380 (Models AE4 and BE4) has 1770 cylinders, each cylinder consisting of 15 tracks, with each track ca-

6.1 WHAT DOES A DASD LOOK LIKE?

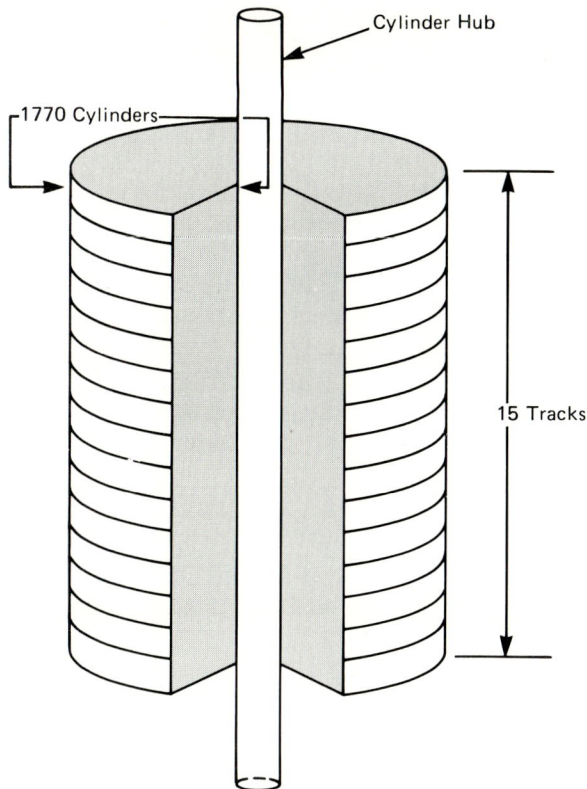

Figure 6.1 Conceptual architecture of a dual-density IBM 3380 (Model AE4 and BE4) disk pack. Each volume has 1770 cylinders, each cylinder having 15 tracks, with each track capable of holding 47,968 bytes of storage.

pable of storing 47,968 bytes. Thus the total capacity of such a disk is 1260 megabytes (or 1.26 gigabytes). Figure 6.1 shows the conceptual architecture of such a disk pack.

We must keep in mind that not all of the storage capacity of a DASD can be used for application data storage. We will see later that effective DASD utilization is a function of CI size, device characteristics, and a number of other factors.

6.1.2 Physical Architecture

Figure 6.2 shows the physical architecture of a typical disk pack. A disk pack does, in fact, consist of stereo-record-like disks that are hung one above the other around a common cylindrical hub. There is a fixed distance between each two consecutive platters. The disks move in unison around the control hub without any independent vertical or rotational movement. Each disk has two recording surfaces, just like a stereo record—top and bottom—so there are twice as many recording surfaces

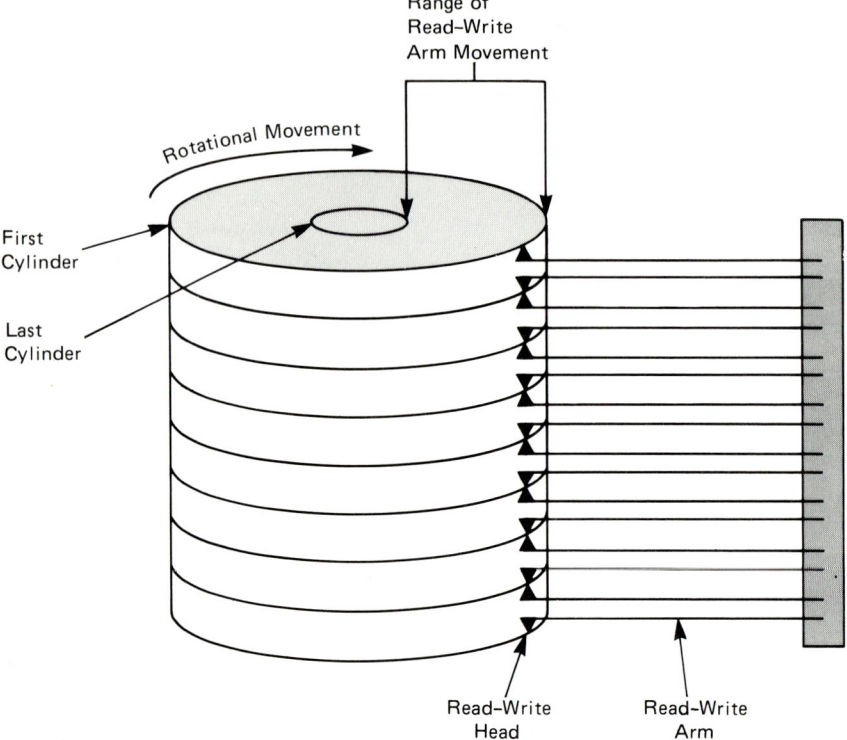

Figure 6.2 Physical architecture of typical disk pack.

as there are platters. By design, not all of the recording surfaces are used for data storage. One is used by the vendor's field engineer (FE), and usually the top surface of the top disk and the bottom surface of the bottom disk are not used. The number of vendor-specified usable surfaces is what determines the number of tracks per cylinder.

Data is transferred to or from the disk pack through a set of read-write arms. A read-write arm can be likened to the stylus of a record player. For application purposes, there are as many read-write arms as there are usable recording surfaces. For example, for an IBM 3380, there are 15 read-write arms. Read-write arms also move in unison; they cannot move independently. If one read-write arm is positioned on the 499th cylinder of an IBM 3380, the other 14 arms are also positioned on the same cylinder. The set of read-write arms ride on the recording surfaces of the disk pack.

The entire set of read-write arms is capable of moving from the first cylinder to the last cylinder of the pack; movement between cylinders is called a *seek*. When the set of read-write arms is positioned on a particular cylinder, all of the data residing on all of the tracks of that cylinder can be read from (or written to) without performing another seek.

All of the physical disks of the disk pack revolve in unison around a common axle (the hub) at a tremendous speed. An IBM 3380 revolves at 3600 revolutions per minute (RPM), or 60 revolutions per second. Once the read-write arms are positioned on a specific cylinder, the data residing on the tracks of the cylinder, revolving with the rotation of the disk pack, has to come under a specific read-write head before an I/O can be started. This kind of delay is referred to as *rotational delay*.

6.2 I/O DELAYS

In order to perform a successful I/O, the following must take place at the DASD end:

1. The read-write arms seek the desired cylinder.
2. The disk rotates until the desired track location is under the read-write head.
3. Data is transferred from or to the DASD.

6.2.1 Seek Time Delay

The seek time delay may be defined as *the time it takes for the read-write arm of the DASD to move from its current position to the desired cylinder*. The maximum seek time delay occurs when the read-write arm moves from the first to the last cylinder. For a single-density IBM 3380, the maximum seek time is 30 milliseconds (30 ms).[1] On the average, however, a seek usually does not traverse more than one-third of the cylinders. So the average seek time for a single-density IBM 3380 is 16 ms. Note that due to startup overhead, the average seek time is more than one-third of 30 ms. For the same device, the seek time delay to move to an *adjacent cylinder* is 3 ms. Always keep in mind that the maximum, the average, and the adjacent cylinder seek time delays do not have a straight-line relationship.

6.2.2 Rotational Delay

Once the seek has been completed, the read-write arm must wait for the data on the revolving tracks to reach the read-write head. This causes a rotational latency or delay. *Rotational delay* may be defined as *the time it takes for the data on a particular track of a cylinder to reach the read-write head*. For an IBM 3380, which revolves at 3600 RPM, a complete revolution takes 16.8 ms. For all practical purposes, one-half of the maximum rotational delay is used to account for the I/O rotational latency. In this particular case, one-half of 16.8 ms is 8.4 ms. For an IBM 3380, av-

---

[1] One millisecond (ms) is one-thousandth of a second.

IBM device*	Max. seek time, ms	Avg. seek time, ms ①	Seek time between adjacent cylinders, ms	Maximum rotational delay, ms	Average rotational delay, ms ②	Data transfer for 4K CI, ms ③	Total of average delays, ms (1+2+3)
3310†	46	27	9	19.1	9.6	4.0	40.6
3330	55	30	10	16.8	8.4	5.0	43.4
3350	50	25	10	16.8	8.4	3.4	36.7
3370†	40	20	5	20.2	10.1	2.2	32.3
3375	38	19	4	20.2	10.1	2.2	31.3
3380 (SD)	30	16	3	16.8	8.4	1.3	25.7
3380 (DD)	31	17	3	16.8	8.4	1.3	26.7
9335†	37	18	4.5	16.6	8.3	1.9	28.2
9332†	50	25	5	19.2	9.6	2.1	36.7

*SD = single-density; DD = double-density.
†IBM 3310, IBM 3370, IBM 9335 and IBM 9332 are fixed block architecture devices used for DOS/VSE environment only.

Figure 6.3 Seek time delay, rotational delay and data transfer delays for some IBM DASDs.

erage seek time delay and average rotational delay account for a total of 24.4 ms (16 ms + 8.4 ms).

6.2.3 Data Transfer Delay

Once a seek and rotational positioning have been successful, the data must be transferred to or from the DASD over the channel. This causes a data transfer delay. The string of DASDs is usually attached to block multiplexer channels, which have data transfer speeds of 2 or 3 megabytes per second (MBS). An IBM 3380 is attached to a 3-MBS channel. In our example, if a 4096-byte CI is transferred to (or from) an IBM 3380 over a 3-MBS channel, the transfer delay will be 1.3 ms.

Therefore, *on an average,* seek time, rotational, and data transfer delays per I/O can add up to a total of 25.7 ms for a single-density IBM 3380. Figure 6.3 gives such delays for other commonly used DASDs assuming that the CI size is 4096 bytes.

6.2.4 Reducing the Delays

The major components of an I/O consist of seek time delay, rotational delay, and data transfer delay. We have considered the averages of these

6.2 I/O DELAYS

IBM DASD	Number of cylinders under fixed heads
2305	All cylinders
3310*	None
3330	None
3344	2 (optional)
3348, Model 70	5 (optional)
3350, Model B2F	2 (optional)
3370*	None
3375	None
3380 (SD)	None
3380 (DD)	None
9332†	None
9335†	None

*IBM 3310 and IBM 3370 are FBA devices supported in DOS/VSE only.
†IBM 9332 and IBM 9335 are FBA devices supported for IBM 9370 seriers of computers for DOS/VSE only.

Figure 6.4 DASDs with fixed-head cylinders.

delays to compute total I/O time. In order to reduce these delays, you have to beat the law of averages.

- Two parallel processed data sets can be placed next to each other on a DASD. This will reduce the seek time because the read-write arm will have to travel a shorter distance. We will see later that *by using the IMBED option, we can reduce the seek time from the sequence set to the data component to zero.*
- *Using the IMBED and REPLICATE option can reduce the rotational delay for the sequence and index sets.* For an IBM 3380, depending upon the index CI size, the delay can be anywhere from 0.4 to 1.4 ms instead of an average of 8.4 ms.
- Channel transfer delay cannot be reduced or eliminated.

As we proceed, these techniques will be analyzed in more detail.

6.2.5 Fixed-Head Cylinders

A few cylinders on *some* DASDs are designated as fixed-head cylinders. Fixed-head cylinders have fixed read-write heads. When an I/O request is made for data residing on a fixed-head cylinder, the seek time is zero because the read-write heads do not move. The only delays incurred are the rotational delay and the data transfer delay. Figure 6.4 lists some IBM DASDs with fixed-head cylinders.

IBM DASD*	Total capacity, megabytes	Cylinders per disk pack	Tracks per cylinder	Bytes per track
3350	317	555	30	19,254
3370	286	750	12	31,744
3375	410	959	12	36,000
3380 (SD)	630	885	15	47,968
3380 (DD)	1260	1770	15	47,968
9335	412	1963	6	36,352
9332	184	1349	4	37,888

*SD = single-density; DD = double-density.

Figure 6.5 Storage capacity of IBM DASDs.

Since fixed-head cylinders are efficient but few in number, their use should be determined with great care. A highly active VSAM or ICF catalog could be considered a candidate for their use. A small but heavily used data set could also be allocated to that space. *One of the best uses of fixed-head cylinders is for index components of KSDS files for HIDAM, HISAM, and secondary indexes of an IMS data base.* All the IMS/DB buffers under CICS are part of a Local Shared Resource (LSR) pool. If they are flushed out, they can be read back with the least delay if they are on fixed-head cylinders.

Keep in mind that IBM 3380 disk packs do not have fixed-head cylinders. In doing a conversion from a fixed-head cylinder DASD to an IBM 3380, alternative techniques must be used to compensate for the loss of performance.

6.3 DASD STORAGE CAPACITY

Figure 6.5 presents data on the storage capacity of some IBM DASDs.

6.4 CONTROL INTERVALS, PHYSICAL BLOCKS, AND LOGICAL RECORDS

6.4.1 Physical Block Size

Although it is common knowledge that a physical sequential (PS) data set consists of many physical blocks, it is a little-known fact that a VSAM data set also consists of physical blocks. In a PS data set, the block size can be anywhere from 9 bytes to 32,768 bytes long. In an MVS/VSAM data set, a block can be one of only four sizes: 512, 1024, 2048, or 4096 bytes.

How does a block fit into the CI architecture? A CI may consist of *one or many* physical blocks. Block size is a function of the CI size of the

6.4 CONTROL INTERVALS, PHYSICAL BLOCKS, AND LOGICAL RECORDS

If the CI size is:	The physical block size is:
4K, 8K, 12K, 16K, 20K, 24K, 28K, or 32K	4K
2K, 6K, 10K, 14K, 18K, 22K, 26K, or 30K	2K
1K, 3K, 5K, or 7K	1K
½K, 1½K, 2½K, 3½K, 4½K, 5½K, 6½K, or 7½K	½K

Figure 6.6 CI sizes and physical block sizes.

DASD	IBG for each physical record, bytes
IBM 3330	135
IBM 3350	185
IBM 3375	384
IBM 3380	512

Figure 6.7 Interblock gaps for few IBM DASDs.

data set. Once you determine the CI size, VSAM determines the block size by successively dividing the CI size by 4096, 2048, 1024, and 512 in that order. Whichever number divides into the CI size first without leaving a remainder becomes the block size. Figure 6.6 lists CI sizes and the corresponding physical block sizes.

Since the CI size for an index component can only be ½K, 1K, 2K, or 4K, the index CI consists of only one block.

For DOS/VSE Only The block size for count key data (CKD) devices in DOS/VSE can be any multiple of ½K from ½K to 8K.

6.4.2 Interblock Gaps

If you have ever noticed DASD space mysteriously disappearing without any visible cause, the culprit might be an interblock gap (IBG). An IBG is a header that precedes *every* physical block, and its size depends upon the device being used. Figure 6.7 lists the IBGs for a few IBM DASDs.

The relationships among CIs, physical blocks, and IBGs, can be summarized as follows:

- A CI, depending upon its size, may consist of one or many physical blocks.
- Each physical block within the CI must be preceded by an IBG.

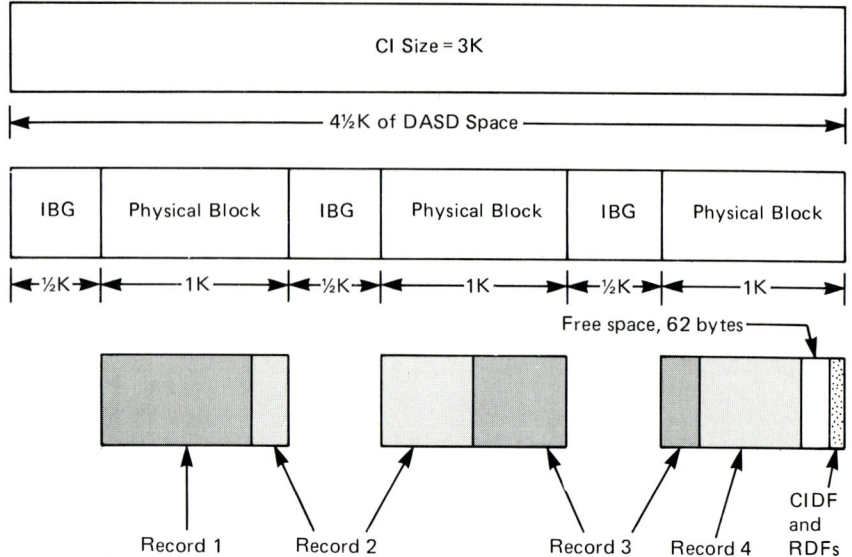

Figure 6.8 Relationship between CI size, physical records, IBGs and logical records for an IBM 3380 for a CI size of 3072 bytes and, logical record length of 750 bytes.

- Therefore, the space occupied by a CI on a DASD consists of IBGs and physical blocks; there will be as many IBGs as there are physical blocks.
- When a CI is read into buffers, the IBGs are not transmitted.

The application program is unaware of the existence of IBGs and physical blocks. Figure 6.8 is a diagram of the relationship of a CI, physical blocks, IBGs, and logical records, assuming that the CI size is 3K, each record is 750 bytes long, and the device is an IBM 3380. This shows that a CI size of 3K occupies, in fact, 4½K of DASD space on an IBM 3380.

Here are a few more examples:

- An 8K CI will have two physical blocks of 4K and two IBGs of ½K each.

  Total DASD space used = 9K

- A 7K CI will have seven physical blocks of 1K and seven IBGs of ½K each.

  Total DASD space used = 10.5K

- A 6K CI will have three physical blocks of 2K and three IBGs of ½K each.

  Total DASD space used = 7.5K

6.4 CONTROL INTERVALS, PHYSICAL BLOCKS, AND LOGICAL RECORDS

Physical block size	Effective DASD utilization, %
4K	88.8
2K	80.0
1K	66.6
½K	50.0

Figure 6.9 Relationship between physical block sizes and effective DASD space utilization for an IBM 3380.

- A 7½K CI will have 15 physical blocks of ½K and 15 IBGs of ½K each.

Total DASD space used = 15K

We can see that as the physical block size is reduced, the effective utilization of a DASD is also reduced. Figure 6.9 gives the effective DASD space utilization for an IBM 3380 for block sizes of ½K to 4K.

6.4.3 Conserving DASD Space

If DASD space conservation is one of your goals, you should strive to keep the physical block size of 4K, especially for an IBM 3380. The main reasons can be summarized as follows:

- A small block size will reduce the effective DASD space utilization. A block size of ½K is the worst choice, because it results in a 50% waste of space due to IBGs.
- Small block sizes also increase the data transfer time to and from the buffers, because the read-write head does not transfer any application-specific data when the IBGs are gliding past it.

We should not draw any drastic conclusions regarding small CI sizes. Sometimes a small CI size has to be chosen because of record size considerations. A small CI size may also be the right choice for installations having virtual storage constraint problems. We will be in a better position to make judgments as we proceed.

chapter 7

Cache DASD Controllers

Since computers have come of age, there have been frequent and dramatic improvements in CPU speed, which is measured in millions of instructions per second (MIPS). There has been steady growth in processor MIPS—a compounded annual rate of more than 40%. Improvements in the I/O speed of DASDs has not been able to keep pace, with the result that a very powerful and expensive resource (the CPU) is often poorly utilized. The data in Fig. 5.6 shows that service time for a random I/O on an IBM 3330 is 43.4 ms, while for an IBM 3880 it is 25.7 ms. Although this represents about a 40% improvement, it is insignificant compared to processor speeds. Since the introduction of *Cache DASD controllers,* performance problems have been alleviated to some extent.

7.1 WHAT IS CACHE?

A *cache* can be roughly defined as *a high-speed buffer between a fast device and a slow device.* Caching (pronounced cashing) is not a totally new concept. A CPU is a fast device, while main memory is relatively slow. If the CPU has to fetch the next sequential instruction to be executed from main memory, it will be a slower process than if it could fetch the same instruction from its high-speed cache buffers. A CPU cycle is much faster than a memory access cycle. The relationship of a CPU, the CPU cache, and the main memory of a system is diagramed in Fig. 7.1.

7.1 WHAT IS CACHE?

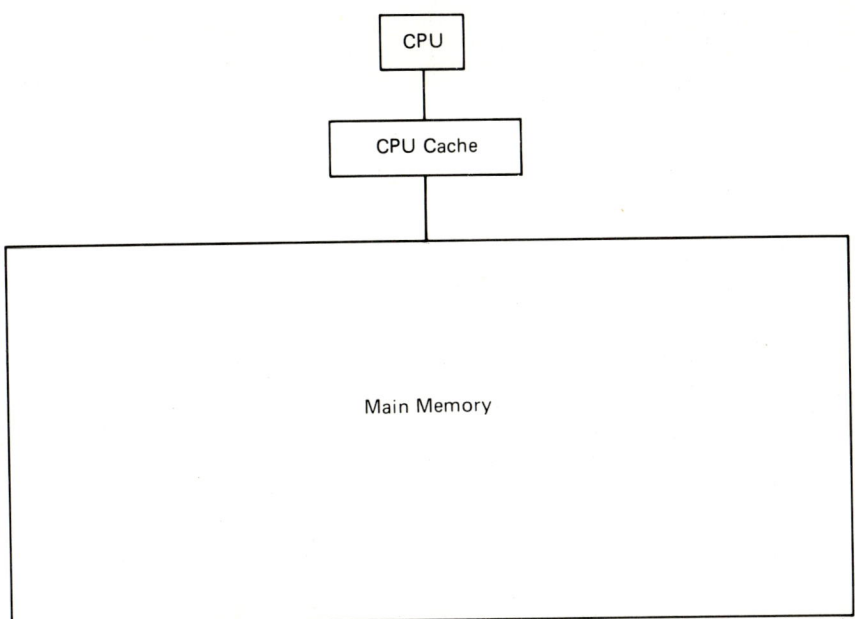

Figure 7.1 Relationship between a CPU, CPU cache, and main memory.

If the CPU does not find the next instruction to be executed in its own cache, it has to follow the slower process of executing in main memory. So an intelligent algorithm is needed to anticipate the CPU's action and transfer the appropriate set of instructions to its cache. A similar principle has been used in the design architecture of cache DASD control units. In a noncached DASD controller, when a program issues an I/O request for a record, the record must be fetched from the DASD. This entails delays due to seek time, rotation, and data transfer. In contrast, a *cache DASD controller* performs a look-aside to its cache buffers to see if it can find the record there. If successful, it transfers the record directly from the cache buffer to the main storage through the channel. The only delay for the I/O is the data transfer delay over the channel. I/O with a cache buffer is a significantly faster operation than I/O without a cache.

7.1.1 Configuration of a Cache DASD Controller

A cache DASD controller has the configuration illustrated in Fig. 7.2. It has the same functions as a noncached controller except that it has buffers to hold data. Figure 7.3 presents some information about IBM cache controllers.

A cache DASD controller consists of two *storage directors*, each of which is a microprocessor that controls a set of DASDs independently of the other. Both storage directors have access to the cache buffers resident

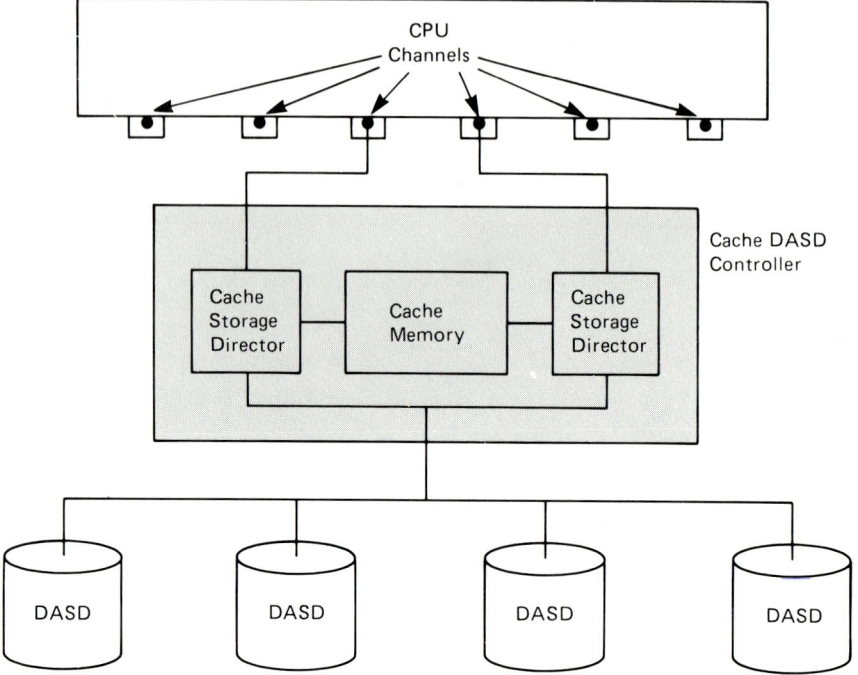

Figure 7.2 Relationship of channels, cache DASD controller, and DASDs.

Cache DASD control unit	Cache buffer size	Use of cache buffer
IBM 3880 Model 11	4 and 8 MB	Page data sets
IBM 3880 Model 13	4 and 8 MB	User data sets
IBM 3880 Model 21	8, 16, 32, 48, and 64 MB	Page data sets
IBM 3880 Model 23	8, 16, 32, 48, and 64 MB	User data sets

Figure 7.3 Characteristics of IBM cache DASD control units.

in the controller (think of it as the controller's memory). The amount of cache memory available depends on the model of DASD controller (see Fig. 7.3).

Cache memory has two components: a directory, which the storage directors scan to find out if the record requested by an application is already in the cache, and the rest of the cache, which is used for the storage of records. A cache directory is a relatively small entity and takes up an insignificant amount of space. In this chapter, we will only talk about the Model 13 and Model 23 control units because Models 11 and 21, although used for high-speed paging, are not within the realm of VSAM fine tuning.

7.1 WHAT IS CACHE?

It is worthwhile mentioning that IBM 3880 Model 21 requires IBM 3350 DASDs, while IBM 3880 Model 23 does not support them. Also, IBM 3880 Model 13 supports standard models of IBM 3380, while IBM 3880 Model 23 supports both standard and extended models. The extended models are single-density (AD4 and BD4; 630 MB per access mechanism) and double-density (AE4 and BE4; 1260 MB per access mechanism).

Cache memory deals with its storage in multiples of *full track sizes only*. One track of an IBM 3380 has 47,968 bytes. Cache can hold 176 such tracks for every 8 MB of memory. A full-blown IBM 3880 Model 23 with 64 MB of memory can hold 1408 tracks of an IBM 3380.

7.1.2 I/O with a Cache DASD Controller

Input Request In a cache configuration, a typical I/O occurs as follows: An input I/O request comes from an application. A channel command word (CCW) is passed to a channel, which directs the cache DASD controller to perform the I/O. The storage director, controlling its own set of DASDs, looks at the cache directory to determine if the track containing that record is already in the cache. If so, it does not go to the DASD; it transfers the record directly through the channel to main memory. In this case, the I/O service time consists of a data transfer delay only. A 4K control interval takes about 1.3 ms to be transferred over a 3 MB/second channel. The overhead of a cache directory search is negligible. Thus, we can see that a cache-serviced DASD can sustain a much higher I/O rate before showing degradation. Finding the track in cache for an input request is called a *read-hit*.

If the storage director does not find the required track in its cache buffers, it performs the following two operations *in parallel*:

1. It reads the requested record and transfers it to main memory through the channel. This is subject to seek delay and rotational delay, as usual.
2. It transfers the entire track to the cache buffers with the record. If there is no free slot available in the cache memory, it flushes out a slot based on a Least Recently Used (LRU) algorithm. The cache directory is updated to record the change. Any future input request involving the same track will be met from the cache buffers until that track is also flushed out on the basis of the LRU algorithm. A heavily used track will tend to stay in cache.

Reading a record from DASD instead of finding it in the cache is called a *read-miss*. A high read-hit ratio reflects effective use of cache.

Output Request Cache does not handle an output request in the same way as it handles an input request. Since cache is a volatile memory (it can disappear with a power failure), an update to a record in a cached track involves a simultaneous update to the DASD record. This operation is synchronous, meaning that your application does not receive control until the DASD update is completed.

If the update request does not find the track in cache, it does not bother to read it into cache. The update operation is performed *as if cache did not exist*. The effective utilization of cache requires that the application have a high read/write ratio, since it is only the input requests that realize the benefits of cache.

Keep in mind that the use of cache *does not* require any application changes. Different cache management modes for different requirements are controlled through Access Method Services (AMS) commands.

7.2 CACHE MANAGEMENT MODES

Various applications have the need to access and process data in a variety of ways. Most on-line (CICS/VS or IMS/DC) applications access data randomly. On-line sequential searches, if any, are brief. Batch application programs may perform file updates in either sequential or random modes. File backups and file restores are usually done in sequential mode. If data is being accessed sequentially, you may not need to access recently read logical records from different control intervals again. It is almost impossible to come up with a universal algorithm to manage cache buffers that will accommodate all these situations.

Managing cache buffers is a function of the application system that is about to issue an I/O to a DASD. AMS commands help you control this function. Some of the system-level IBM utilities make use of cache buffer management through the use of a new channel command word called DEFINE EXTENT CCW.

There are five cache management modes:

- *Bypass cache mode:* Cache is not used at all in this mode. Data is retrieved directly from the DASD. The majority of applications should issue I/O requests without the use of cache, because cache memory is a limited resource. IBM's Data Facility Data Set Services (DF/DSS) uses bypass cache mode for its dump and restore functions.
- *Normal cache mode:* In this mode, the storage director checks the cache directory to see if the DASD track is already cache-resident. If so, it does not do any I/O but passes data on to the channel directly from the cache. If the track is not resident in cache (referred to as a read-miss), the required application data is read from the DASD, and simultaneously the entire track containing that data is transferred to the cache. If the cache does not have a free slot in which to place the track, it invalidates another track on the basis of an LRU algorithm. In the future, all I/O requests referencing that

track will be satisfied from the cache until the LRU algorithm logic invalidates that track. Each request to a cache-resident track updates the time stamp for that slot. It is on the basis of this time stamp that the LRU logic marks track slots eligible for invalidation and replacement. Frequently accessed data will tend to keep that track in the cache buffers.

- *Inhibit cache loading mode:* On a read-hit, data is accessed from the cache. On a read-miss, the data is accessed from the DASD, but in this mode the track containing the data is *not* transferred to cache.
- *Bound track mode:* In this mode, the BINDDATA command of Access Method Services binds tracks in cache so that the LRU logic will ignore them as it looks for candidate slots for invalidation. As we will see later, this is an excellent mode for cache-fixing (making cache-resident) the sequence set records of the index component of a response-time-sensitive, highly active KSDS. When not needed, these tracks can be unbound with the TERMINATE option of the BINDDATA command.
- *Sequential access mode:* The sequential access mode uses only two track buffers in the cache. It does a pretransfer of tracks into these buffers in alternating sequence. When the application needs access to these tracks, they get transferred directly from the cache. As soon as the track has been transferred to the application buffers in the host, it is marked as an invalid slot so that the next DASD track can replace it. QSAM and BSAM access methods have the ability to use this mode in DEFINE EXTENT CCW. VSAM uses this mode for sequential access to an ESDS. The SORT/MERGE product of IBM also uses sequential access mode for SORTIN and SORTOUT.

The two AMS commands SETCACHE and BINDDATA are used to turn modes on or off and are fully controlled by the user. The LISTDATA command is used to get statistics about cache utilization and helps in fine tuning the use of cache controllers. Some IBM utilities use DEFINE EXTENT CCW to effectively control cache to their advantage, but it is transparent to the user.

7.3 AMS COMMANDS USED WITH CACHE

7.3.1 SETCACHE

SETCACHE is an AMS command that helps to make a device or a subsystem eligible for or disable it from the use of cache.

We already know that a mainframe has many channels. A channel may have may devices (DASD volumes) attached to it through DASD control units. A DASD control unit may also be connected to many channels to facilitate multiple data paths and increase its availability. For this

(a)

```
//SETCACHE  JOB  (ACCTINFO),'JAY RANADE',
//STEP1     EXEC PGM=IDCAMS
//ABC       DD   UNIT=3380,VOL=SER=VSAM01,DISP=SHR
//SYSPRINT  DD   SYSOUT=A
//SYSIN     DD   *
            SETCACHE                           -
            FILE(ABC)                          -
            DEVICE                             -
            ON
/*
//
```

(b)

```
//SETCACHE  JOB  (ACCTINFO),'JAY RANADE',
//STEP1     EXEC PGM=IDCAMS
//SYSPRINT  DD   SYSOUT=A
//SYSIN     DD   *
            SETCACHE                           -
            VOLUME(VSAM01)                     -
            UNIT(3380)                         -
            DEVICE                             -
            ON
/*
//
```

Figure 7.4 (a) and (b) JCL to enable a device for the use of cache. Both JCL listings produce *identical* end results.

discussion, we will use the word *device* to identify a volume serial (volser) number. A subsystem may consist of many devices attached to the DASD control unit.

The JCL in Fig. 7.4 may be used to enable a device for the use of cache. Note that both the JCL listings of Fig. 7.4 perform *exactly* the same job. If you choose not to use the FILE parameter, the UNIT and VOLUME information must be provided in the command itself (Fig. 7.4b). It is a matter of personal preference as to which way you choose to code. The parameters are self-explanatory.

You might want to enable one or more devices for cache before bringing up an on-line system (CICS/VS or IMS/DC). To make effective utilization of this limited resource, only those devices having very high I/O activity should be considered eligible. For a random access data set, the index set of the index component of a KSDS should be kept in the appli-

7.3 AMS COMMANDS USED WITH CACHE

cation buffers in the host. Cache should not be considered a substitute for the index set of a KSDS. Since the index set control intervals are probably the most heavily used area of a KSDS, better results can be achieved if they are in the host buffers. Transferring such CIs from cache takes a few milliseconds, while host buffers are searched in microseconds. The technique of putting index set records in core is discussed in Chaps. 15 and 16.

The following JCL will enable cache for an entire subsystem.

```
SETCACHE              -
    VOLUME(VSAM01)    -
    UNIT(3380)        -
    SUBSYSTEM         -
    ON
```

Volume VSAM01 specifies just one device in the entire subsystem. Note that the only syntax difference between this JCL and those in Fig. 7.4 is the use of the keyword SUBSYSTEM in place of DEVICE.

Once you have used cache to accomplish your purpose and applications no longer require its use for a particular device, the following JCL may be used to disable cache for that device:

```
SETCACHE              -
    VOLUME(VSAM01)    -
    UNIT(3380)        -
    DEVICE            -
    OFF
```

If the intent is to disable cache for the entire subsystem, the keyword DEVICE may be replaced with SUBSYSTEM. Note that disabling cache does not impede access to the DASD.

When cache is enabled for a particular device or subsystem, *normal cache mode* (Section 7.2) is used to promote or invalidate cache buffers.

7.3.2 BINDDATA

Cache memory deals with data at the whole track level only. You cannot put only one part of the track (e.g., control interval) into cache. Cache treats all the tracks belonging to a device or subsystem made eligible through the SETCACHE command equally. If a track contains heavily accessed data, that track tends to stay in cache by virtue of the LRU algorithm.

There may be times when certain tracks require preferential treatment. These tracks can be made immune to the LRU algorithm and become cache-eligible through the BINDDATA command. This places cache in the bound track mode discussed in section 7.2. This mode is used for applications that are highly sensitive to response time.

In many installations, some files are accessed by almost all on-line applications. These files may contain, for example, data security and authorization information that must be accessed to make a user eligible for certain transactions and data. Since all applications may funnel through a security routine, response time may degrade due to heavy I/O activity. If the data set is a KSDS, the following technique may be used to reduce I/O's:

1. Place the index set CIs in core through the proper use of the BUFNI parameter. BUFNI is one of the parameters in the DFHFCT macro for File Control Table in CICS/VS. This will be discussed in detail in Chap. 16.
2. Bind the sequence set CIs by using the BINDDATA command. Remember that sequence set CIs cannot *normally* be put into core by increasing the index buffers (i.e., using BUFNI).[1] Binding them in cache will eliminate I/O's to the sequence set CIs.

Using this technique, each retrieval request to the KSDS will involve only one I/O to the data component and none to the index component. If you use only step 1, each retrieval request will cause two I/O's—one to the sequence set and one to the data component.

Examples Consider the following command:

```
BINDDATA                    -
   ESTABLISH                -
   VOLUME(VSAM01)           -
   UNIT(3380)               -
   LOWCCHH(00030002)        -
   HIGHCCHH(00030004)       -
   DEVICE
```

The values of the LOWCCHH and HIGHCCHH are eight-digit hexadecimal numbers. LOWCCHH represents the lower bounds and HIGHCCHH the upper bounds of a cylinder-track address, where the first four digits are the hexadecimal number of the cylinder and the last four the hex address of the track. All tracks between these addresses are bound after the execution of the command. Remember that the first cylinder of a device is the zeroth cylinder, and the first track of a cylinder is

---

[1]Sequence set CIs can, in fact, be placed into core by using the LSR buffer pool. However, LSR pool buffers are governed by the LRU algorithm. More on this in Chap. 17.

7.3 AMS COMMANDS USED WITH CACHE

the zeroth track. For an IBM 3380, the tracks on each cylinder are addressed from hex 0000 to hex 000E (i.e., 0 to 14). Similarly, the cylinders of a single-density IBM 3380 are addressed from hex 0000 to hex 0374 and those of a double-density 3380 from hex 0000 to hex 06EA. This corresponds to a capacity of 885 cylinders for single density and 1770 cylinders for double density.

In the given example, tracks 2, 3 and 4 of cylinder 3 are bound in cache after the successful execution of the command.

After the application needing access to the bound tracks has completed its processing, you may wish to free the slots in cache for other applications. The following command will release the tracks and make them eligible for normal cache mode:

```
BINDDATA                   -
    TERMINATE              -
    VOLUME(VSAM01)         -
    UNIT(3380)             -
    LOWCCHH(00030002)      -
    HIGHCCHH(00030004)     -
    DEVICE
```

Note that the keyword ESTABLISH has been replaced with TERMINATE. If you were to substitute the keyword DEVICE with SUBSYSTEM, all bound tracks for that DASD subsystem would be unbound.

How to Find CCHH   Listings produced by the execution of LISTCAT command provide the CCHH information for some of the key components and the extents of a data set. Let's look at the listing in Fig. 7.5. It is a listing for a KSDS defined with the NOIMBED and NOREPLICATE parameters. The data and index components are defined on VOL001. The physical extents of the index component are highlighted and their values are

```
LOW-CCHH X'00000004'
HIGH-CCHH X'00000004'
```

It means that the index component records (or CIs) are on the 4th track of the zeroth cylinder.

NOREPLICATE and NOIMBED   Since cache deals with data at the track level only, it is important to use techniques that will pack cache-eligible logically related data into as few tracks as possible. To bind the sequence set records of an index component, we *must use* the NOREPLICATE and NOIMBED parameters of DEFINE CLUSTER or DEFINE AIX. However, since these are the default options, you may choose to leave them

```
LISTCAT ENT(TEST.KSDS2.CLUSTER) ALL
CLUSTER ------- TEST.KSDS2.CLUSTER
     IN-CAT --- SYS1.ICFUCAT.RANADE
     HISTORY
       OWNER-IDENT-----(NULL)          CREATION--------87.082
       RELEASE---------------2         EXPIRATION------00.000
     PROTECTION-PSWD-----(NULL)        RACF-----------------(NO)
     ASSOCIATIONS
       DATA-----TEST.KSDS2.DATA
       INDEX----TEST.KSDS2.INDEX

DATA ------- TEST.KSDS2.DATA
     IN-CAT --- SYS1.ICFUCAT.RANADE
     HISTORY
       OWNER-IDENT-----(NULL)          CREATION--------87.082
       RELEASE---------------2         EXPIRATION------00.000
     PROTECTION-PSWD-----(NULL)        RACF-----------------(NO)
     ASSOCIATIONS
       CLUSTER--TEST.KSDS2.CLUSTER
     ATTRIBUTES
       KEYLEN----------------17        AVGLRECL--------------80        BUFSPACE-----------5120
       RKP-------------------0         MAXLRECL--------------80        EXCPEXIT---------(NULL)
       SHROPTNS(1,3)   RECOVERY   UNIQUE          NOERASE              INDEXED        NOWRITECHK
       UNORDERED       NOREUSE    NONSPANNED
     STATISTICS
       REC-TOTAL---------15000         SPLITS-CI-------------0         EXCPS---------------222
       REC-DELETED-----------0         SPLITS-CA-------------0         EXTENTS---------------1
       REC-INSERTED----------0         FREESPACE-%CI---------0         SYSTEM-TIMESTAMP:
       REC-UPDATED-----------0         FREESPACE-%CA---------0                 X'9C7646EC0016F401'
       REC-RETRIEVED---------0         FREESPC-BYTES----604160
     ALLOCATION
```

CISIZE----------512
CI/CA-----------460
NOIMBED   NOREPLICAT

```
      SPACE-TYPE------------TRACK              HI-ALLOC-RBA------1884160
      SPACE-PRI---------------80               HI-USED-RBA-------1648640
      SPACE-SEC---------------80
   VOLUME
      VOLSER-------------X'301C0C01
      DEVTYPE------------X'3010200C'           PHYREC-SIZE----------512    EXTENT-NUMBER--------1
      VOLFLAG--------------PRIME               PHYRECS/TRK-----------46    EXTENT-TYPE-------X'40'
      EXTENTS:                                 TRACKS/CA-------------10
      LOW-CCHH-------X'00C6000C'               LOW-RBA----------------0
      HIGH-CCHH------X'00C8000C4'              HIGH-RBA--------1884159                TRACKS--------------80

INDEX ------- TEST.KSDS2.INDEX
   IN-CAT ---- SYS1.ICFUCAT.RANADE
   HISTORY
      OWNER-IDENT--------(NULL)                CREATION----------87.082
      RELEASE-----------------2                EXPIRATION--------00.000
   PROTECTION-PSWD-------(NULL)                RACF----------------(NO)
   ASSOCIATIONS
      CLUSTER----TEST.KSDS2.CLUSTER
   ATTRIBUTES
      KEYLEN----------------17                 AVGLRECL--------------0     CISIZE------------4096
      RKP--------------------0                 MAXLRECL-----------4089     CICA/CI----UNORDERED
      SHROPTNS(1,3)    RECOVERY                UNIQUE          NOERASE     NOREPLICAT    NOIMBED
      NOREUSE
   STATISTICS                                                              INDEX:
      REC-TOTAL-------------11                 SPLITS-CI-------------0     LEVELS/SECT----------2
      REC-DELETED-----------0                  SPLITS-CA-------------0     ENTRIES/SECT---------21
      REC-INSERTED----------0                  FREESPACE-%CI---------0     SEQ-SET-RBA----------0
      REC-UPDATED-----------0                  FREESPACE-%CA---------0     HI-LEVEL-RBA------8192
      REC-RETRIEVED--------32                  FREESPC-BYTES--4294963200
                                               EXCPS-----------------76
                                               EXTENTS---------------1
                                               SYSTEM-TIMESTAMP:
                                                X'9C7646EC0015F401'
   ALLOCATION
      SPACE-TYPE---------TRACK                 HI-ALLOC-RBA------40960
      SPACE-PRI-------------10                 HI-USED-RBA-------32768
      SPACE-SEC--------------0
   VOLUME
      VOLSER-------------X'301C0C01
      DEVTYPE------------X'3010200C'           PHYREC-SIZE---------4096    EXTENT-NUMBER--------1
      VOLFLAG--------------PRIME               PHYRECS/TRK----------10     EXTENT-TYPE------X'00'
      EXTENTS:                                 TRACKS/CA-------------1
      LOW-CCHH-------X'000C0004'               LOW-RBA----------------0
      HIGH-CCHH------X'000C0004'               HIGH-RBA----------40959               TRACKS---------------1
```

Figure 7.5 A data set listing for a KSDS generated by the execution of the LISTCAT command.

out of your DEFINE. Using the example in Fig. 7.5, the following command will bind the index component in cache.

```
BINDDATA                            -
    ESTABLISH                       -
    VOLUME(VSAM01)                  -
    UNIT(3380)                      -
    LOWCCHH(00000004)               -
    HIGHCCHH(00000004)              -
    DEVICE
```

REUSE Parameter KSDS files are usually deleted, reallocated, and loaded at regular intervals for the purpose of reorganization. Reallocation of data sets may cause their index component to be placed at a physically different location than previously. If that happens, you will have to change the values of LOWCCHH and HIGHCCHH to provide the new track locations. This is an operational nightmare, requiring human involvement in producing new data set listings and modifying the CCHH values after each KSDS reorganization. This problem can be alleviated by using the REUSE parameter when you allocate a KSDS (or an alternate index) for the first time. A REUSEable data set does not have to be deleted or redefined. Opening the data set as follows will logically delete the previous records and treat the file as newly defined:

- Use the REUSE option with the REPRO command.
- In Cobol, open the file as OUTPUT with ACCESS MODE IS SEQUENTIAL.
- In Assembler, define the ACB macro with MACRF=RST. Thus, when the file is opened, the RST option will reset the high used RBA (HURBA) to zero, logically deleting all the records.

7.3.3 LISTDATA

The LISTDATA command of Access Method Services provides a facility for printing cache-related counters, status, and statistics maintained within the subsystem. It aids a performance analyst in determining whether the cache is being used and whether any changes are required to use it more effectively. This command does not change or affect any subsystem usage characteristics. Consider the command

```
LISTDATA                            -
    COUNTS                          -
    VOLUME(VSAM01)                  -
    UNIT(3380)                      -
    DEVICE                          -
    LEGEND
```

7.4 CACHE RATIOS

The COUNTS parameter will print the various counters accumulated within the subsystem. VOLUME and UNIT specify the device and the device type, respectively. When first using LISTDATA, you may want to use the LEGEND option. This will display the meanings of various headings and abbreviations used in producing the listings. Once you feel comfortable in reading the report, you can omit this parameter. Figure 7.6 provides a sample listing produced by the execution of the LISTDATA command shown above. Figure 7.7 is a legend listing produced by the use of the LEGEND parameter in the LISTDATA command.

STATUS Listing The *status* of a cache may be determined by using the following command:

```
LISTDATA              -
    STATUS            -
    SUBSYSTEM         -
    VOLUME(VSAM01)    -
    UNIT(3380)        -
    LEGEND
```

Execution of this command will produce a listing that gives the status of the subsystem in which VSAM01 is a device. LEGEND will generate a listing describing the various headings and abbreviations. Figure 7.8 shows a sample listing produced by the STATUS parameter of this command.

7.4 CACHE RATIOS

7.4.1 Read/Write Ratio

The read/write ratio may be defined as follows:

$$\text{Read/write ratio} = \frac{\text{read operations}}{\text{write operations}}$$

Cache is more effective for read operations than for write operations. A write operation has additional overhead with cache because the record has to be updated in cache as well as on the DASD. For effective cache use, the read/write ratio should be greater than 2/1. Data sets may be placed on different DASDs so that cache-eligible DASDs have a high read/write ratio.

7.4.2 Read-Hit Ratio

The read-hit ratio may be defined as follows:

$$\text{Read-hit ratio} = \frac{\text{number of reads where record is found in cache}}{\text{total number of read requests}}$$

```
IDCAMS SYSTEM SERVICES                      338C SUBSYSTEM COUNTERS REPORT
VOLUME VSAM01  DEVICE ID X'60'
CHANNEL COMMAND CHAINS          CSD ID

                                             SEARCH/READ REQUESTS         WRITE CACHING REQUESTS
                                            TOTAL     NO DASD ACCESS       TOTAL     NO DASD READS
    NORMAL CACHING              X'12'       61137          46909           44607         35685
                                X'13'       51393          38544           34026         27219

    SEQUENTIAL                  X'12'       46116           3781           29529          N/A
                                X'13'       47439           3795           23943          N/A

    INHIBIT CACHE LOADING       CSD ID     REQUESTS
                                X'12'       44904
                                X'13'       45543

    REQUESTS TO BOUND TRACKS    CSD ID    SEARCHES/READS    WRITES
                                X'12'        19542           5448
                                X'13'        19848           4941

DASD TC CACHE TRANSFERS         CSD ID    INTERNAL COMMAND CHAINS
                                X'12'            21339
                                X'13'            19767

CONTROL UNIT UTILIZATION        CSD ID                     BYTES                              BYTES
    DUE TO DATA TRANSFER                CACHE TO CHANNEL    DASD TO CHANNEL       CACHE TO DASD    DASD TO CACHE
                                X'12'      26813250           17108424              10954437         20255481
                                X'13'      48011184           17351883              11601444         41682798
```

Figure 7.6 A sample listing produced by using the COUNTS parameter in the LISTDATA command.

```
IDCAMS SYSTEM SERVICES          LEGEND          3380 SUBSYSTEM COUNTERS LEGEND

VOLUME ID                    VOLUME SERIAL NUMBER FOR WHICH THE DATA IS GATHERED
DEVICE ID                    DEVICE IDENTIFICATION ID.  DATA IS GATHERED FOR BOTH CSD'S ATTACHED TO A DEVICE
CSD ID                       CACHE STORAGE DIRECTOR ID.

CHANNEL COMMAND CHAINS       A CCW CHAIN WHICH CONTAINS AT LEAST ONE SEARCH, READ OR WRITE
  NORMAL CACHING             CCW CHAINS WHICH DO NOT INCLUDE A DEFINE EXTENT CCW OR SPECIFY NORMAL CACHE
                             REPLACEMENT WHICH THE DEFINE EXTENT CCW

SEQUENTIAL                   CCW CHAINS WHICH SPECIFY SEQUENTIAL ACCESS IN THE DEFINE EXTENT CCW
  SEARCH/READ REQUESTS       CCW SEARCH/READ CCW CHAINS CONTAINING AT LEAST ONE SEARCH OR READ BUT NO WRITE CCW
  TOTAL                      CCW CHAINS REQUIRING NO DATA TO BE MOVED TO/FROM THE 3380
  NO DASD ACCESS             CCW CHAINS CONTAINING AT LEAST ONE WRITE CCW
  WRITE CACHING              CCW CHAINS NOT REQUIRING DATA MOVEMENT TO THE CACHE FROM THE 3380. THIS DATA IS NOT
  TOTAL                      KEPT FOR SEQUENTIAL
  NO DASD READS

INHIBIT CACHE LOADING        CCW CHAINS WHICH SPECIFY INHIBIT CACHE LOADING IN THE DEFINE EXTENT CCW
REQUESTS TO BOUND TRACKS     CCW CHAINS WHICH SPECIFY A TRACK PREVIOUSLY BOUND BY THE BINDDATA COMMAND
  SEARCH/READS               SEARCH READ REQUESTS WHICH REFERENCE A BOUND TRACK
  WRITES                     WRITE REQUESTS WHICH REFERENCE A BOUND TRACK

DASD TC CACHE TRANSFERS      THE NUMBER OF INTERNAL COMMAND CHAINS WHICH MOVE DATA FROM THE 3380 TO THE CACHE

CONTROL UNIT UTILIZATION     MEASURED IN BYTES TRANSFERRED
CACHE TO CHANNEL             NUMBER OF BYTES TRANSFERRED FROM CACHE TO THE CHANNEL
CSD ORIENTATION WITH DASD DATA
  CACHE TO DASD              NUMBER OF BYTES TRANSFERRED FROM THE 3380 TO THE CHANNEL
                             NUMBER OF BYTES TRANSFERRED FROM CACHE TO 3380. THIS ALSO REPRESENTS CHANNEL TO
                             CACHE
  DASD TO CACHE              NUMBER OF BYTES TRANSFERRED FROM THE 3380 TO THE CACHE
```

Figure 7.7 A sample legend listing explaining the meaning of various headings and abbreviations used in counters report.

```
IDCAMS SYSTEM SERVICES                    3380 SUBSYSTEM STATUS REPORT
CACHING STORAGE DIRECTOR ID               X'12'
DEVICE ID                                 X'60'
IN BYTES
   CONFIGURED SUBSYSTEM STORAGE                         4194304
   AVAILABLE SUBSYSTEM STORAGE                          4189232
   BOUND SUBSYSTEM STORAGE                              0
   OFFLINE SUBSYSTEM STORAGE                            0
OVERALL CACHING STATUS                    ACTIVE
FOR DEVICES
```

Figure 7.8 Sample subsystem status listing produced by the use of the STATUS parameter in the LISTDATA command.

For effective use of cache, 75% of the read requests should be met from cache. So the ratio in the equation should be 3/4 or higher. Again, data sets should be placed on DASDs so that a desirable read-hit ratio can be achieved.

If the read-hit ratio and read/write ratio create a conflict, preference should be given to the read-hit ratio. A higher read-hit ratio will have a more significant effect on response time than a higher read/write ratio.

IBM's Cache Analysis Aid (CAA) can be used to analyze the Generalized Trace Facility (GTF) CCW trace data and produce reports on read-hit ratios and read/write ratios.

7.5 SUMMARY

While we have demonstrated that cache can be very effective, it should be used selectively. Caching the most frequently used data will ensure a high read-hit ratio. Using cache for the sequence set of the index component (using BINDDATA) is a nice way of cutting I/O's in half. However, this feature should be used only for very active data sets.

Excessive use of BINDDATA will reduce cache storage for the normal cache mode, because bound tracks are not governed by the LRU algorithm invalidation process. Expanded memory in the IBM's Sierra Series (IBM 3090 series) is *not* a substitute for Model 13 and 23 cache controllers. (Expanded memory will be discussed in Chap. 8.)

In this chapter, we have considered the use of cache for application VSAM data sets only. In fact, cache may be used for any data set organizations. Some other prime candidates for caching are PROCLIB, ICF catalogs, RACF and HSM control data sets, and the RECON data set for IMS. Further details are beyond the scope of this book, which is limited to VSAM.

chapter 8

Expanded Memory, Mass Storage System, and Solid State Devices

8.1 EXPANDED MEMORY

IBM has provided another level of memory for the users of its Sierra series of computers, which consist of a variety of IBM 3090 computer models. *Expanded memory* is a semiconductor memory that can be used only for paging purposes, is *not* addressable or directly accessible by user applications, and has the same performance characteristics as main memory. Figure 8.1 lists the amount of expanded memory that is supported on various IBM models.

All page faults occurring in the expanded storage are serviced at a memory transfer speed that is extremely fast compared to that of a page being serviced from a DASD. Although it increases throughput considerably, expanded memory *does not directly affect* VSAM processing. It is beneficial to have expanded memory if the system is doing a lot of DASD paging, but there are no tricks or techniques you can use to directly influence VSAM performance.

8.2 MASS STORAGE SYSTEM (MSS)

Mass Storage System is a mass storage facility whose price and performance characteristics fall between those of DASD and tape. Its capacity is equivalent to that of a large tape library. The smallest unit of the storage

CHAPTER 8 / EXPANDED MEMORY, MSS, AND SOLID STATE DEVICES

IBM 3090 model	Maximum configuration, megabytes
Model 150E	128
Model 180E	256
Model 200E	512
Model 300E	512
Model 400E	1024
Model 600E	1024

Figure 8.1 Maximum amounts of expanded memory supported on IBM Sierra Series models.

facility consists of a data cartridge capable of storing 50 megabytes (MB) of data. MSS can have a storage capacity of 472 gigabytes (1 GB = 1000 MB). Data can be organized in any of the traditional storage organizations such as KSDS, ESDS, RRDS, or PS. The cost per megabyte of storage is higher than that of a tape subsystem but lower than that of a DASD system. Figure 8.2 shows the flow of data in an MSS-configured facility.

Data is stored on the Mass Storage Facility in DASD format, and when data is needed by the DASD it is read from the MSS cartridge(s) and moved to the DASD. No operator intervention is required. This movement of data from MSS to DASD is called *staging*. After the data on the DASD is processed by the application and is no longer active, it is transferred back to the MSS; this process is called *destaging*. Staging and destaging occur independently of the application code and are transparent to the end user *except for the delays caused by them*. IBM 3380s have considerably reduced the cost of DASD storage, causing many users to consider reducing their dependence on MSS. Bear in mind that MSS is used for MVS and not for DOS/VSE.

The IBM 3850 Mass Storage System supports IBM 3330 disk storage only. If you are using an IBM 3350 DASD, it must be operating in the 3330 Model 11 compatibility mode. IBM 3380 is *not* supported by MSS.

Two data cartridges, each capable of holding 50 MB of data, are called a mass storage volume (MSV). IBM 3330s, which participate in the MSS configuration, are called *virtual volumes*. One MSS holds 4720 MSVs or 472,000 MB (472 GB) of data. IBM's Hierarchical Storage Manager (HSM) program product supports MSS. HSM software automates backup, recovery, and space-management requirements in an installation.

It is safe to say that MSS is to a DASD what virtual storage is to an operating system. MSS gives a real DASD more virtual storage capability by staging and destaging data on demand. However, there is a price associated with this enhanced capability, which is a reduced level of performance. Sections 8.2.1 and 8.2.2 discuss the AMS parameters that affect VSAM performance in an MSS environment.

8.2 MASS STORAGE SYSTEM (MSS)

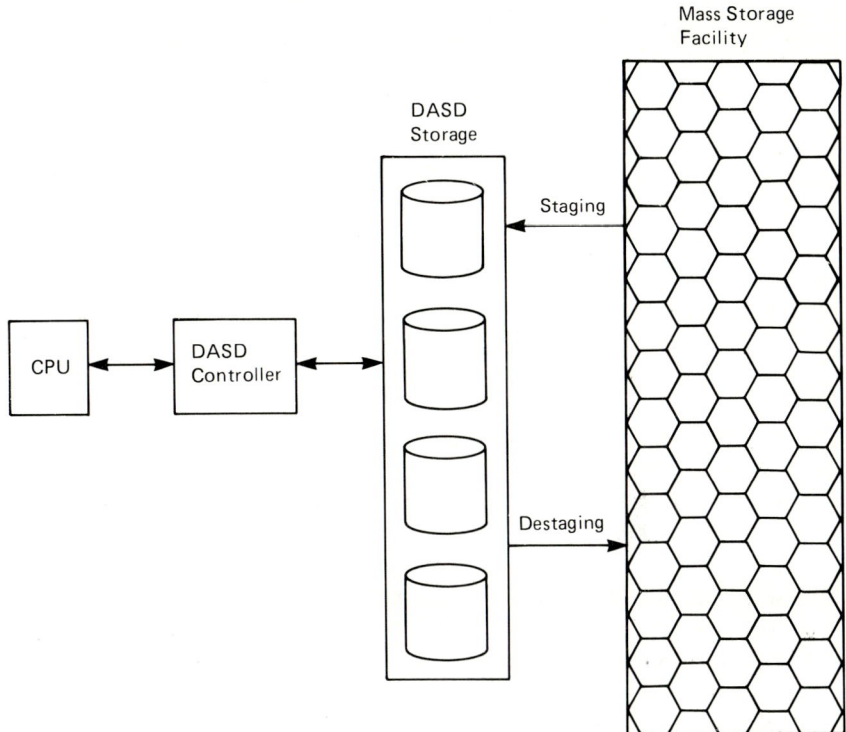

Figure 8.2 Flow of data in an MSS configured facility.

8.2.1 DESTAGEWAIT Parameter

DESTAGEWAIT is an AMS parameter that may be specified in the DEFINE CLUSTER or DEFINE ALTERNATEINDEX commands. It is effective only if the data set is stored on a mass storage volume. This parameter comes into play when an application issues a CLOSE macro (or CLOSE verb in Cobol programs). DESTAGEWAIT specifies that the program issuing the CLOSE will get control when the data set close *and* the destaging process have been successfully completed. In a Cobol program you will receive a file status of 00 when both processes have been finished. This helps you by executing the close, the destaging, and the program notification process synchronously. If destaging is unsuccessful owing to an I/O error, system error, power failure, or any other reason, the application can take steps to apply corrective measures.

If NODESTAGEWAIT was specified at the time of data set allocation, the application is notified as soon as the close is successful, and the application does not wait for the destaging process to complete successfully. If the destaging process results in an error, the application will be unaware of it because it will probably have long since ended. However, a message of unsuccessful destaging is sent to the console, where the operator may (if he or she knows how!) take appropriate action. NODE-STAGEWAIT is the default.

An application program will run for a *longer time* if the cluster it is closing has been defined with the DESTAGEWAIT parameter. On the other hand, if it is not defined with that parameter you risk other problems. Depending upon the application requirements, the pros and cons of DESTAGEWAIT and NODESTAGEWAIT should be kept in mind when defining a VSAM data set that will be stored on MSS. Needless to say, if the data set was opened for read-only purpose, destaging does not occur on close. Under these circumstances, these parameters have no effect.

8.2.2 STAGE, BIND, and CYLINDERFAULT

As with the parameter DESTAGEWAIT, the specification of these three mutually exclusive parameters is effective only if the data set is on a mass storage volume. They affect the staging characteristics of data sets at the time of their open.

STAGE This specifies that the data set is to be staged as soon as the open request has been issued. If it is not possible to stage it because of heavy activity on other data sets, the staging is deferred until the first I/O request is issued for that file. The data set is then eligible for automatic destaging if the space is needed to stage other objects. This automatic destaging may occur at any time. Afterwards, it is restaged on an as-needed basis.

If such a data set is staged and destaged owing to low activity between CICS/VS tasks, it could have an adverse effect on transaction response time.

BIND BIND goes one step further than STAGE. The data set is not only staged on open, it is marked ineligible for destaging unless the application issues a close. Thus, if the data set is open under CICS/VS, it cannot be destaged between tasks. However, the staging process is deferred until the first I/O request if there is heavy MSS activity on other objects at the time of the open.

CYLINDERFAULT This implies that the data set is not to be staged on open, but on the issuance of the first I/O request. During heavy MSS activity, the STAGE parameter acts like CYLINDERFAULT.

If you intend to put CICS/VS-accessed data sets on an MSS, you may want to define them with CYLINDERFAULT. Otherwise they will all be staged when CICS is opening them initially, which could severely delay the CICS initialization process. On the other hand, data sets defined with CYLINDERFAULT can be destaged between tasks, thus increasing transaction response time. This can be prevented if you use BIND instead. But BIND, like STAGE, will slow down the CICS initialization process. The choice depends upon your installation priorities.

8.2.3 Recommendations

Large data sets that are accessed only during batch processing are good candidates for MSS. Do not put CICS/VS or other on-line data sets on MSS, because you will either pay for slow CICS initialization due to massive staging (STAGE, BIND) or slow transaction response time due to destaging of data sets between tasks (STAGE, CYLINDERFAULT). Also, do not define a CICS data set with DESTAGEWAIT. This could slow down the normal CICS termination process because each close will be done synchronously with the destaging process. However, you must then have a data set recovery plan in case the data set was not destaged properly on CICS shutdown.

8.3 SOLID STATE DEVICES (SSDs)

Solid state devices (SSDs) are DASDs with extremely fast I/O service times. They use semiconductor memory and have no electromechanical moving parts like conventional disk packs and drives. Their seek time and rotational delay are zero. Needless to say, these devices are more expensive than conventional DASDs. However, application programs require no modifications; they access data from the solid state devices as if the devices were conventional DASDs.

All the currently available solid state devices are manufactured by non-IBM vendors. Storage Technology Corporation (STC) was the pioneer, with Memorex, Amdahl, and National Advanced Systems (NAS) joining the bandwagon later. Figure 8.3 gives the storage characteristics of these devices. Since their I/O service time is quite low, these devices can sustain a high I/O rate without degradation in response time.

The storage memory of solid state devices is rather volatile; a power failure can destroy the data. Therefore, most vendors (Amdahl, NAS, Memorex) provide a battery-powered disk backup in their units. As soon as a power failure is detected, the contents of the semiconductor memory are transferred to the backup disk pack. Upon restoration of power, the contents are transferred back from the disk to the solid state memory.

Vendors have made the solid state devices emulate standard IBM DASDs. They may emulate an IBM 3350, 3380, or 2305. Also, multiple logical volumes (volsers) can be emulated in a single physical SSD module. Multiple SSD modules can be combined to provide increased storage capacity. For example, six modules of 128-MB capacity each may be put together for a storage capacity of 768 MB.

Since SSDs are a new technology, we can expect to see increased storage capacities and enhanced functional capabilities in the future.

Vendor	Device model	Capacity per storage module, MB	Protocol overhead, ms	Data transfer delay for a 4K CI, ms	I/O service time, ms
Amdahl	6880	128	0.3	1.3	1.6
Memorex	6880	128	0.3	1.3	1.6
NAS	7990	128	0.3	1.3	1.6
STC	4305	96	0.3	1.3	1.6

Figure 8.3 Storage capacity and I/O service time of currently available solid state devices.

Check with the vendors to learn about new SSD product line developments and plans.

8.3.1 Comparison of SSDs and DASDs

It is interesting to compare the performance characteristics of an SSD with conventional DASDs. Since an SSD has no electromechanical moving parts, the seek time delay and rotational delay are absolutely zero. The only major I/O service time delay is in the channel transfer delay. Figure 8.4 compares I/O services times for some conventional DASDs and SSDs. As you can see, the I/O service time for a 4K CI in an SSD is only 1.6 ms. Since there are no moving parts, rotational position sensing (RPS) miss doesn't exist. An SSD is approximately 16 times faster than an IBM 3380, and about 4½ to 5 times faster than an IBM 2305 drum. An SSD can also sustain higher device busy and channel busy rates. The queue wait for an I/O is also minimal because of the low I/O service time.

Besides other uses, an SSD can be useful for a small VSAM data set that has an extremely high I/O rate. Usually, such a data set is spread over multiple conventional disk packs (using KEYRANGES), and each disk pack is only partially used. An SSD device may not only provide excellent I/O service time; it can also be cost effective.

SSDs are also good candidates for alternate indexes. Upgrade set alternate indexes are small data sets compared to the base cluster, but their use is impractical due to the numbers of I/O's required to keep the upgrade set is synchronization. Upgrade set alternate indexes placed on an SSD can be maintained at a very fast rate, and their use will not cause any performance problems. This can open up a wide range of possibilities, maintaining multiple views of a data set without the I/O considerations usually associated with such features. SSDs are recommended for the KSDS portion of an IMS/HIDAM data base and for secondary indexes in IMS data bases for the same reasons.

8.3 SOLID STATE DEVICES (SSDS)

IBM DASD	Average seek time, ms	Average rotational delay, ms	Data transfer delay for a 4K CI, ms	I/O service time, ms
3310	27	9.6	4.0	40.6
3330	30	8.4	5.0	43.4
3340	25	10.1	4.6	39.7
3350	25	8.4	3.4	36.8
3370	20	10.1	2.2	32.3
3375	19	10.1	2.2	31.3
3380 (SD)*	16	8.4	1.3	25.7
3380 (DD)*	17	8.4	1.3	26.7
2305	0	5.0	2.7	7.7
SSD	0.3†	0	1.3	1.6

*SD = single-density; DD = double-density.
†Protocol overhead only. SSDs have no seek time.

Figure 8.4 Comparison of I/O service times for conventional DASDs and solid state devices (SSDs).

8.3.2 SSD and CACHE

Cache DASD controllers serve as fast I/O devices for a large number of DASDs. If data is very heavily accessed, it will tend to stay in cache on the basis of an LRU algorithm. The I/O service time is therefore faster for records that happen to be on heavily accessed DASD tracks. The I/O service time of an SSD is the same whether the data is heavily accessed or not. The only data in cache that can meet the performance characteristics of an SSD is data that has been bound by the BINDDATA command of Access Method Services.

An IBM 3380 Model 23 has a maximum cache storage of 64 MB, while SSDs can have 128 MB for each module—a total of 768 MB for a configuration of six modules. Relatively large data sets can be allocated on an SSD that cannot be bound in a DASD cache controller.

Whether or not a record will be found in cache is a function of what else is happening in the system at that moment. If the record is found in cache (a read-hit), its I/O service time is comparable to that of an SSD I/O service time. On a read-miss, the I/O service time is almost the same as if there were no cache. On an SSD, there is never a read-miss.

An IBM 3880 Model 23 supports only IBM 3380 DASDs. An SSD can emulate an IBM 3380, 3350, or 2305.

SSDs are recommended for very heavily accessed data sets where the I/O service time must be guaranteed to be uniform. A consistently low I/O service time will also ensure a good response time for on-line systems.

8.3.3 SSD and Expanded Memory

Expanded memory is used for paging purposes only and has no direct effect on VSAM performance. An SSD may also be used for page data sets. Expanded memory can deliver a page of data to real memory at a much faster rate than an SSD. While the limiting factor in an SSD is the channel speed, there is no such limitation for expanded memory data transfer. If transfer speed is the only consideration, expanded memory is the obvious choice for Sierra series mainframes. For other IBM mainframes, where expanded memory is not supported, other techniques may have to be used to reduce page service times. One option might be the use of SSDs.

three

ACCESS METHOD SERVICES PARAMETERS

The AMS parameters of DEFINE CLUSTER (or DEFINE AIX) play a significant role in achieving optimum VSAM performance. It has been my experience that these parameters are coded without an understanding of their effect in the context of an application or of the whole-system environment. The next six chapters are devoted to the understanding and effective utilization of those parameters. Chapter 9 includes a detailed discussion of the CI size for the data and index components. Chapter 10 enumerates the pros and cons of the various space allocation parameters. IMBED and REPLICATE are the subject matter of Chap. 11, while Chap. 12 is devoted to the use of the FREESPACE parameter and its effect on VSAM performance. Some miscellaneous but important parameters are included in Chap. 13. Chapter 14 discusses procedures for estimating space requirements for VSAM data sets.

Wherever applicable, the use of AMS parameters is discussed in the context of other topics in the book such as hardware, design considerations, buffer requirements, batch jobs, CICS performance, and IMS/DB performance.

chapter 9
CI Size and Record Size

The sizes of the control interval and control area have a profound effect on VSAM performance. They directly affect CI/CA splits, buffer management, processing efficiency, and DASD space utilization, for example. There is no single rule of thumb that can be applied to determine an ideal CI or CA size. External factors such as the availability of particular resources in your particular environment can affect the size. Don't jump to any conclusions by reading only one or two sections of this chapter. You need a complete picture, which can only come from an understanding of all the important considerations.

9.1 DATA CI SIZE

First of all, let's look at the basic rule that determines the data CI size. A data CI must have a value derived from the following formula:

$$\text{Data CI size} = 512 \times n \quad \text{or} \quad 2048 \times n$$

where the value of n may vary from 1 to 16.

Substituting in the possible values of n, the data component CI size may be ½K, 1K, 1½K, 2K, 2½K, 3K, 3½K, 4K, 4½K, 5K, 5½K, 6K, 6½K, 7K, 7½K, 8K, 10K, 12K, 14K, 16K, 18K, 20K, 22K, 24K, 26K, 28K, 30K, or 32K.

CI size, bytes	Data transfer delay, ms
512	0.17
2,048	0.66
4,096	1.33
8,192	2.66
16,384	5.33
32,768	10.66

Figure 9.1 Data transfer time over a 3-MBS channel for some representative CI sizes with an IBM 3380.

9.1.1 Type of Processing

Random Reads If a KSDS is used only for random reads, a small CI size may be appropriate. If all you have to do is read a record of 100 bytes, it is immaterial whether it is contained in a 512-byte CI or a CI of 32,768 bytes. With this kind of processing, a larger CI will not only require more buffer space but also will have a longer data transfer time after the seek and rotational delay have been completed. Figure 9.1 gives the data transfer time for some selected CI sizes. Note that it takes longer to transfer a 32K CI than the rotational delay of 8.4 ms incurred to locate it.

Sequential Reads It may be more appropriate to use relatively large CI sizes for files that are *read only sequentially*. If the record size is 100 bytes, you may sequentially read 40 records in a 4096-byte CI and 81 records in a 8192-byte CI. Although you process double the number of records, the 8192-byte CI will require half the number of physical I/O's.

In Chap. 15, you will learn that you don't have to increase the CI size to reduce the I/O's in sequential processing. In batch processing, you can reduce the number of physical I/O's by increasing the data buffers through the BUFND parameter, making use of the read-ahead feature instead. In CICS/VS, it may be inappropriate and difficult to do a read-ahead of data CIs, so a larger CI size may be the only choice that will allow you to read more records in a single browse operation. But remember that on-line systems like CICS/VS are not normally used for heavy browse operations.

Mixed Processing If a data set is used for random as well as sequential access, the CI size may be determined on the basis of the distribution of the random and sequential requests. Our ultimate goal is to reduce the number of physical I/O's.

9.1.2 Record Size and Insert Activity

The record size should influence your choice of data CI size. Let's say that the logical record size for a data set is 1000 bytes and that the data set is subject to heavy update activity. Most of the activity for the data set is the addition of new records. If you select a CI size of 2048 bytes, a CI can contain only two records. Once the CI has the maximum of two records, the addition of another record in that CI will result in a CI split. We already know that a CI split will cause 6 to 8 I/O's instead of the 3 to 5 I/O's of a normal update. If you opted, instead, to use a CI size of 4096 bytes, the CI could contain a maximum of four 1000-byte records. With free space of 75%, 50%, or 25% left at the time of initial load, you could insert one, two, or three records, respectively, before expecting a CI split. CI splits could potentially be reduced in half with the 4K CI size.

In a nutshell: A data set with larger logical records and heavy insert activity will require a larger CI size with more free space in it. Definitely, a larger CI will require larger buffers too.

9.1.3 DASD Type and Physical Records

In Chap. 6 we noted that a CI consists of one or more physical blocks. In MVS/VSAM, the physical blocks may be ½K, 1K, 2K, or 4K in size. Some CI sizes force VSAM to select a physical block size that leaves an excessive number of wasted interblock gaps (IBGs) within the CI. This results in

- Poor utilization of DASD space
- Increased data transfer delay due to intervening interblock gaps

This problem is most critical on IBM 3380s because the interblock gap between the physical records of a CI is 512 bytes. If you select a data CI size of 3½K, it will result in every CI consisting of 7 physical records of 512 bytes each and 7 IBGs also of 512 bytes each. So the data CI of 3½K will occupy 7K of DASD space. If, instead, the CI size is 4K, the physical block will also be 4K and there will be only one IBG of 512 bytes. A 4K data CI will occupy 4½K of DASD space. It is clear that a 4K CI will use 2½K less DASD space than a 3½K CI! The problem is less acute with IBM 3330 and IBM 3350 models because their IBGs are 135 bytes and 185 bytes, respectively. Figure 9.2 illustrates the relationship between the CI size, the physical block size selected by VSAM, and the effective DASD utilization for IBM 3330, 3350, 3375, and 3380 DASDs.

It is evident that a 4K block provides the best and a ½K block size the worst DASD utilization. Unless there are valid reasons not to do so,

CI sizes	Physical block size	Effective DASD utilization, %			
		IBM 3330	IBM 3350	IBM 3375	IBM 3380
½K, 1½K, 2½K, 3½K, 4½K, 5½K, 6½K, 7½K	½K	79.1	73.5	57.1	50
1K, 3K, 5K, 7K	1K	88.3	84.7	72.7	66.6
2K, 6K, 10K, 14K, 18K, 22K, 26K, 30K	2K	93.8	91.7	84.2	80.0
4K, 8K, 12K, 16K, 20K, 24K, 28K, 32K	4K	96.8	95.7	91.4	88.8

Figure 9.2 Relationship between CI size, physical block size, and DASD utilization for IBM 3330, IBM 3350, IBM 3375, and IBM 3380. It is assumed that the environment is MVS.

(e.g., virtual storage constraint), it is recommended that a data CI size that is a multiple of 4K be selected.

9.1.4 Virtual Storage Constraint

Non-MVS/XA As we discussed in Chap. 1, a non-MVS/XA environment does not have much virtual storage left for running very large applications. Thus, all the VSAM performance-related techniques that make heavy use of buffer allocation to speed up processing may not be feasible in such an environment. Because of the addressability limitation, you may have to use small data CI sizes to conserve the buffer space. A batch job may not pose a virtual storage problem, but a CICS region will definitely require prudent use of virtual storage.

MVS/XA Since VSAM buffers in an MVS/XA environment reside above the 16-MB line, you may not have to worry much about the virtual storage constraint. The buffer space allocation can therefore be fairly liberal. You may have relatively large data CIs to speed up browse operations under CICS/VS.

9.2 INDEX CI SIZE

Index CI size can have a major impact on VSAM performance. Each record of the lowermost level of the index component, the sequence set, has pointers to the data CIs of the data CA, one pointer for each data CI. The example in Fig. 9.3 illustrates this concept.

Let's assume that the data CA size in this case is one cylinder of the IBM 3380 and that the CI size is 4096 bytes. The cluster is defined with the IMBED option, and the CI size for the index component is 1024 bytes. Each data CA (one cylinder) can have up to 140 data CIs. The sequence

9.2 INDEX CI SIZE

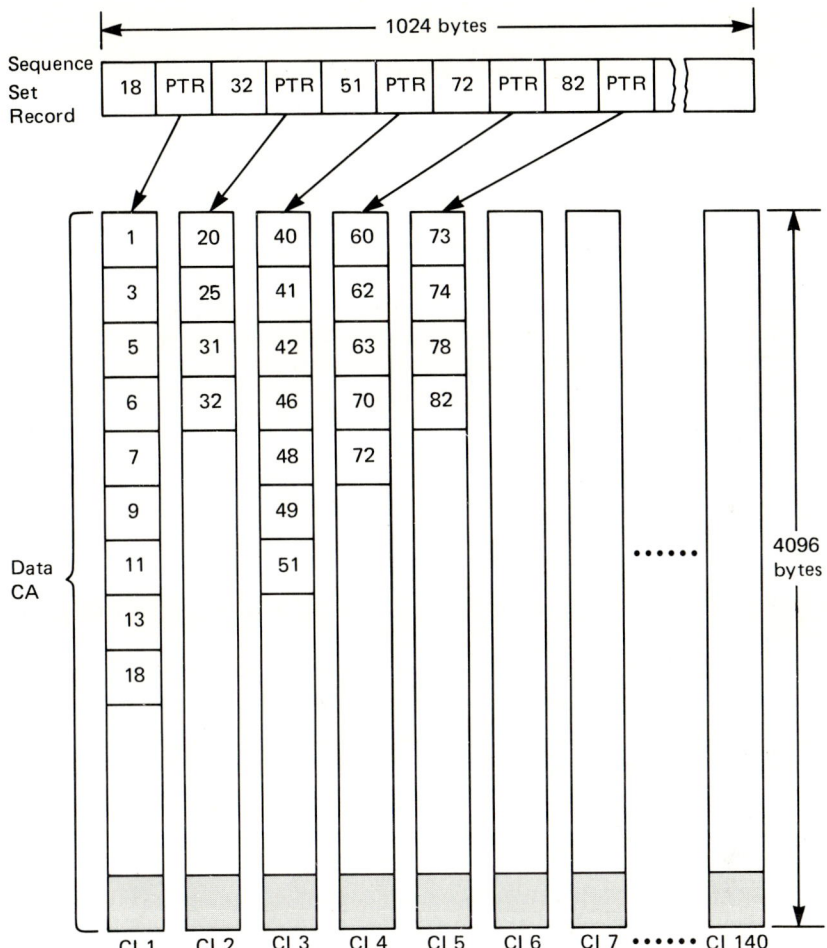

Figure 9.3 In this example a KSDS cluster is defined on an IBM 3380. The CA is one cylinder and the CI is 4096 bytes in size. The index CI is 1024 bytes. Since the cluster is defined with the IMBED option, there are 140 data CIs in one cylinder of data CA.

set record must contain at least 140 pointers to the data CIs to establish their addressability. If it is too small to contain all these pointers, some data CIs will become unusable. Following causes contribute to the unusability of data CIs:

- The index CI is too small to contain all the pointers.
- The key compression algorithm is not working effectively.
- The data CI size is too small, so there are too many data CIs. Even the largest possible index CI (4096 bytes in MVS) may not be able to contain pointers to all of them.

Whatever the cause, the net effect is the underutilization of the data CA.

9.2.1 Implications of a Small Index CI

A small index CI size can have adverse consequences:

- *Premature data CA splits:* As soon as the sequence set record is unable to contain another pointer, the remaining data CIs in that CA lose their usefulness. This will not only result in an underutilized data CA but may also cause premature CA splits. An increase in the number of CA splits will increase I/O activity and adversely affect performance.
- *Increased DASD requirement:* Since the data CAs will be underutilized, more DASD space will be required.
- *Slower sequential processing:* Since the same amount of data will be spread over a much larger DASD area, it will take longer to process it sequentially.

9.2.2 Testing for Index CI Utilization

In the index component, the keys are stored in a compressed format. If you dump the sequence set records, it will be difficult to decipher the information and determine whether the index CI has run out of pointer space. Therefore it is recommended that you let VSAM calculate the correct index CI size. This can be done by omitting the CISZ parameter for the index component in the DEFINE CLUSTER and DEFINE ALTERNATEINDEX. Access Method Services will calculate what it considers to be the ideal index CI size based on the key length, data CI size, data CA size, and features of its key compression algorithm.

Under MVS, the only index CI sizes supported are ½K, 1K, 2K, and 4K. In a majority of cases, the CI size calculated by AMS will be large enough to contain all the pointers. Various techniques discussed here can be used to determine those few cases where AMS erred in estimating the capabilities of VSAM's key compression algorithm. In these cases, redefine the VSAM data set and hard code the index CI size to the next higher figure. For example, if a 2K index CI could not hold all the pointers, increase the index CI to 4K. If a 4K index CI cannot hold the pointers either, you can either reduce the data CA size or increase the data CI size. Either technique will reduce the pointer requirements in the sequence set record.

The following techniques can be used to determine if a problem exists.

Data Load Technique   Allocate a KSDS cluster with a primary space allocation of one cylinder, secondary space allocation of zero, and FREE-

9.2 INDEX CI SIZE

SPACE parameter (0,0). Do not code the index CI size; let AMS determine it for you. The parameters you will use will be

CYLINDERS(1,0)
FREESPACE(0,0)

The record size, the data CI size, and other parameters (e.g., IMBED) should be coded as you would in a real environment. This will help you to determine how many records this one-cylinder data set is capable of holding under ideal circumstances.

Let's take an example. If the data CI size is 4096 bytes and the IMBED parameter is used, one cylinder of an IBM 3380 will hold 140 data CIs. If the record size is 500 bytes, each data CI can contain a maximum of 8 records with no free space left. Therefore 140 CIs can potentially contain 140×8 or 1120 records in total. Now all you have to do is create 1120 records of real data, sort them on key field, and load them (e.g., REPRO) into the one-cylinder data set. If the load is successful and there are no error messages, the index CI size is sufficient. If you detect an out-of-space condition, the index CI record is too small. Increase it to the next higher value (if possible), and reallocate the data set. Repeat this procedure until the load completes successfully.

Binary Zeros Technique You can use this technique if the data set you intend to analyze is already in a production environment. It is a two-step procedure. First, get a hex dump of the sequence set index records. Second, visually analyze them to detect any abnormal situation. Let's find out how to print the sequence set records. First of all, use LISTCAT to get a listing of the data set; then, using the formulas given below, calculate the value of N after substituting the appropriate values from the listing. There are four formulas for data sets defined with different combinations of IMBED/NOIMBED and REPLICATE/NOREPLICATE options:

1. *IMBED and NOREPLICATE:* If the data set was defined with the IMBED and NOREPLICATE parameters, use the formula

$$N = \frac{\text{HURBA of index set}}{\text{CI size of index}}$$

2. *NOIMBED and NOREPLICATE:* If NOIMBED and NOREPLICATE were specified or implied, the formula will be

$$N = \frac{\text{HURBA of index component}}{\text{CI size of index}} - \frac{\text{HURBA of data}}{(\text{CI size of data}) \times (\text{number of data CIs per data CA})}$$

3. *IMBED and REPLICATE:* If IMBED and REPLICATE were specified, the formula will be

$$N = \frac{\text{HURBA of index set}}{(\text{CI size of index}) \times (\text{PHYRECS per TRK for the index})}$$

Number of PHYRECS per TRK for the index are listed under the heading PHYRECS/TRK in the LISTCAT produced listing.

4. *NOIMBED and REPLICATE*: If the data set was defined with the NOIMBED and REPLICATE parameters, use the formula

$$N = \frac{\text{HURBA of index component}}{(\text{CI size of index}) \times (\text{PHYRECS per TRK for the index})}$$
$$- \frac{\text{HURBA of data}}{(\text{CI size of data}) \times (\text{number of data CIs per data CA})}$$

The result should be an integer (no fractions!). This value is, in fact, the number of *index set* records (or CIs) in the index component and should vary between 0 and 20. Note that the HURBA of index set used in formulas 1 and 3 is given by EXTENT-TYPE X'00' (and not X'80') in the listing.

Now dump the index component of the data set with the PRINT command of Access Method Services. The command to use will be

```
PRINT                                   -
    IDS(EMPLOYEE.KSDS.INDEX)    -
    HEX SKIP(N)
```

In this example, EMPLOYEE.KSDS.INDEX is the name of the index component for the cluster in question, and *N* is the number of index set records calculated above. Visually scan a few records of the dump. *You will be looking for imbedded binary zeros somewhere in the middle of the hex dump of each sequence set record. The presence of binary zeros indicates good key compression and adequate index CI size.* The absence of binary zeros indicates that the sequence set CI size is too small to contain all the pointers for its data CA. In that case, you may use the recommendations of Section 9.2.3 to correct the situation.

Example 1: Figure 9.4 is a LISTCAT-produced listing for the data set named 'TEST.KSDS1.CLUSTER'. As you can see, the data set was defined with the IMBED and NOREPLICATE options. The values of the appropriate variables may be substituted in formula 1 as follows:

$$\frac{\text{HURBA of index set}}{\text{CI size of index}} = \frac{4096}{4096} = 1$$

9.2 INDEX CI SIZE

The value of the result, 1, is the number of index set records that must be skipped to get to the first sequence set record. The following command was executed to skip the index set records and print the sequence set records:

```
PRINT          -
    IDS(TEST.KSDS1.INDEX)    -
    HEX         -
    SKIP(1)
```

Part of the hex listing produced is shown in Fig. 9.5.

Note that there are plenty of binary zeros imbedded in the middle of the sequence set record. This is indicative of good key compression and adequate index CI size.

Example 2: Figure 9.6 is a LISTCAT-generated listing for the data set named 'TEST.KSDS2.CLUSTER'. The data set was defined (or implied) with the NOIMBED and NOREPLICATE options. The appropriate values may be substituted in formula #2 as follows:

$$\frac{\text{HURBA of index component}}{\text{CI size of index}} - \frac{\text{HURBA of data}}{(\text{CI size of data}) \times (\text{number of data CIs per data CA})}$$

$$= \frac{32{,}768}{4096} - \frac{1{,}648{,}640}{512 \times 460}$$

$$= 8 - 7$$

$$= 1$$

The value of the result, 1, is the number of index set records that must be skipped to get to the first sequence set record. The following command was executed to skip the index set records and print the hexadecimal dump of the sequence set records:

```
PRINT          -
    IDS(TEST.KSDS2.INDEX)    -
    HEX         -
    SKIP(1)
```

Part of the listing produced is shown in Fig. 9.7. Notice that there are no binary zeros imbedded in the middle of the sequence set record. This is indicative of either poor key compression or an index CI size that is too small. Corrective measures must be taken to rectify the situation. Such recommendations are listed in Section 9.2.3.

```
IDCAMS  SYSTEM  SERVICES

LISTCAT ENT(TEST.KSDS1.CLUSTER) ALL
CLUSTER ------- TEST.KSDS1.CLUSTER
     IN-CAT --- SYS1.ICFUCAT.RANADE
     HISTORY
       OWNER-IDENT------(NULL)     CREATION--------87.082
       RELEASE----------2          EXPIRATION------00.000
     PROTECTION-PSWD----(NULL)     RACF------------(NO)
     ASSOCIATIONS
       DATA-----TEST.KSDS1.DATA
       INDEX----TEST.KSDS1.INDEX

DATA ------- TEST.KSDS1.DATA
     IN-CAT --- SYS1.ICFUCAT.RANADE
     HISTORY
       OWNER-IDENT------(NULL)     CREATION--------87.082
       RELEASE----------2          EXPIRATION------00.000
     PROTECTION-PSWD----(NULL)     RACF------------(NO)
     ASSOCIATIONS
       CLUSTER--TEST.KSDS1.CLUSTER
     ATTRIBUTES
       KEYLEN----------17          AVGLRECL--------80         BUFSPACE--------12288        CISIZE----------4096
       RKP--------------0          MAXLRECL--------80         EXCPEXIT--------(NULL)       CI/CA-----------140
       SHROPTNS(1,3)  RECOVERY     UNIQUE       NOERASE       INDEXED      NOWRITECHK      IMBED       NOREPLICAT
       UNORDERED      NOREUSE      NONSPANNED
     STATISTICS
       REC-TOTAL-------35700       SPLITS-CI-------0          EXCPS----------154
       REC-DELETED-----0           SPLITS-CA-------0          EXTENTS--------1
       REC-INSERTED----0           FREESPACE-%CI---0          SYSTEM-TIMESTAMP:
       REC-UPDATED-----0           FREESPACE-%CA---0            X'9C764493C764DF01'
       REC-RETRIEVED---0           FREESPC-BYTES---0
     ALLOCATION
       SPACE-TYPE----CYLINDER      HI-ALLOC-RBA----2867200    HI-ALLOC-RBA----2867200
       SPACE-PRI-------5           HI-USED-RBA-----2867200    HI-USED-RBA-----2867200
       SPACE-SEC-------0
     VOLUME
       VOLSER------X'301C001'      PHYREC-SIZE-----4096
       DEVTYPE-----X'301C000'      PHYRECS/TRK-----10
       VOLFLAG---------PRIME       TRACKS/CA-------15
       EXTENTS:
       LOW-CCHH----X'0001000C'     LOW-RBA---------0          TRACKS----------75           EXTENT-NUMBER---1
       HIGH-CCHH---X'000500CE'     HIGH-RBA--------2867199                                 EXTENT-TYPE-----X'40'

INDEX ------- TEST.KSDS1.INDEX
     IN-CAT --- SYS1.ICFUCAT.RANADE
     HISTORY
       OWNER-IDENT------(NULL)     CREATION--------87.082
       RELEASE----------2          EXPIRATION------00.000
     PROTECTION-PSWD----(NULL)     RACF------------(NO)
     ASSOCIATIONS
```

```
CLUSTER---TEST.KSDS1.CLUSTER
     ATTRIBUTES
       KEYLEN-----------------17              AVGLRECL----------------0          BUFSPACE------------(NULL)
       RKP-------------------0              MAXLRECL---------------4089          EXCPEXIT-----------(NULL)
       SHROPTNS(1,3)      RECOVERY           UNIQUE             NOERASE          NOWRITECHK           IMBED
       NOREUSE
     STATISTICS
       REC--TOTAL---------------6            SPLITS-CI----------------0          EXCPS------------------50
       REC--DELETED------------0            SPLITS-CA----------------0          EXTENTS-----------------2
       REC--INSERTED-----------0            FREESPACE-%CI-----------0          SYSTEM-TIMESTAMP:
       REC--UPDATED------------0            FREESPACE-%CA-----------0                X'9C764493C764DF01'
       REC--RETRIEVED---------18            FREESPC-BYTES-------36864
     ALLOCATION
       SPACE-TYPE--------TRACK              HI-ALLOC-RBA--------61440
       SPACE-PRI---------------1            HI-USED-RBA--------61440
       SPACE-SEC---------------0
     VOLUME
       VOLSER-----------X'301'VOL001        PHYREC-SIZE----------4096          HI-ALLOC-RBA--------40960
       DEVTYPE---------X'3010200E'          PHYRECS/TRK-------------10          HI-USED-RBA---------4096
       VOLFLAG----------PRIME               TRACKS/CA---------------1
       EXTENTS:                                                                   TRACKS-----------------1
       LOW-CCHH--------X'00CC00C3'          LOW-RBA---------------------0
       HIGH-CCHH-------X'00CC00C3'          HIGH-RBA-------------40959
     VOLUME
       VOLSER----------X'301'VOL001         PHYREC-SIZE----------4096          HI-ALLOC-RBA--------61440
       DEVTYPE---------X'3010200E'          PHYRECS/TRK-------------10          HI-USED-RBA---------61440
       VOLFLAG----------PRIME               TRACKS/CA---------------15
       EXTENTS:                                                                   TRACKS----------------75
       LOW-CCHH--------X'00C1000C'          LCW-RBA--------------40960
       HIGH-CCHH-------X'00C500CE'          HIGH-RBA-------------61439
```

CISIZE------------------4096
CI/CA--------------------10
NOREPLICAT   UNORDERED
INDEX:
 LEVELS------------------1
 ENTRIES/SECT------------2
 SEQ-SET-RBA---------40960
 HI-LEVEL-RBA------------0

EXTENT-NUMBER-----------1
EXTENT-TYPE---------X'00'

EXTENT-NUMBER-----------1
EXTENT-TYPE---------X'80'

Figure 9.4 A data set listing produced by the LISTCAT command. Note that the sequence set is IMBEDed.

```
F50087C82C0154020D3CF4F1F50087079C014120C60A3BF2F0F3F3F7F90087076C011310030D3AF1F1F5F3F3F7020639F5F90087077C070638F9F8F0
F20087C78C0144050A370C8AF3F0F2F0F6F8F6F6C087076C0165010E36F2F0F0F6F7F10087076C030A35F3F0F1F5F9F7F9F60087082C0120010E34F8
F2F0F4F6F4F20C87076C020B33F2F0F9F9F9F80087078C012145030D32F7F1F5F4F8F8020631F6F2F0F9F6F0F40087078C017243020E30F405012FF5
F2F0F2F9F3F70087079C0143020D2EF5F60087078C07062DF2F0F6F0F1F10087072C030A2C0093F2F4F1F5F6F0F5F90087082C0135010E2BF6F90087
075C07C62AF3F2F0F8F7F2F800087076C020B29F2F2F0F6F2F5F70087077C0143020D28F2F0F2030327F0F0F5F3F7F0F60085020926F2C1F1F5F6F7F3
F20087C82C014323010F25F8F30087078C070624F8F2F0F9F2F3F50087076C020B23F7F2F0F8F9F4F20087078C020B22F9F6F4F30087076C05082100
8CF1F6F2F0F0F3F0F40087077C01CC20F5F2F0F6F7F3F002071FF4F2F0F2F5F1F20087077C010433020E1EF3F2F0F7F9F702061DF6F7F606031CF2F2
F0F8F5C2051BF7F9F9F405041AF3F0F2F605C419F2F0F2F8F8F10087076C030A18F1F0F1F5F3F0F2F60087082C0125010E17F2F0FCF4F2F80087078C
018450C30D16007EF9F0F5F8F0F1F80087007C02CB15F2F0F0F6F4F40087078C030A14F8F1F5F0F6F3F2020713F4F90087077C012131070912F1F2F7
060311F7F2F0F9F0F6F40087C78CC1531402CE10F6F2FCF9F3F102060FF5F2F0F1F9F6F60087076C020BCEF4F2F0F4F1F4F40087C78C020B0DF3F2F0
F8F6F2F90087078C01516302CE0CF2F2F0F1F0F0F302070B008FF2F0F0F1F5F1F0F2F80087079C0174030C100AF9F1F5F1F0F1F8C20709F7F2F0F8F5
F5F5C087077CC140020D08F2FCF1FCF0F30087076C015022030D07F9F3F1F5F0F7F1F60087082C015385010F06F4F5F2F0F7F3F1FC0087076C012401
0E05F1F1F1F0F8F0F1F800870501CB04F9F3F5F2C087076C0143050A03F2F2F0F2F0F1F20087075C020B02F2F00087078C00070701F1F0F1F2F0F1F0
F0F30087077CCC0D00
```

Figure 9.5 Hexadecimal dump of the sequence set of the index component 'TEST.KSDS1.INDEX' of the base cluster 'TEST.KSDS1.CLUSTER'. Note the presence of binary zeros in the middle of the sequence set record.

```
LISTCAT ENT(TEST.KSDS2.CLUSTER) ALL
CLUSTER ------- TEST.KSDS2.CLUSTER
     IN-CAT --- SYS1.ICFUCAT.RANADE
     HISTORY
       OWNER-IDENT------(NULL)      CREATION--------87.082
       RELEASE----------------2     EXPIRATION------00.000
     PROTECTION-PSWD-----(NULL)     RACF------------(NO)
     ASSOCIATIONS
       DATA----TEST.KSDS2.DATA
       INDEX---TEST.KSDS2.INDEX

DATA ------- TEST.KSDS2.DATA
     IN-CAT --- SYS1.ICFUCAT.RANADE
     HISTORY
       OWNER-IDENT------(NULL)      CREATION--------87.082
       RELEASE----------------2     EXPIRATION------00.000
     PROTECTION-PSWD-----(NULL)     RACF------------(NO)
     ASSOCIATIONS
       CLUSTER--TEST.KSDS2.CLUSTER
     ATTRIBUTES
       KEYLEN-----------------17    AVGLRECL---------------0    BUFSPACE------------5120    CISIZE--------------512
       RKP--------------------0     MAXLRECL--------------80    EXCPEXIT----------(NULL)    CI/CA----------------460
       SHROPTNS(1,3)      RECOVERY  UNIQUE             NOERASE  INDEXED       NOWRITECHK    NOIMBED      NOREPLICAT
       UNORDERED          NOREUSE   NOSPANNED
     STATISTICS
       REC-TOTAL----------15000     SPLITS-CI--------------0    EXCPS----------------222
       REC-DELETED------------0     SPLITS-CA--------------0    EXTENTS----------------1
       REC-INSERTED----------0     FREESPACE-%CI----------0    SYSTEM-TIMESTAMP:
       REC-UPDATED-----------0     FREESPACE-%CA----------0         X'9C7646EC0016F401'
       REC-RETRIEVED---------0     FREESPC-BYTES-----604160
     ALLOCATION
```

```
        SPACE-TYPE--------TRACK              HI-ALLOC-RBA-----1884160
        SPACE-PRI------------80              HI-USED-RBA------1648640
        SPACE-SEC-------------0
      VOLUME
        VOLSER------X'301O200E'VOLC01        PHYRECS-SIZE---------512
        DEVTYPE-----X'301O200E'               PHYRECS/TRK-----------46
        VOLFLAG----------PRIME                TRACKS/CA-------------10
        EXTENTS:
          LOW-CCHH----X'00060000'             LOW-RBA----------------0
          HIGH-CCHH---X'0008O004'              HIGH-RBA--------1884159
    INDEX ------ TEST.KSDS2.INDEX
      IN-CAT --- SYS1.ICFUCAT.RANADE
      HISTORY
        OWNER-IDENT----(NULL)                 CREATION--------87.082
        RELEASE------------2                  EXPIRATION------00.000
      PROTECTION-PSWD-----(NULL)              RACF---------------(NO)
      ASSOCIATIONS
        CLUSTER--TEST.KSDS2.CLUSTER
      ATTRIBUTES
        KEYLEN-------------17                 AVGLRECL-----------4089
        RKP-----------------0                 MAXLRECL--------NOERASE
        SHROPTNS(1,3)  RECOVERY                UNIQUE
        NOREUSE
      STATISTICS
        REC-TOTAL----------11                 SPLITS-CI--------------0                 BUFSPACE-------------(NULL)
        REC-DELETED---------0                 SPLITS-CA--------------0                 EXCPEXIT------------(NULL)
        REC-INSERTED--------0                 FREESPACE-%CI----------0                 NOWRITECHK        NOIMBED
        REC-UPDATED---------0                 FREESPACE-%CA----------0
        REC-RETRIEVED------24                 FREESPC-BYTES--429496320                EXCPS-----------------68
                                                                                        EXTENTS----------------1
      ALLOCATION                                                                        SYSTEM-TIMESTAMP:
        SPACE-TYPE------TRACK                 HI-ALLOC-RBA-------40960                  X'9C7646EC0016F401'
        SPACE-PRI-----------1                 HI-USED-RBA--------32768
        SPACE-SEC-----------0                                                         INDEX:
      VOLUME                                                                            LEVELS-----------------2
        VOLSER------X'301O200E'VOLC01         PHYREC-SIZE---------4096                  ENTRIES/SECT----------21
        DEVTYPE-----X'301O200E'               PHYRECS/TRK-----------10                  SEQ-SET-RBA------------0
        VOLFLAG----------PRIME                TRACKS/CA--------------1                  HI-LEVEL-RBA--------8192
        EXTENTS:
          LOW-CCHH----X'00000004'             LOW-RBA----------------0                EXTENT-NUMBER----------1
          HIGH-CCHH---X'00000004'             HIGH-RBA-----------40959                EXTENT-TYPE--------X'00'
                                              TRACKS-----------------1
```

Figure 9.6 A data set listing produced by the LISTCAT command. Note that the sequence set is NOIMBEDed.

```
5E0700C05DF1F5F1F0F10305CC5CF5008608C30058F2F0F0F0F5F1F0F2F00009005AF8F0F1F80087077C0124050A0059F6F1F8F10087076C05080058
F70087C76C08050057F2F0F1F0F1F60087078C03CA005605000055F9F1F5F1F0F1F60207005400CBF802010053F5CC87077C0164C508080052F1F300
87077CC7060051F2F0F1F0F0F303C6005C0B00004FF8F0F1F80087069C012250050B004EF50501004DF8F1F5F1F0F0F70207004CF5F10702004B0C00
004AF2F0F8F5F1F40087077CC130C30CC049F7F1F5F8F5F5F102070048F10087078C080500470D000C46F1F00087079C00922007C90045F808010044
F30087C76C015022C8080C43F1F0F0F1C504C042F5F3C0087078C009535070900410D000040F4F20087078C0094040709003F00CDF9F3F2F0F0F7F2F9
0087076C0111010E003EF1F0F0F30504CC3DF40701003CF9F3F1F5F0F7F1F60087082C015414010F003B0700003A08000039F50087076C08050038F4
F00087C78C014C1507090037F3F5C702CC36F2F6C087070C07060035F30087077C080500349C01220C030C33F3F1F00087076C012406090032080000
31F7F20087076C01520207090030F2F0F7F2F4F9C087C76C030A002FF4F50087082C015207080002EF5F1F5F7F3F1F30087082C015445020E002DF4F0
0102002C05000C2BF8F305020C2ACCC3F1F1F1F0F501050029F3F7F5F50086281C05080028F1F1F1F0F001050027F1F107020026F60087076C080500
25F2F0F1F0F0F50087078C030A0024F1F5F1F0F0C305CC23F3F0F5F1F0F0F50087064C0103020D0022F5F20087076C0143070800218C0C010020F900
87077CC1030807001F8C0C01CC1EF9F3F4F5C087C76CC508CC1DF7F2F80087079C011410060A001CF8F0C502C01B0800001AF1F3C087077C07060019
F2F0F0F505040018F2F0F1F0F0F4C087C76CC1431303CD0017F80501C016F2F0F1F50087082C0100050A0C1500D5F1F0F2F1F5F1F0F0000800140E00
00138CC10502CC040012F4F8F0F1C087C76CC113C50AC011F2F00087078C0007070010F90087077C0805CC0FF80087077C080500CE0C00000DF60087
076C01130807000C0C000C0BF1F20087C72CC706C00AF70087076C01500807000 9F308010008F20087077C01504208080007F2F0F1F0F0F10087079C
0140C3CC0006F4F8F0F10087C82CC155C50AC005F80087082C016508070004F1F207020003F1F5F1F0F0F703060002F1F0F5F1F0F002060001F1F0F0
F2F0F0F0F100080000
```


Figure 9.7 Hexadecimal dump of the sequence set of the index component 'TEST.KSDS2.INDEX' of the base cluster 'TEST.KSDS2.CLUSTER'. Note that there are no binary zeros in the middle of the sequence set record.

Bear in mind that you may use AMS commands under TSO or option 6 of ISPF and then examine the contents of the sequence set CIs by dumping them onto the CRT.

9.2.3 Recommendations

First of all, let Access Method Services determine the index CI size. On the basis of the data CI size, CA size, key length, and record length, AMS will select the appropriate index CI size for you. In the majority of cases, this will work just fine. You can verify it by using the techniques discussed in Section 9.2.2. If you spot a problem, use the following tips in the listed order to correct the situation. In extreme cases, you may have to use more than one technique.

Increase Index CI Size You may define the data set with a larger index CI size. You will have to code the CISZ parameter of the INDEX portion of DEFINE CLUSTER and thus override the AMS-determined value. However, if the AMS-determined value was 4096 (in MVS), you have already reached the limit, because 4K is the largest index CI size possible.

Increase Data CI Size If the sequence set CI cannot hold enough pointers for all the data CIs, reduce the number of data CIs. This can be accomplished by increasing the data CI size. For example, an IBM 3380 cylinder may contain 150 data CIs of 4K each but only 75 data CIs of 8K size. If the number of data CIs is reduced, the pointer requirements within the sequence set CI are also reduced. Remember the following rule: *A small data CI needs a large index CI, while a large data CI needs a small index CI.* Don't ignore the increase in buffer requirements resulting from the increase in the data CI size.

Reduce Data CA Size One sequence set record has pointers to the data CIs of one and only one data CA. If the data CA size is reduced, the number of data CIs per data CA will also be reduced. Thus the pointer requirements within the sequence set record will decrease. However, if the IMBED option is specified with a reduced data CA size, DASD requirements will increase. This is due to the fact that IMBED uses the first track of the data CA for the sequence set regardless of the data CA size. For example, if the data CA size is one cylinder (15 tracks) of an IBM 3380, IMBED will require one track out of 15 (6.6%), while in a data CA of 10 tracks, IMBED will require one track out of 10 (10%).

DOS/VSE Considerations In DOS/VSE, the index CI size can be as large as 8192 bytes (8K) for Count Key Data (CKD) devices. Therefore you may have fewer of these problems than in an MVS environment.

9.3 RECORD SIZE

Usually, the only deciding factor for a record size should be the application requirements. However, performance considerations require that you keep a few things in mind. Consider the following examples.

Example 1: The largest nonspanned record that can be held by a CI is the CI size minus 7 bytes. If the CI size is 4096 bytes, the largest possible record is 4089 bytes. Let's say that the application requires a record size of 3500 bytes. 589 bytes of storage in each CI will be wasted.

Example 2: If there is more than one fixed length record in a CI, 10 bytes of control information are needed. Thus the usable space in a 4096-byte data CI available to an application will be 4086 bytes. Let's say that the application indicates a record length of 2044 bytes. You will be left with 2042 bytes of free space per CI, which, again, will be useless. This means that 50% of the DASD space is wasted. Under these circumstances, you might want to reduce the record length to 2043 bytes, leaving 2043 bytes of free space for another record.

While designing a record format, you must also consider how efficiently it will use the data CI space.

9.3.1 Support for Spanned Records

If a record cannot fit into one CI, it must span over more than one. This can be accomplished by coding the SPANNED parameter of DEFINE CLUSTER. CICS/VS did not support spanned records up to CICS release 1.6.1. The only way to get around the problem was to use a larger CI, but this also increased the buffer requirements. With CICS release 1.7, the restriction no longer exists.

Although CICS 1.7 fully supports spanned records, there are several performance considerations. If a spanned record spans over, say, four CIs, reading the complete record will require four *separate* I/O's. There are no chained channel command words (CCWs) involved. This increases the I/O activity. Also, a CICS task that is processing a spanned record will grab more data buffers and thus affect the performance of other CICS tasks. A spanned record always starts on a CI boundary and can also increase DASD space requirements. It is therefore recommended that you not use spanned records for a highly active data set in an on-line environment.

chapter 10

Space Allocation Parameters

Space allocation may be specified in CYLINDERS, TRACKS, OR RECORDS under MVS and also for the CKD devices of DOS/VSE. But for the FBA devices under DOS/VSE, space allocation is specified in RECORDS or BLOCKS (FBA blocks). The data set may be suballocated in a previously defined VSAM space (for VSAM catalogs only) or it may have a unique space of its own (VSAM and ICF catalogs). The secondary extents allocation parameter specified at the time of cluster allocation is helpful in extending the data set when additional space is required. KEYRANGES may be used to disperse various data set extents over different volumes and thus use more than one read-write arm to execute the I/O's. All these parameters have a direct or indirect effect on VSAM performance.

10.1 CYLINDERS, TRACKS, AND RECORDS

In defining a VSAM cluster, you can use the space allocation parameters CYLINDERS, TRACKS, OR RECORDS. These parameters are mutually exclusive. Consider the following coding examples:

```
CYLINDERS(10,5)    or
TRACKS(6,2)    or
RECORDS(1000,250)
```

10.1 CYLINDERS, TRACKS, AND RECORDS

In these examples, AMS will make an initial allocation of 10 cylinders, 6 tracks, or 1000 records of space, respectively. When the allocation is used up, VSAM will make secondary allocations of 5 cylinders, 2 tracks, or 250 records of space, respectively. The secondary extents may be allocated up to a maximum of 123 times. The only exception occurs with UNIQUE data sets under MVS/VSAM (not ICF) catalogs, where the limitation is 15 times. Under DOS/VSE, however, UNIQUE data sets *cannot be extended*. Data sets defined with the REUSE parameter also may not have more than 15 secondary extents.

10.1.1 Data CA Size

Unlike the CI size, there is no parameter for you to use for CA size as you allocate a VSAM data set. Access Method Services determines the data CA size at the time of the data set allocation. *If the space allocation is made in cylinders, the data CA size is always 1 cylinder.* It is recommended that you always make space allocations in cylinders for the following reasons:

- The larger the CA size, the fewer the number of CA splits. Since 1 cylinder is the largest possible data CA size, it will cause the least number of CA splits.
- When a CA split acquires the first free CA at the end of the data set, it also writes a Software End of File (SEOF) to the first CI of the next CA. The VERIFY command uses the SEOF pointers to correct the HURBA value in the catalog. In a system with a large number of VSAM files (e.g., CICS), it will take longer to issue VERIFY commands (explicitly or implicitly) after a system failure. In other words, a smaller CA size will slow down the process of a CICS/VS restart.
- A small CA size will increase the number of sequence set records, and since index set records have pointers to the sequence set records, it will also increase the number of index set records. In Chaps. 15, 16, and 17, we will discuss placing the index set records in core to reduce I/O's. An increase in the number of index set records will also increase the buffer requirements. This could be critical in non-MVS/XA environments, which usually have virtual storage constraint problems.
- An IMBEDed sequence set acquires the first track of a data CA. If the data CA is small, the effective DASD utilization will be reduced. Consider an extreme case: Let's say that the data component is allocated in tracks and the data CA happens to be two tracks in size. The IMBED parameter will use one of the two tracks for the sequence set and the other track for the data CIs. 50% of the data set will be the sequence set, making the effective utilization of the data set 50%.

10.2 INDEX SPACE ALLOCATION

It is common practice to specify the space allocation parameters for the data component only. If you omit these parameters for the index component, AMS determines them for you on the basis of the data component size, data CI size, key length, IMBED/REPLICATE specifications, DASD considerations, and so on. In most cases, AMS calculates these values in tracks and substitutes them *implicitly* as an index space allocation parameter. An example of the equivalent hard-coded explict value is:

```
INDEX                                    -
    (NAME(EMPLOYEE.KSDS.INDEX)    -
    TRACKS(3,2))
```

The AMS-determined values work just fine as far as the functioning of the data set is concerned. However, when it comes to VSAM performance, there may be serious side effects. Consider the following example:

Example: We'll start with an empty volume called VOL001. A KSDS, named A, is defined on that volume. Its data component has a primary allocation of 10 cylinders, and AMS determines the allocation of its index component to be 2 tracks. Both of the cluster's components are allocated as shown in Fig. 10.1.

Data set B, with a primary allocation of 18 cylinders, is defined afterwards, and 4 tracks are allocated for its index component. The VSAM space management algorithm determines that the 4 tracks will fit on the remaining tracks of the cylinder already containing the index component for data set A. Note that the index and data components of data set B are more distant physically than if they were allocated adjacent to each other. Similarly, a data set C is defined with a primary allocation of 7 cylinders, and its index is allocated 2 tracks. While the 7 cylinders of the data component fit right after the data component of B, the space-management module allocates the index component on the same cylinder as those of A and B. This causes the index and the data components of C to be further apart than is desirable. Remember that we started with an empty disk pack, but the same result could occur if the disk had had other preallocated files.

Now consider the performance impact. Since the index components are small in size, they tend to be clustered on one cylinder of the DASD. Because KSDS file requests are usually routed through the index components, the seek time for the read-write arms between the two components of B and C is greater than that of A. If we could somehow force the constituent components of a KSDS cluster to be

10.2 INDEX SPACE ALLOCATION

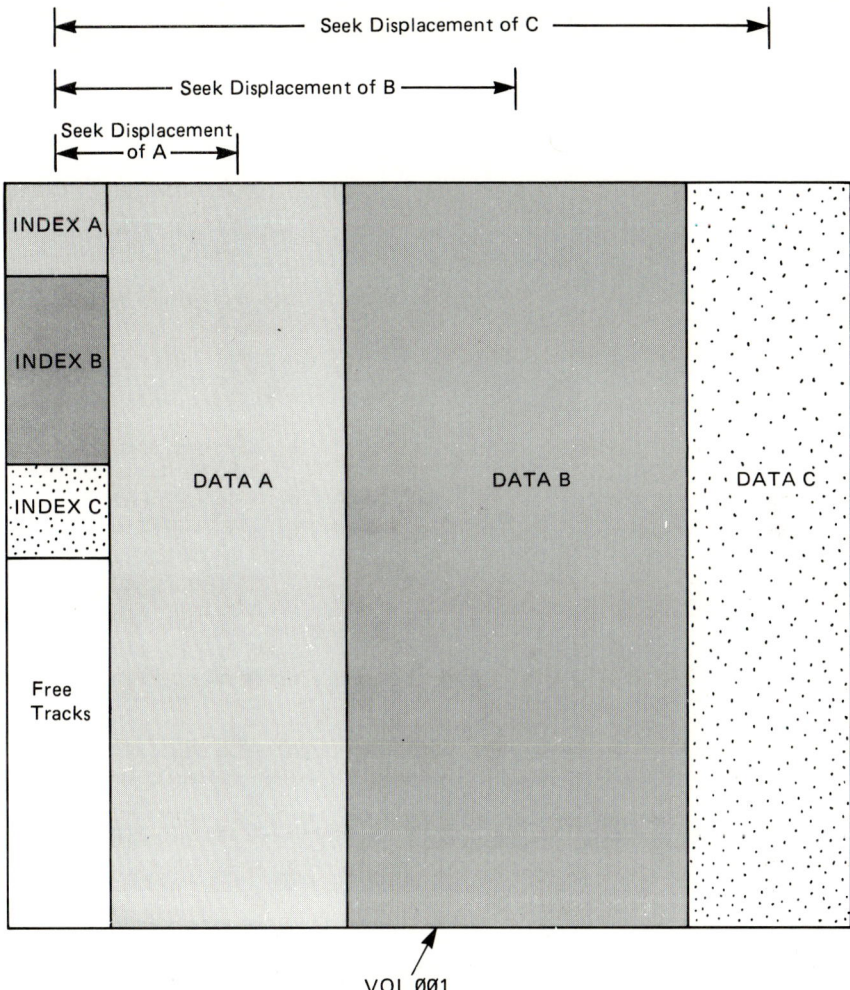

Figure 10.1 An example of the physical location of the index and data components for three data sets, A, B, and C, when AMS determined their index space allocation.

adjacent to each other, the seek time delay could be reduced significantly.

Since index clustering is caused by leaving empty tracks on a cylinder, the solution is to make sure that there are no empty tracks on any cylinder of the DASD. This can be achieved by hard coding the index component allocation parameters in cylinders. Normally, a primary and secondary allocation of one cylinder each should suffice. An example of the coding syntax is

```
INDEX                              -
    (NAME(EMPLOYEE.KSDS.INDEX)     -
    CYLINDERS(1,1))
```

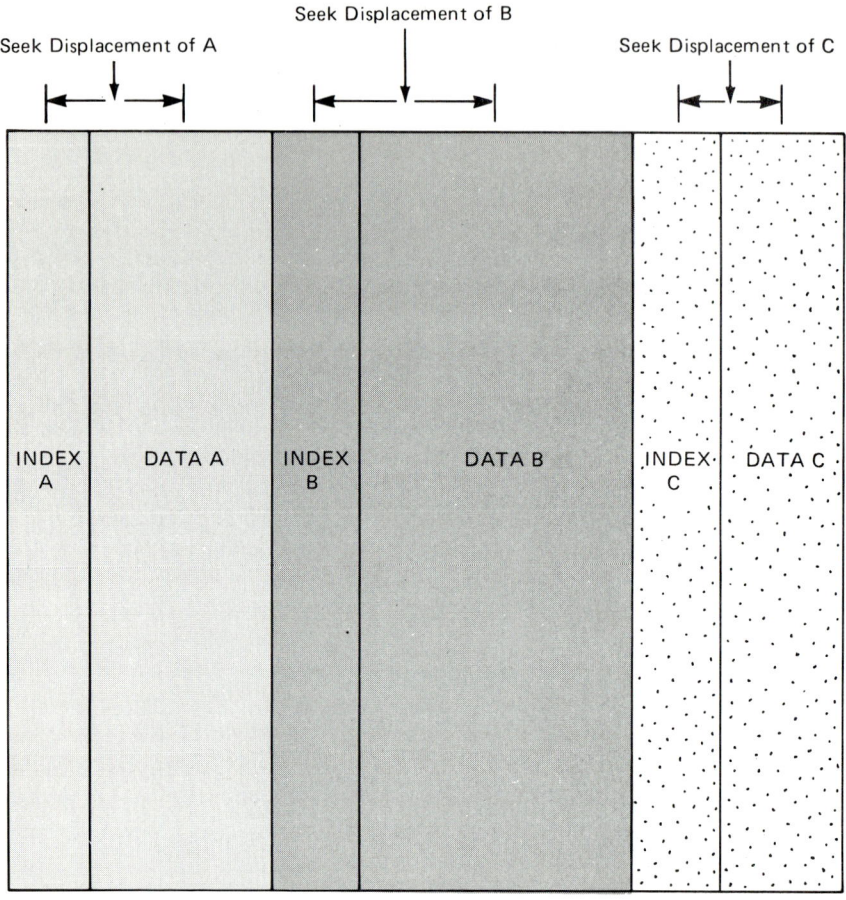

Figure 10.2 An example of the physical locations of the index and data components for three data sets A, B, and C when the AMS-allocated index sizes of 1 cylinder each is based on the index space-allocation parameters.

This will ensure the index component size of 1 cylinder and thus the space-management algorithm will not cause any index clustering. Be aware that this technique will overallocate the size of the index components for small data sets. While this means wasted DASD space, it is a very small price to pay for the improvement in I/O performance. The techniques suggested here are used for production systems where I/O performance is one of the major considerations.

If the index components of data sets A, B, and C were allocated with the index space allocation parameters of CYLINDERS(1,1), the physical location of the index and data components in the example would appear as in Fig. 10.2. Note that the seek displacements between the index and data components of data sets B and C have been reduced significantly.

10.3 FBA DEVICES (DOS/VSE ONLY)

There are two types of DASDs. One is the Count Key Data (CKD) device; examples are the IBM 3330, IBM 3350, and IBM 3380. Such devices are supported by both the MVS and DOS/VSE operating systems. For allocating VSAM data sets on these DASDs, the allocation parameter CYLINDERS is recommended; this will ensure the data CA size of one cylinder.

The second type of DASD is known as Fixed Block Architecture (FBA). Examples are the IBM 3310, IBM 3370, IBM 9335, and IBM 9332, the last two of which became available with the introduction of IBM 9370 computers. FBA devices are used only for DOS/VSE systems. When allocating a VSAM data set, you may not specify CYLINDERS or TRACKS for FBA devices; the only parameters supported by the AMS syntax are RECORDS and BLOCKS. Each FBA block represents 512 bytes of application-usable data.

Although the concept of DASD cylinders is not applicable to FBA devices, the physical hardware *does* consist of cylinders and tracks. Ensuring a data CA size of one cylinder is slightly tricky in this case. You have to make sure that the primary and secondary space allocation values are exact multiples of the number of FBA blocks per hardware cylinder. Figure 10.3 lists some attributes of selected FBA devices.

Example: We want to allocate a KSDS on an IBM 3370. The requirement is for 100 cylinders of primary and 10 cylinders of secondary space allocation. Since each cylinder of an IBM 3370 contains 744 blocks, the space allocation parameter of DEFINE CLUSTER will be

> BLOCKS(74400,7440)

> *We must make sure that every data set defined on that FBA device uses multiples of 744 blocks.* Since the index component of a

FBA DASD	Number of FBA blocks per track	Number of tracks per cylinder	Number of FBA blocks per cylinder	Cylinders per volume
IBM 3310	32	11	352	358
IBM 3370	62	12	744	750
IBM 9335	71	6	426	1963
IBM 9332	74	4	296	1349

Figure 10.3 Some FBA devices and their storage characteristics.

KSDS is a separate entity, its space allocation parameter will be coded as follows:

BLOCKS(744,744)

This will also prevent index clustering as discussed in Section 10.2. If all the files on an FBA device are not allocated in multiples of one-cylinder blocks, some components may start from a noncylinder boundary. This could nullify some of the performance characteristics of IMBEDed sequence set files.

10.4 UNIQUE VS SUBALLOCATION

UNIQUE and SUBALLOCATION are mutually exclusive parameters of the data set allocation commands. SUBALLOCATION is applicable only to data sets defined in VSAM catalogs; the concept has no relevance in ICF catalogs. Data sets thus defined are allocated in VSAM space previously defined with the DEFINE SPACE or DEFINE USERCATALOG commands. UNIQUE is applicable to both VSAM and ICF catalogs. Data sets defined with UNIQUE are allocated in VSAM space that is unique to them alone. Each of the two KSDS components will have VSAM space of its own. SUBALLOCATEd data sets are not known to the DASD Volume Table of Contents (VTOC), whereas the individual components of UNIQUE data sets have different data set control blocks (DSCBs) in the VTOC. Therefore if the VTOC entries are listed under TSO/SPF option 3.7, SUBALLOCATEd VSAM data sets are not displayed.

10.4.1 First Available VS Best Fit Algorithms

First Available Algorithm A request for the allocation of UNIQUE data sets is managed by the Direct Access Device Storage Management (DADSM) software of MVS. DADSM will allocate the VSAM data set as follows:

1. It receives the primary space request value from the command parameters.
2. It scans the DASD from beginning to end and allocates the unique data set to the *first available space* that is large enough to contain it.

Let's consider an example. Suppose an IBM 3380 (double density) with 1770 cylinders of space is as shown in Fig. 10.4a. It has two data sets, file A and file B. There are two separate blocks of empty DASD space of 200 cylinders and 180 cylinders, respectively. Allocation is requested for a third unique data set, file C, with a primary space value of 160 cylinders. DADSM will scan the DASD and try to find the first empty

10.4 UNIQUE VS SUBALLOCATION

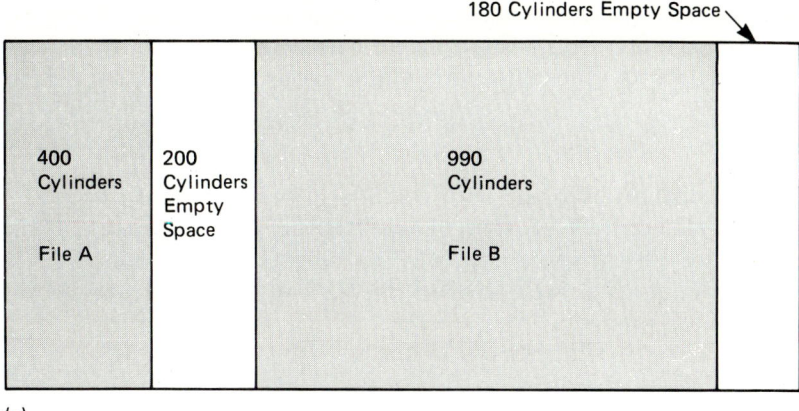

(a)

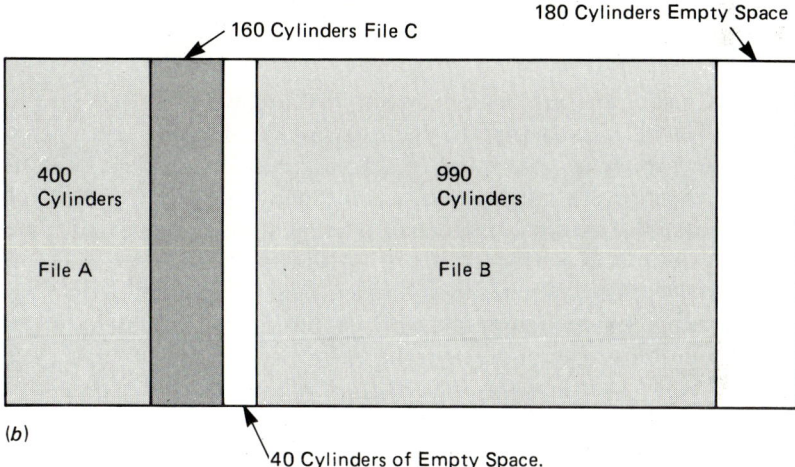

(b)

Figure 10.4 An example of the allocation of a UNIQUE data set. DADSM uses the first available space algorithm to allocate the unique data set (a) Before; (b) after.

space equal to or larger than 160 cylinders. In this scan, it happens to come across 200 cylinders of empty space. It will allocate 160 cylinders of that for file C. After proper allocation, the DASD will look like Fig. 10.4b.

Now consider the performance impact. If file A and file C are two parallel-processed data sets,[1] they will be processed in the least possible run time because of their close physical proximity. The seek displacement for the read-write arm as it jumps from file A to file C will be minimal.

[1]Parallel-processed data sets are those that are read and/or updated by reading them alternately on a Common Key Value. A master file and a transaction file are examples of such data sets.

Remember that no special technique has been used to put file A and file B next to each other. DADSM happened to do so although it was unaware of the impact of its space allocation algorithm on an application performance.

Best Fit Algorithm A request for the allocation of SUBALLOCATEd data sets is managed by VSAM and not DADSM. DADSM plays its role only while the VSAM space itself is being allocated. Afterwards, VSAM is responsible for managing its own space. VSAM will allocate the VSAM data sets as follows:

1. It receives the primary space request value from the command parameters.
2. It scans only the VSAM space on the DASD and identifies all unallocated spaces within it. It then allocates the data set on the unallocated area that *best fits the space request and causes the least amount of fragmentation.*

Let's consider the previous example in the context of our current discussion. We will assume that the entire IBM 3380 (double-density) consists of VSAM space as shown in Fig. 10.5a. It has two data sets, file A and file B. There are two separate blocks of empty VSAM space of 200 cylinders and 180 cylinders, respectively. Allocation is requested for a third SUBALLOCATEd data set, file C, with a primary space value of 160 cylinders. VSAM will determine that the least fragmentation will occur by allocating 160 cylinders of file C within the 180 cylinders of the empty block. After proper allocation, the VSAM space (the entire DASD, in this case) will be as shown in Fig. 10.5b.

Now consider the performance impact. If file A and file C are two parallel-processed data sets, it will take longer to process them compared to the data sets in Fig. 10.4b, because they are physically farther apart than in the other example.

Do not conclude that SUBALLOCATEd data sets perform poorly. The intent here is to describe the functions of two separate softwares and how they use their respective algorithms; which data set will be allocated where depends entirely upon what else is allocated on the DASD and the locations of unallocated free space areas. The best fit algorithm could have performed better if the VSAM space configuration had been different from the start and it might have been able to put files A and C closer to each other.

Conclusion If a program that has to do parallel processing of two or more data sets performs in a different way at different times, it could be due to differences in the physical locations of the data sets. Every time you de-

10.4 UNIQUE VS SUBALLOCATION

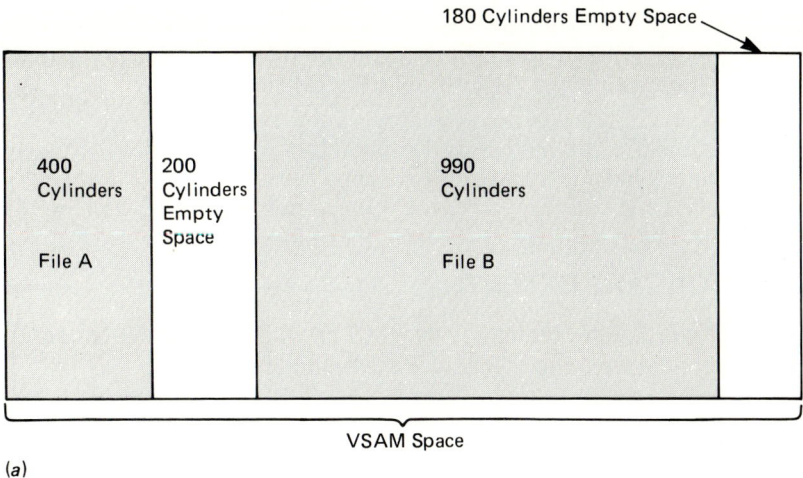

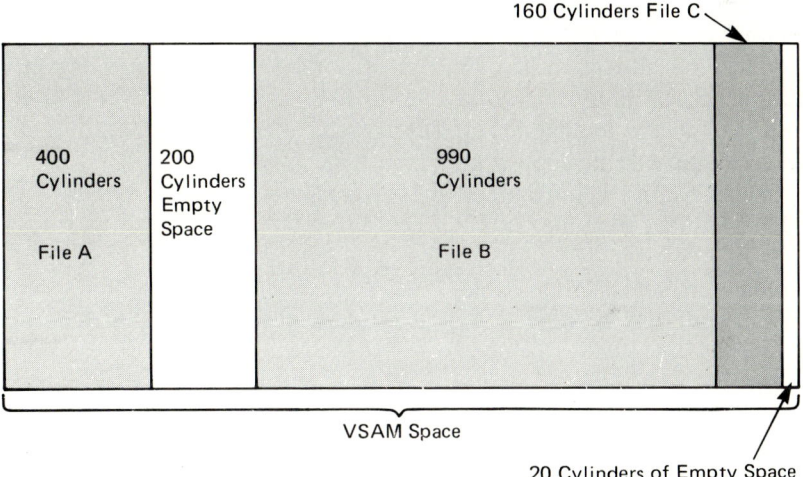

Figure 10.5 An example of the allocation of a SUBALLOCATEd data set. VSAM uses the best fit algorithm to allocate such a data set (a) Before; (b) after.

lete and redefine a VSAM file, it can be moved to a different location on the DASD.

10.4.2 Recommendation

One of the techniques that can be used to bind a VSAM file to one physical location is to define it with the REUSE parameter. You may never have to delete and reallocate such a file again. A REUSEable file, if opened for OUTPUT, will logically delete all of its existing records and act as if it is newly allocated. However, you should also be aware of some of the major limitations of a REUSEable VSAM file:

- A reusable file can have only 15 secondary extents, not 123.
- You cannot have alternate indexes on a reusable file.
- Under VSAM catalogs, a reusable file cannot be UNIQUE.

10.5 SECONDARY EXTENTS

The data set allocation commands of AMS provide for the allocation of space for secondary extents. Consider the command

CYLINDERS(100,10)

A DEFINE CLUSTER with this space allocation parameter will allocate 100 cylinders of DASD space at the time of the initial data set allocation. When all 100 cylinders of space have been used, secondary extents will be allocated 10 cylinders at a time. Under most circumstances, a VSAM data set may have up to 123 secondary extents. Therefore, subject to the availability of DASD space, the data set in our example could grow to be 1330 cylinders in size.

Under certain circumstances, a VSAM data set may be eligible for only 15 secondary extents. Two examples are:

- The data set is REUSEable.
- The data set is UNIQUE and is cataloged in a VSAM catalog (rather than an ICF catalog).

A major advantage to having the ability to extend a data set is that you can keep an application program running smoothly when additional file space requirements cannot be met from the existing allocated extents. Once it is determined that a data set requires secondary extents on a regular basis, the primary space allocation should be increased accordingly. Try to avoid having any secondary extent allocations in an on-line (e.g., CICS/VS) system. Data set allocations should be monitored on a regular basis using LISTCAT-generated listings. If any secondary extents are detected, the data set should be reallocated with a larger primary extent.

VTOC Update Overhead Each secondary extent allocation of UNIQUE data sets requires the system to update the Volume Table of Contents (VTOC) and the VSAM/ICF catalog. A VTOC update in an on-line environment could carry significant overhead in terms of elapsed time spent to effect the update. Therefore, the allocation of secondary extents, especially in a CICS/VS environment, should be avoided by allocating a larger primary extent.

EDB Overhead When a VSAM file is opened or extended dynamically, an extent data block (EDB) is created for each extent. Since VSAM deals with a relative byte address (RBA) rather than the physical address on the DASD, the EDBs keep track of the beginning and ending RBAs for each extent. When an application file request is converted to an RBA request, it must be further converted to the physical address on the DASD for each extent. The greater the number of extents, the greater the overhead to determine that value and the longer the path length (more machine instructions) for an I/O. Note that the VTOC update overhead occurs only when an extent is being allocated, while the EDB overhead occurs for every I/O request that is met from the secondary extents.

Secondary Volumes Consider the following parameters of a DEFINE CLUSTER example:

```
CYLINDERS(400,50)              -
VOLUMES(VSAM01,VSAM02,VSAM03)  -
```

When this command is executed, 400 cylinders will be allocated on the volume VSAM01. Later, as the data set grows in size and all 400 cylinders have been used, secondary allocations will be made in increments of 50 cylinders each on VSAM01. What happens when VSAM01 can no longer accommodate the secondary extents for lack of sufficient DASD space? VSAM will look for space on the next volume specified, VSAM02. Now comes the tricky part. How much space will VSAM look for and allocate on VSAM02, 50 cylinders or 400 cylinders? If you guessed 50 cylinders, you were wrong. VSAM will try to allocate 400 cylinders, i.e., the primary space allocation value, on each of the new volumes. If it cannot find enough space to allocate that amount (400 cylinders in our example), the data set extension will be unsuccessful. VSAM will notify your application of this condition. In batch Cobol, you can expect to receive a file status of 24 or 34, while CICS/VS will invoke the NOSPACE condition. This is a little-known fact and is often the source of great frustration. *When a CICS application is returning a NOSPACE condition while the VTOC listing of the secondary volumes shows enough space available to accommodate the secondary allocations, VSAM is, in fact, looking for space sufficient for the primary allocation.*

10.6 KEYRANGES

Use of KEYRANGES is an excellent technique for spreading a highly active data set over multiple volumes based on the values of the keys. By distributing the data over many volumes, you are making use of a multiple number of read-write heads on different DASDs to service the I/O re-

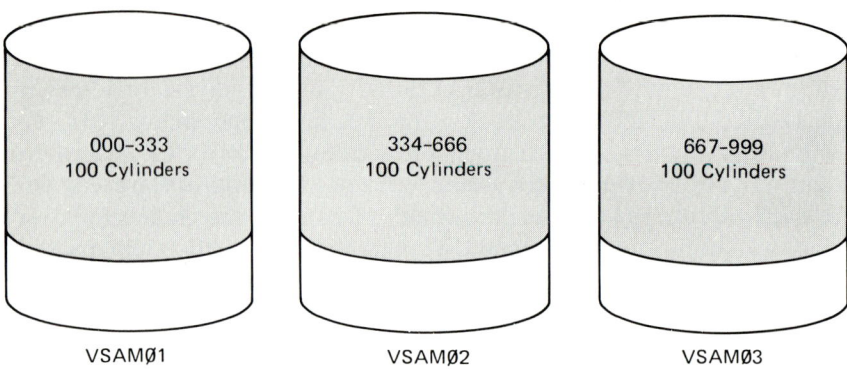

Figure 10.6 An example of allocation of a KSDS on the volumes VSAM01, VSAM02, and VSAM03 based on KEYRANGES.

- Allocate space for the data component in cylinders. This will ensure a data CA size of one cylinder.
- Allocate space for the index component in cylinders to reduce chances of index clustering.
- Allocate space for FBA devices in exact multiples of the number of FBA blocks per hardware cylinder.
- Be aware of the first available and best fit algorithms of UNIQUE and SUBALLOCATION space management.
- VSAM tries to allocate primary space first on each additional volume eligible for data set extension.
- Avoid allocation of secondary extents in on-line systems.
- Use KEYRANGES for highly active data sets to distribute I/O's over multiple volumes.

Figure 10.7 Recommendations for the use of space allocation parameters.

10.7 SUMMARY 139

quests. This may, depending upon the activity of other data sets on those volumes, provide better I/O service time. Consider the following example of a DEFINE CLUSTER:

```
KEYRANGES((000 333),(334 666),(667 999))      -
VOLUMES(VSAM01,VSAM02,VSAM03)                 -
CYLINDERS(100,15)
```

Upon successful executions of the command, space of 100 cylinders *each* will be allocated on VSAM01, VSAM02, and VSAM03 (see Fig. 10.6). When the data set is initially loaded, all the records in the key range 000 to 333 will be loaded into the 100 cylinders of space on VSAM01. When the load program encounters records with key 334, it will begin loading them on VSAM02, up to a key value of 666. Similarly, the records from 667 to 999 will only be eligible for VSAM03. In fact, the load program does not need any special coding to direct records to any particular key range. Once they have been defined at the time of data set allocation, the key ranges are transparent to the load, the update, and the data retrieval programs.

Note that the primary and secondary space allocation parameters apply to each segment of a key range. Also be aware that the key ranges don't have to be evenly divided over different volumes. For example, the following is a valid command syntax:

```
KEYRANGES((000 100),(101 800),(801 999))      -
VOLUMES(VSAM01,VSAM02,VSAM03)                 -
CYLINDERS(100,15)
```

IBM's Access Method Services manual provides more details about KEYRANGES.

10.7 SUMMARY

We conclude that the space allocation parameters play a significant role in the performance design of VSAM files. Major recommendations for their use are summarized in Fig. 10.7.

chapter 11

Imbed and Replicate

In Chap. 6 we learned that seek time delay and the rotational delay are the major components of I/O service time. We can gain significant improvements in I/O service time by using techniques to reduce these delays. IMBED and REPLICATE are two such techniques.

The IMBED and REPLICATE options are applicable only to the index component of a KSDS or an alternate index. IMBED relates to the sequence set, while REPLICATE is applicable to the index set of the index component. These options, while improving I/O performance, also *increase* the DASD requirement to some extent. The default options are NOIMBED and NOREPLICATE. Remember that these four options are *not* applicable to an ESDS or RRDS.

The use and effect of these options can be better explained by using a sample case. Figure 11.1 shows a KSDS with three levels of index. As you already know, the first two levels are the index set, while the third, lowermost level is the sequence set. There are three records (or index CIs) in our index set. For reference, we will name them ISR-1, ISR-2, and ISR-3. There are six records (or index CIs) in the sequence set. We will refer to them as SSR-1, SSR-2, SSR-3, SSR-4, SSR-5, and SSR-6. Note that ISR-2 points to SSR-1, SSR-2, and SSR-3, while ISR-3 points to SSR-4, SSR-5, and SSR-6. In real life, a two-level index would have been sufficient for our test case, because one index set record (ISR) would have provided enough space to contain pointers for six sequence set records (SSR). We are purposely creating a three-level index to make this example

11.1 IMBED AND NOREPLICATE

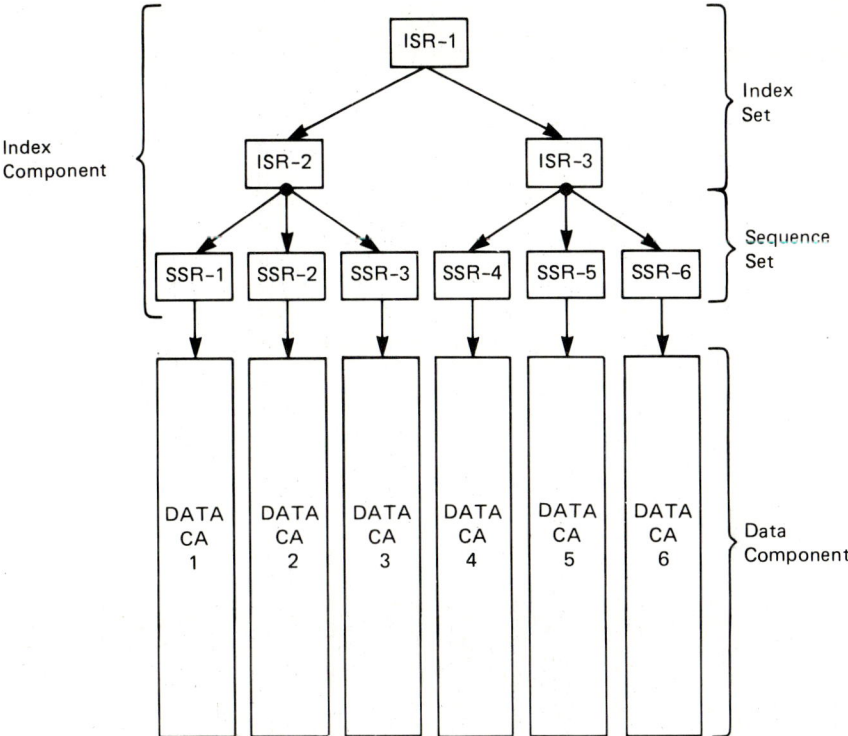

Figure 11.1 Configuration of a typical three-level index KSDS. There are three records (or index CIs) in the index set and six records (or index CIs) in the sequence set of the index component. Each sequence set record points to one data CA.

more interesting. Note that each sequence set record contains pointers to the data CIs of *one and only one* data CA.

Let's assume that the space allocation for the data component is in cylinders, making the data CA size one cylinder. In this example, the data CI size, as well as the index CI size, is 4096 bytes. With these assumptions in mind, let's move on to our first example.

11.1 IMBED AND NOREPLICATE

In our first case, the KSDS in Fig. 11.1 is defined with the IMBED and NOREPLICATE options. Since NOREPLICATE is also the default, we need not include it in the DEFINE CLUSTER. IMBED, however, must be coded explicitly, since it is not the default option. After the data set was defined, it was loaded sequentially, and it may have been randomly updated later. It is currently using six data CAs with the index architecture depicted in Fig. 11.1. Figure 11.2 represents the physical placement of the index set records, sequence set records, and data CAs.

Since IMBED was used, the sequence set records occupy the first physical track of the data CA. In other words, the sequence set record is

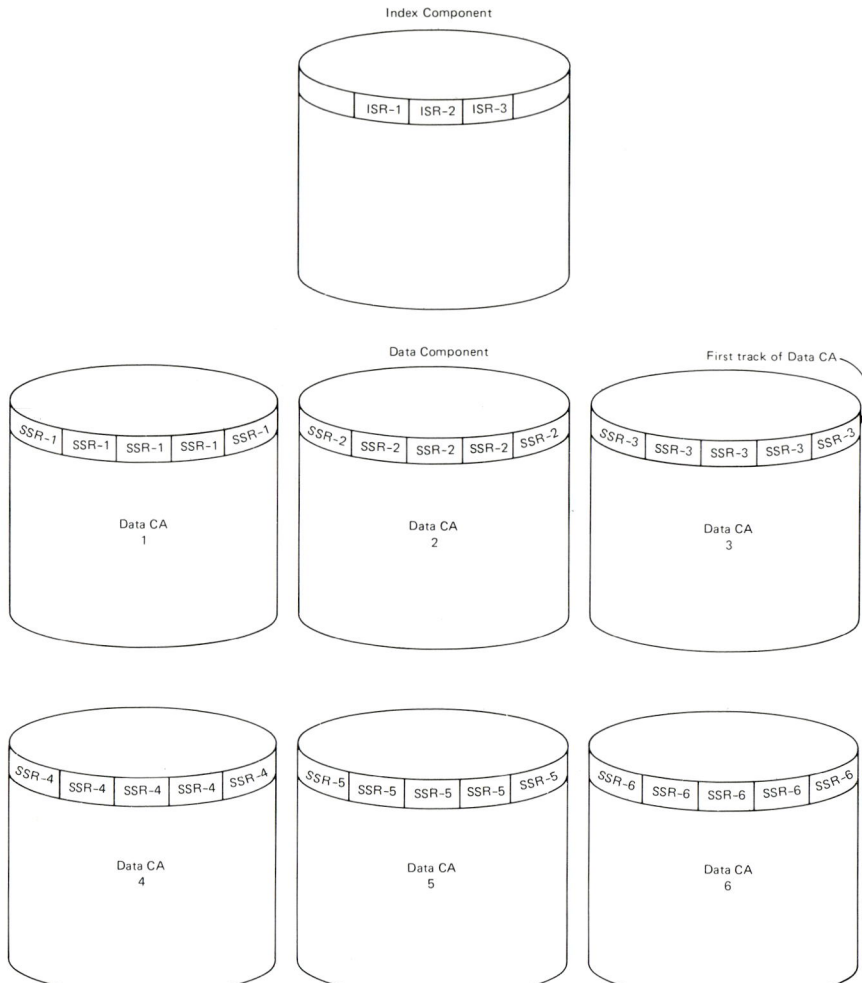

Figure 11.2 Layout of the KSDS in Fig. 11.1 defined with IMBED and NOREPLICATE options.

IMBEDed in the first track of the data CA, and it is repeated there as many times as possible. For example, if the device is an IBM 3380 and the index CI size is 4096 bytes, the sequence set CI will be repeated on the DASD track 10 times. Notice that SSR-1 is on the first track of data CA 1, SSR-2 is on the first track of data CA 2, and so on.

Since NOREPLICATE was also used, the index set records (three of them in this case) reside in the space allocated for the index component of the data set. ISR-1, ISR-2, and ISR-3 use up the three control intervals of the index component. If the device is an IBM 3380, it is capable of carrying seven more ISRs on the same track in the future.

11.1 IMBED AND NOREPLICATE

11.1.1 Increased DASD Space Requirement

Since the IMBED option uses one track of *each* data component for the sequence set, it reduces the effective DASD utilization. The corresponding increase in the DASD space requirement is lowest if the data CA is one cylinder in size, i.e., if space allocation is made in cylinders. Figure 11.3 tabulates effective data CA utilization assuming that the data CA is one cylinder in size.

The data CA utilization will be the lowest if the data CA size is two tracks. In that case, the IMBEDed sequence set will use one of the two tracks for itself, reducing the effective data CA utilization to 50%. Therefore, *it is recommended that the space allocation for the data component be made in cylinders if the IMBED option is used for data set allocation.*

11.1.2 Effect on I/O Performance

Consider a typical file request scenario. Suppose a read request is issued to the data set in Fig. 11.2. Let's also assume that by proper allocation of index buffers (see Chaps. 15 and 16), the index set records are kept in core. The index set records in our example are ISR-1, ISR-2, and ISR-3. Since the index set records are in real storage, no physical I/O will be performed to retrieve them. For all practical purposes, the read request will retrieve the appropriate sequence set record and then the appropriate data CI. Note that in our example the SSRs and the data CI are on the *same cylinder*. Also, the SSRs are repeated on the first track a multiple

IBM DASD	Tracks per cylinder	Tracks used for data component (with IMBED)	Effective DASD utilization, %
3330	19	18	95
3340	12	11	92
3350	30	29	97
3375	12	11	92
3380	15	14	93
3310*	11	10	91
3370*	12	11	92
9335*	6	5	83
9332*	4	3	75

*IBM 3310 and 3370 are FBA DASDs used with the 4331 and 4341 series. IBM 9335 and 9332 are FBA DASDs used only with the IBM 9370 seriers of computers.

Figure 11.3 Effective data CA space utilization for DASDs with the use of the IMBED option and a data CA size of one cylinder.

number of times. This will have a favorable effect on I/O performance for two reasons:

- After the proper seek is done to the sequence set cylinder, the *rotational delay will be reduced* because the same SSR is repeated on the track a number of times.
- After the SSR is read into the buffers and VSAM determines the correct pointers for the data CI, there is a high probability that the read-write arm will be stationed at the same cylinder. *If it is, the seek time for the data component will be zero.* However, keep in mind that the seek can be stolen by another I/O on the same DASD if there was a pending I/O executed between the sequence set record I/O and the data CI I/O.

In a nutshell: *IMBED reduces the rotational delay for the SSR and increases the possibility of eliminating the seek delay for the data CI.* Figure 11.4 tabulates the effect of IMBED on I/O services times for various IBM DASDs.

Let's consider the example in Fig. 11.4 for the IBM 3380 (double-density). If NOIMBED was specified, the I/O's for the SSR and the data CI will be executed with average seek and rotational delays. Thus, both of the I/O's for a record read will be executed in 53.2 ms. The itemized breakdown is given in the figure. Now let's analyze the same DASD with the IMBED option. The rotational delay for the SSR is 0.8 ms instead of 8.3 ms. (Since a 4096-byte SSR is repeated 10 times on a track of an IBM 3380, the rotational delay will be $1/10 \times 8.3$ ms, or 0.8 ms.) The seek time delay for the data CI is zero, because we are assuming that the seek is not stolen by another pending I/O on the same DASD. Thus the total service time for the two I/O's is 28.7 ms. Compared with 53.2 ms, this shows a 46% improvement. A casual perusal of Fig. 11.4 shows improvements of 41 to 46% for the listed IBM DASDs.

Device Busy and Stolen Seek In the example just discussed, the I/O performance improvement would not be so dramatic if the seek had been stolen by another I/O between the SSR read and the data CI read. What causes a stolen seek? Consider the example of the double-density IBM 3380 in Fig. 11.4. Following the necessary seek delay and rotational delay for the SSR, it will take 1.3 ms to transfer the data to the index buffers in main storage. VSAM will then determine the pointers to the data CI that is likely to contain the desired record. During this process, if another I/O for the same DASD is queued up, the read-write arm will be directed to the new cylinder to satisfy the requirements of that I/O. The I/O request could be for the same file (e.g., another CICS/VS task) or for a different file on the same DASD. Therefore, whether the seek will be stolen or not depends upon whether an I/O for the same DASD is queued up at that particular moment. The busier the device, the greater the likelihood of a

			I/O for sequence set**				I/O for data CI**				Total time for two I/O's, ms	Percent reduction
IBM DASD	Index option	Seek time, ms	Rotational delay, ms	Data transfer, ms	Total I/O, ms	Seek time,* ms	Rotational delay, ms	Data transfer, ms	Total I/O, ms			
3330	NOIMBED	30	8.4	5.0	43.4	30	8.4	5.0	43.4	86.8	41
	IMBED	30	2.8	5.0	37.8	0	8.4	5.0	13.4	51.2	
3350	NOIMBED	25	8.4	3.4	36.8	25	8.4	3.4	36.8	73.6	42
	IMBED	25	2.1	3.4	30.5	0	8.4	3.4	11.8	42.3	
3375	NOIMBED	19	10.1	2.1	31.2	19	10.1	2.1	31.2	62.4	44
	IMBED	19	1.2	2.1	22.3	0	10.1	2.1	12.2	34.5	
3380 (SD)	NOIMBED	16	8.3	1.3	25.6	16	8.3	1.3	25.6	51.2	45
	IMBED	16	0.8	1.3	18.1	0	8.3	1.3	9.6	27.7	
3380 (DD)	NOIMBED	17	8.3	1.3	26.6	17	8.3	1.3	26.6	53.2	46
	IMBED	17	0.8	1.3	19.1	0	8.3	1.3	9.6	28.7	
3310†	NOIMBED	27	9.6	3.9	40.5	27	9.6	3.9	40.5	81.0	42
	IMBED	27	2.4	3.9	33.3	0	9.6	3.9	13.5	46.8	
3370†	NOIMBED	20	10.1	2.2	32.3	20	10.1	2.2	32.3	64.6	44
	IMBED	20	1.4	2.2	23.6	0	10.1	2.2	12.3	35.9	
9335†	NOIMBED	18	8.3	1.9	28.2	18	8.3	1.9	28.2	56.4	44
	IMBED	18	1.0	1.9	20.9	0	8.3	1.9	10.2	31.1	
9332†	NOIMBED	24	9.6	2.1	35.7	24	9.6	2.1	35.7	71.4	45
	IMBED	24	1.1	2.1	27.2	0	9.6	2.1	11.7	38.9	

*It is assumed that the seek is not stolen by another I/O waiting in the queue.
**Assumptions: Data CI size = 4096 Bytes, Index CI size = 4096 bytes.
†3310, 3370, 9335, and 9332 are FBA devices

Figure 11.4 Effect of index options IMBED and NOIMBED on the I/O service times for sequence set and the data CI for KSDS.

stolen seek due to a queued-up I/O. Omegamon/CICS and Omegamon/MVS are good tools for measuring the device busy and queue depth (pending I/O's) for a particular DASD. *An excessively busy DASD will negate the effect of an IMBEDed sequence set through stolen seeks.*

IMBED and Device Busy Since an IMBEDed sequence set reduces the average service time for an I/O, it also reduces the device busy percentage. Moreover, a low device busy figure reduces the I/O queue and helps in reducing the stolen seeks for an IMBEDed sequence set data set. Thus we can see that a reduction in the device busy percentage and the reduced I/O service time resulting from the use of IMBED go hand in hand. It is very important to keep the queue length to a minimum to derive the real benefits from the use of the IMBED parameter.

IMBED and CI Split A CI split updates the contents of a sequence set record. A CI split of an IMBEDed sequence set will take a little longer because VSAM has to update all the copies of the SSRs on the first track of the data CA. Since, for an IBM 3380, a full track rotation takes 16.7 ms, it will take 16.7 ms to update all the copies of the SSRs on the track. In a majority of cases, this additional overhead may be ignored because of a low number of CI splits.

There are some circumstances in which only one record is contained in each data CI (these are called single-record CIs). For example, if the data CI size is 4096 bytes and the record size is 4000 bytes, there will be only one logical record per data CI. *Each addition of a new record to the data set will cause an update of the SSR.* Each record-add under these circumstances will cause full track update overhead of 16.7 ms. In such cases, the advantages of an expedited read request must be weighed against the slower add requests to justify the use of IMBED. *Under DF/EF (or DFP), a delete request erasing the last and only record in a CI also updates the SSR.* This should be considered in the context of the IMBED parameter. However, a record update (read and rewrite) does not update the SSR.

11.1.3 Summary

Figure 11.5 summarizes the characteristics of an IMBED/NO-REPLICATE data set.

11.2 IMBED AND REPLICATE

Figure 11.6 shows the data set structure created with the use of the IMBED and REPLICATE options for the data given in Fig. 11.1.

The manner in which the IMBED option that is applicable to the sequence set works was explained in Section 11.1. The SSRs are imbed-

11.2 IMBED AND REPLICATE

- IMBED reduces effective DASD utilization.
- IMBED significantly improves I/O performance for data sets with low I/O queue length.
- An excessively busy DASD will negate the effect of IMBED because of stolen seeks.
- CI splits take longer for an IMBEDed sequence set.
- IMBED slows down record adds and deletes for single-record-CI data sets.
- NOREPLICATE is recommended if the index set records are kept in core using NSR buffers (Chaps. 15 and 16).

Figure 11.5 Summary of characteristics of an IMBED/NOREPLICATE data set.

ded in the data component and are repeated on the first track as many times as possible. The *REPLICATE option* puts each *index set record* on a *separate track of the index component* and *replicates it as many times as possible*. While the NOREPLICATE option puts all the index set records on one track (Fig. 11.2), REPLICATE uses as many tracks as there are index set records.

11.2.1 DASD Space Requirement

The index set of the index component is always a small entity. In a three-level index structure, the number of records at the second level determines the size of the index set, because the top level always has one record. It is rare to have more than 20 ISRs even in the index set of a very large data set. Therefore the index set of a fairly large data set will fit on one or two cylinders of the DASD. For all practical purposes, *the increase in the DASD requirement due to the use of REPLICATE is insignificant and can be ignored.*

11.2.2 I/O Performance

The effect of IMBED on I/O performance was discussed in Section 11.1. The effect of REPLICATE depends upon:

- Whether NonShared Resource (NSR) or Local Shared Resource (LSR) buffers are being used (Chaps. 16 and 17)

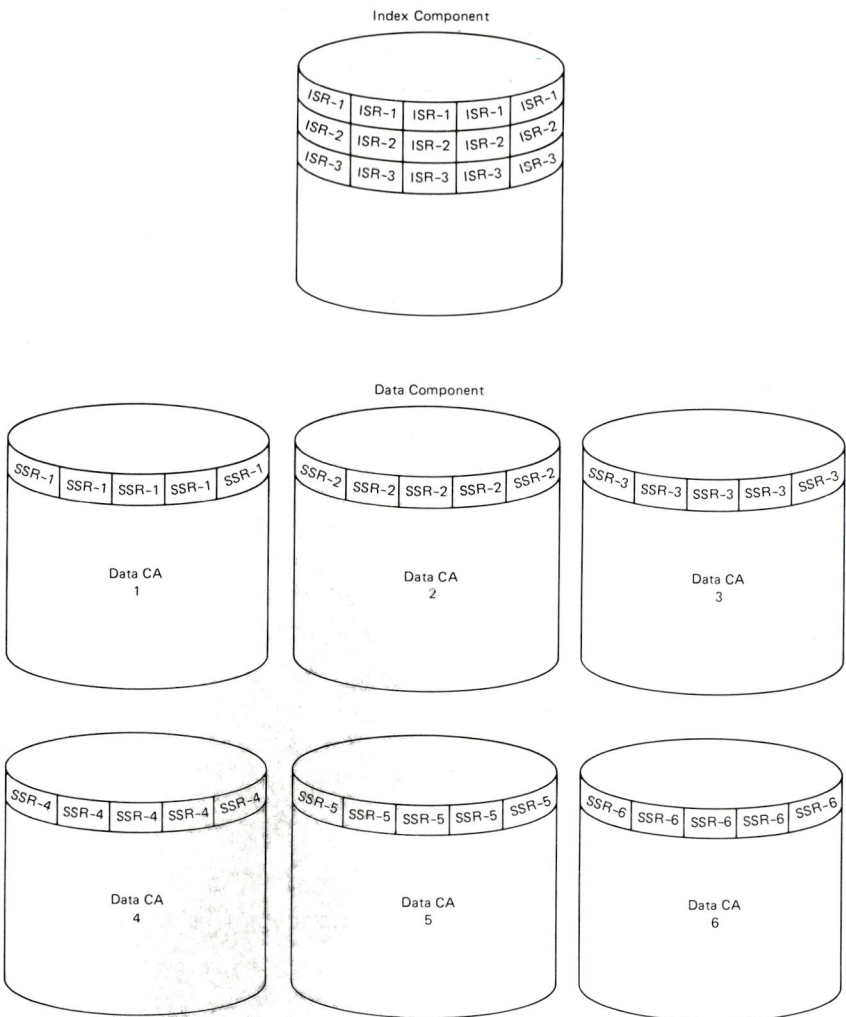

Figure 11.6 Layout of the KSDS in Fig. 11.1 defined with the IMBED and REPLICATE options.

- Whether the buffer allocation for NSR is sufficient to contain the index set in core
- Whether the KSDS is being used for IMS/DB data bases

NSR and Good Index Buffer Allocation Buffer allocation under NSR is considered to be good if the allocation of index buffers is sufficient to place the *entire index set* into core and also provide one additional index buffer for each string. Consider the index structure in Fig. 11.1. There are three records in the index set. If this file is being used for CICS/VS and the value of string number (STRNO) is 4, the total number of index buff-

11.2 IMBED AND REPLICATE

ers (BUFNI) allocated should be 7, i.e., three for the index set plus one for each string. With this kind of buffer allocation, only one I/O is performed to retrieve each record of the index set *on its first reference*. After that, no I/O to the index set is necessary until the data set is closed or the index set record itself is updated. We can see, then, that *the REPLICATE option does not have any effect on a data set using NSR buffers with sufficient buffer allocation to keep the index set in core.*

NSR and Poor Index Buffer Allocation A data set is considered to have poor index buffer allocation if, after one index buffer is allocated for each string, there are not enough buffers left to put the index set records into core. Let's consider an example for the KSDS shown in Fig. 11.1. Suppose the value of STRNO is 4 and the value of BUFNI is 6. Four index buffers of the six will be allocated for the four strings. There are only two buffers remaining to be used for the index set. Since the index set has three records, all of them cannot remain in those two buffers all the time. Under these circumstances, VSAM will make use of those two buffers on the basis of a least recently used (LRU) algorithm. The two most frequently used ISRs of the three will tend to stay in core. Since the top-level ISR is always the most highly referenced buffer, it will always stay in core, leaving only one index buffer for the second-level ISRs. Now we will see the advantages of having REPLICATEd index set records for poor buffer allocation situations.

Since VSAM will use the remaining index set buffer to read in the second-level ISRs on *each random file request*, it would be advantageous to have that I/O executed as quickly as possible. Since REPLICATE will repeat each ISR on a separate track, the rotational delay will be far less than if the ISRs were not replicated. Figure 11.7 tabulates rotational delays for REPLICATEd and NOREPLICATEd records for a number of IBM DASDs. We can see that REPLICATE will *reduce* the rotational delay for ISRs anywhere from 66%, for an IBM 3330, to 90%, for an IBM 3380 (double-density). This is a tremendous performance improvement for index set I/O's. It is worth repeating that the default index buffer allocation (if BUFNI is not coded) is the value of STRNO. Since this represents the worst index buffer allocation, the use of REPLICATE will give relatively better results.

Remember that the best performance results are achieved by keeping the ISRs in core. In that case, the use of REPLICATE does not provide any improvement in performance. However, if it is not possible to keep the ISRs in core (e.g., virtual storage constraint problem in a non-MVS/XA environment), the use of REPLICATE is highly recommended.

LSR and REPLICATE We learned in Chap. 4 that buffers are shared among data sets in an LSR environment. Index and data buffers may use the same buffer pool in an LSR allocation, and the only criterion used is

IBM DASD	Rotational delay†, ms		Reduction in rotational delay, %
	NOREPLICATE	REPLICATE	
3330	8.4	2.8	66
3350	8.4	2.1	75
3375	10.1	1.2	88
3380 (SD)	8.3	0.8	90
3380 (DD)	8.3	0.8	90
3310*	9.6	2.4	75
3370*	10.1	1.4	86
9335*	8.3	1.0	87
9332*	9.6	1.1	88

*IBM 3310, 3370, 9335, and 9332 are FBA DASDs.
†It is assumed that the index CI size is 4096 bytes.

Figure 11.7 Rotational delay for index set record reads with and without the use of REPLICATE option.

the CI size. The data and index buffers are part of the buffer pool and may be invalidated at any time on the basis of the LRU principle. Thus, there is absolutely no way to ensure that the index set records will stay in the buffers. It is impossible to predict whether the I/O request will cause a physical I/O or a successful look-aside to read the records from the buffer pool. *To make sure that the index component I/O's, if required, are executed efficiently, the use of REPLICATE is highly recommended in an LSR environment.*

11.2.3 Summary

Figure 11.8 summarizes the use of REPLICATE in a IMBED/REPLICATE environment for a KSDS.

11.3 NOIMBED AND REPLICATE

Figure 11.9 shows the data set structure that would be created with the use of the NOIMBED and REPLICATE options for the data in Fig. 11.1.

11.3 NOIMBED AND REPLICATE

> - REPLICATE causes an insignificant increase in DASD space requirements for the index component.
> - REPLICATE does not improve performance in an NSR environment if index buffer allocation is sufficient to keep the ISRs in core.
> - REPLICATE significantly improves I/O performance in an NSR environment if index buffer allocation is insufficient to keep the ISRs in core.
> - REPLICATE is *always* recommended in an LSR environment.
> - REPLICATE is always recommended for the KSDS portions of IMS data bases.

Figure 11.8 Summary of the implications of the use of REPLICATE in an IMBED/REPLICATE environment.

Note that the SSRs are not IMBEDed on the first track of the data component. Rather, they are placed in the *index component* along with the ISRs. The REPLICATE option causes both the ISRs and SSRs to use one track per record and to be replicated on the tracks as many times as possible.

DASD Space Requirement *The DASD space requirement for NOIMBED and REPLICATE is the same as for IMBED and REPLICATE.* The only difference is that with NOIMBED and REPLICATE the SSRs are kept in the index component, while in the latter case the SSRs are imbeded on the first track of their respective data components.

Performance The overall performance effects of NOIMBED and REPLICATE are *almost the same* as those of IMBED and REPLICATE. However, IMBEDed sequence set records are always preferred for a device with a small I/O queue length in order to save on a possible seek when reading the data CI. *The only situation where NOIMBED and REPLICATE might be preferred over IMBED and REPLICATE is when you wish to put the index component on a separate DASD (preferably a high-performance disk drive) from the data component.*

NOIMBED and REPLICATE is recommended for underallocated

CHAPTER 11 / IMBED AND REPLICATE

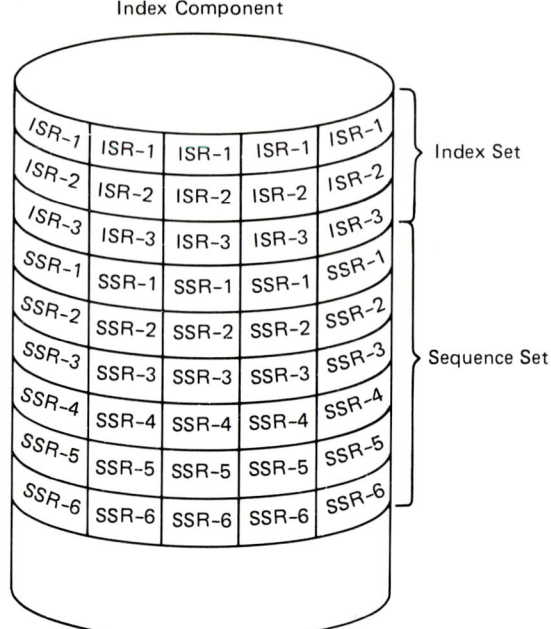

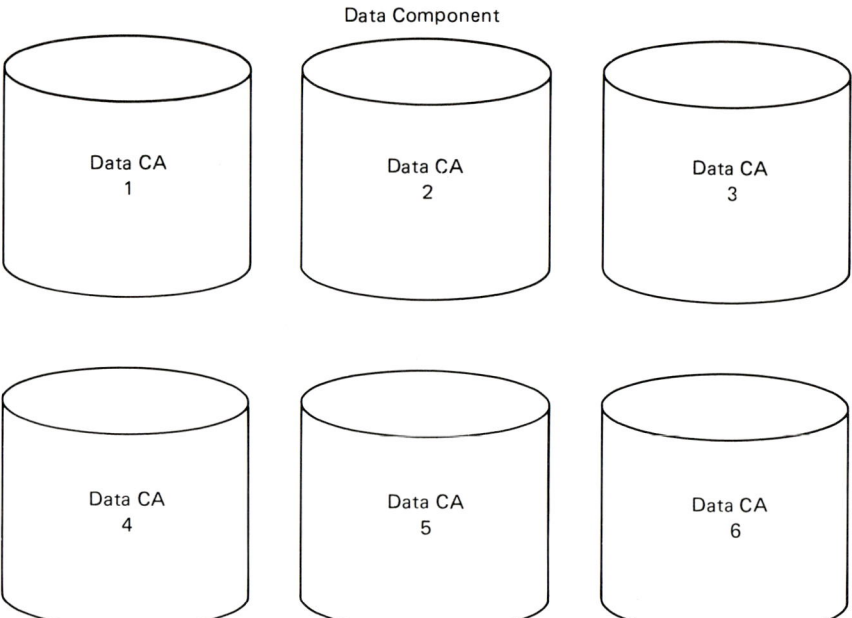

Figure 11.9 Layout of the KSDS in Fig. 11.1 defined with the NOIMBED and REPLICATE options.

NSR buffer data sets, all the LSR buffer pool eligible data sets, and the KSDS portions of IMS data bases.

11.4 NOIMBED AND NOREPLICATE

NOIMBED and NOREPLICATE are the default index options for a DEFINE CLUSTER or DEFINE AIX. Figure 11.10 shows the data set structure created with these options for the data of Fig. 11.1. As you can see, all nine records of the index component (three ISRs and six SSRs) are placed on a single track of an IBM 3380. Use of these options requires the least amount of DASD space for the index component. *Use of these options is recommended only for data sets with low I/O activity when performance is not critical.*

11.4.1 Cache DASD Controllers

Cache DASD controllers were discussed in detail in Chap. 7. You will recall that cache memory deals with data in terms of full DASD tracks only. For example, cache will consider a 47,968-byte track of an IBM 3380 as one entity for caching purposes. In order to make full use of this characteristic, you must use index options that pack the maximum amount of index records on one track. NOIMBED and NOREPLICATE are the options that will make the most efficient use of DASD space for the index component. Remember that IMBED and REPLICATE increase the I/O performance for electromechanical DASDs by reducing rotational delay. Since cache is a solid state memory without moving parts, these options have no impact on I/O performance. However, they do have a negative impact on performance by requiring the allocation of more DASD space and thus more cache slots. Therefore, *in a cache DASD controller environment, only the use of the NOIMBED and NOREPLICATE options is recommended.*

11.5 IMS/DB AND REPLICATE

CICS/VS *always* uses LSR buffer pools for IMS data bases. IMS/DC may use LSR or Global Shared Resource (GSR) buffer pools. In either case, the buffers are subject to being flushed out by an LRU algorithm. The following IMS data base access methods may use VSAM/KSDS as the underlying physical file architecture:

- The KSDS portion of the Hierarchical Indexed Sequential Access Method (HISAM) or SHISAM
- The KSDS portion of the Hierarchical Indexed Direct Access Method (HIDAM)
- The IMS secondary index

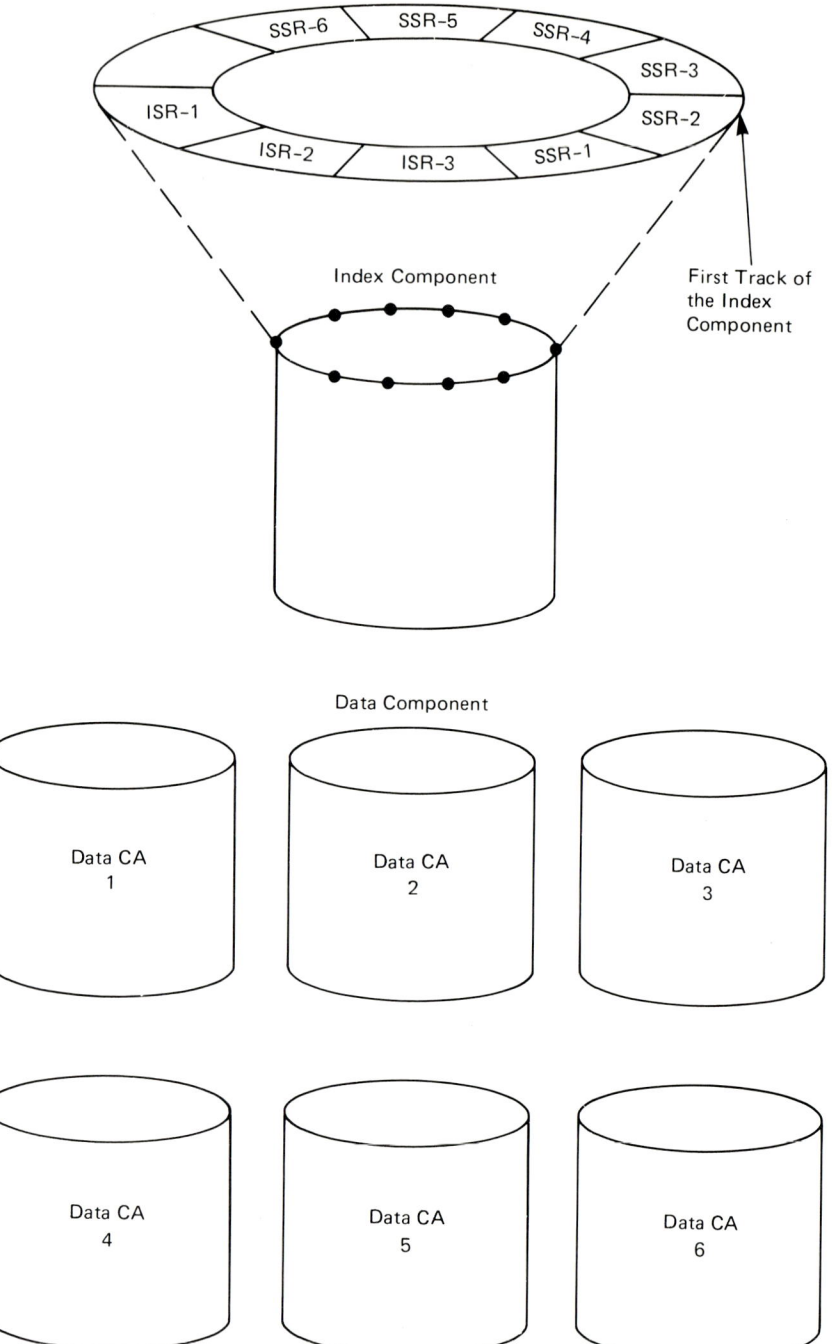

Figure 11.10 Layout of the KSDS in Fig. 11.1 defined with the NOIMBED and NOREPLICATE options. These are the default options.

In all these cases, the use of REPLICATE is highly recommended to improve I/O performance. Whether IMBED or NOIMBED is used is immaterial, because REPLICATE will ensure the replication of the sequence set records as well as the index set records. Since all the index records are replicated, rotational delay will be minimal if any one of them has to be read into the LSR/GSR buffers after it has been flushed out.

11.6 ALTERNATE INDEXES

Alternate indexes are, in fact, KSDS in architecture. Therefore all the rules that apply to the index options discussed in this chapter also apply to alternate indexes.

Alternate index clusters are usually a small subset of the base cluster. In most cases, they should fit onto one DASD cylinder. If they do, it is important that you specify IMBED when allocating them. An IMBEDed sequence set will expedite the I/O and reduce the overhead associated with alternate indexes.

If an alternate index cluster is greater than one cylinder in size, make sure that the index buffer allocation for the alternate index itself is sufficient to place its index set in core.

Before release 1.6.1 of CICS/VS, the alternate indexes of the upgrade set[1] could not be defined in the LSR buffer pool.[2] Beginning with CICS/VS 1.7, alternate indexes are eligible to be part of the LSR buffer pool. Also remember that with CICS/VS 1.7, LSR is the default File Control Table (FCT) option unless it is overridden by NSR at assembly time. *If you inted to use LSR for alternate indexes, make sure to define the indexes with the REPLICATE option for performance reasons.*

---

[1]Alternate indexes allocated with the UPGRADE option become members of the upgrade set of the base cluster. Any update to the base cluster is automatically communicated to the members of the upgrade set by VSAM.

[2]IBM supplied some fixes to CICS/VS 1.6.1 to support LSR for alternate indexes. However, this feature was not part of the base product.

chapter 12

Techniques for Using FREESPACE

The FREESPACE parameter may be specified at the time of DEFINE CLUSTER or DEFINE AIX as follows:

FREESPACE(CI-percent,CA-percent)

Although this parameter is coded at the time of data set allocation, it is applicable *only* when the file is *sequentially* loaded later. The two integer values CI-percent and CA-percent may vary from 0 to 100. CI-percent indicates the percentage of free space that will be left empty in each data component control interval at the time of initial load or resume load.[1] CA-percent specifies the percentage of CIs within each CA that will be left empty at the time of the initial load or resume load. Let's consider an example.

Example: A KSDS is defined with the NOIMBED option on an IBM 3380. The space allocation is done in cylinders so that the data CA is one cylinder in size. The data CI size is specified to be 8192 bytes

---

[1] In Cobol, the *initial load* occurs when the file is opened as OUTPUT, and *resume load* is done when it is opened as EXTEND.

12 TECHNIQUES FOR USING FREESPACE

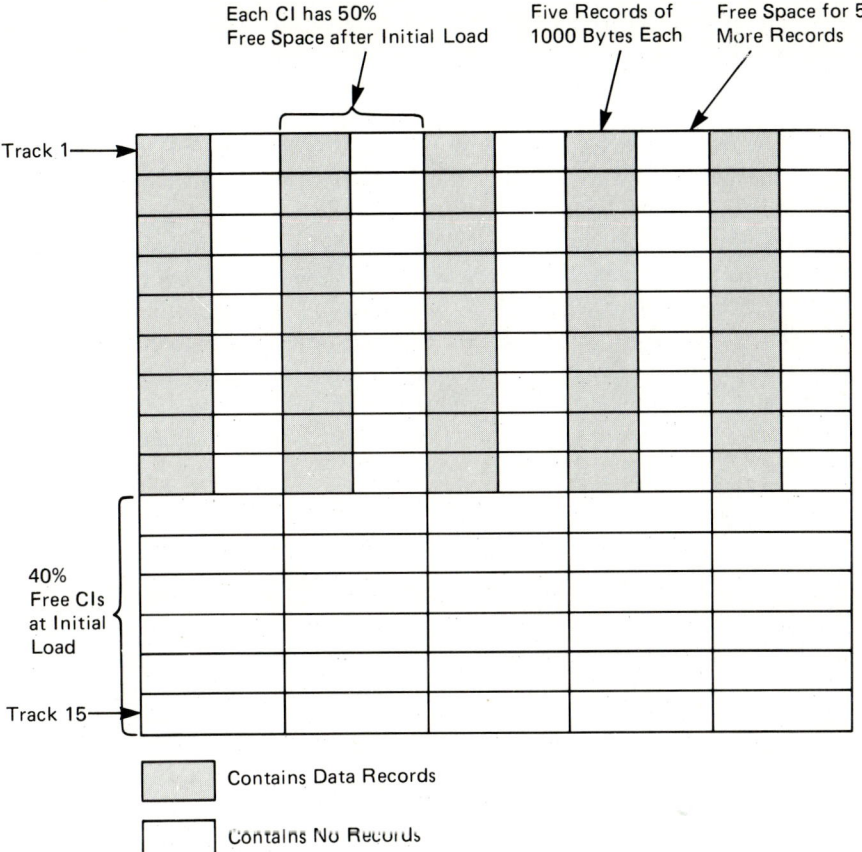

Figure 12.1 Configuration of one cylinder (one CA) of a KSDS after the initial load of records. It is defined on an IBM 3380 with NOIMBED, CI size of 8192 bytes, record size of 1000 bytes, and FREESPACE(50,40). The CA has 75 CIs in it.

and the record size is 1000 bytes. Each data CA will contain 75 data CIs. FREESPACE is coded

FREESPACE(50,40)

When the records in this data set are initially loaded (sequentially), 50% of each CI will be left empty. Since each CI is 8192 bytes long, it will contain 4 data records of 1000 bytes each and have free space for 4 more data records that can be added later. The CA-percent figure of 40% indicates that 30 CIs (40% of 75 CIs in each CA) will be left *completely* empty in each CA at initial load. Figure 12.1 shows what the data set will look like after the records are sequentially loaded. Free space within the CIs will be used for the addition of new records to minimize CI splits. Thirty free CIs will be used to take care of CI splits and to minimize CA splits.

The free space value of a data set may be changed by using the ALTER command of Access Method Services. However, remember that *the altered free space value will apply to resume load only; it has no meaning for random updates*. Many systems designers initially allocate a data set with low free space values, and after sequentially loading it with records, alter the free space to a higher value. If the file is never subsequently opened for resume load but is used only for random updates, the increased value of the free space does not help to minimize CI and CA splits. *It is the physical free space in the data set that affects CI/CA splits, not the value of the FREESPACE parameter in the catalog.*

The only purpose of the FREESPACE parameter is to direct the free space allocation at the time of initial or resume load. The only purpose of free space thus allocated is to reduce or eliminate CI and CA splits when the data set is randomly updated. The FREESPACE parameter is not applicable to ESDS or RRDS files.

12.1 FACTORS AFFECTING FREE SPACE

The values of the FREESPACE parameters should not be arbitrarily specified if we are concerned about DASD space utilization and/or CI or CA splits. The following considerations should be kept in mind when determining their values.

CISIZE/RECORDSIZE Ratio This ratio determines the number of records that will fit into a data CI. For fixed-length records, the procedure given in Fig. 12.2 may be used to determine the value of CI-percent. If you have variable length records in the data set, use the value of average record length in the RECORDSIZE parameter. Let's consider an example.

Example: A data set has fixed length records of 300 bytes each. The data CI size is 4096 bytes. As shown in Fig. 12.2, the value of N will be $(4096 - 10)/300$, or 13.62. Ignoring the fractional part, each data CI is capable of containing 13 complete records of 300 bytes each. Depending upon other factors (discussed later), let's decide to leave 4 records worth of free space at the time of the initial load. According to step 3 of Fig. 12.2, the value of CI-percent will be:

$$\text{CI-percent} = \frac{4}{13.62} \times 100 = 29.3\%$$

If you ignore the fractional part, the value of CI-percent will be 29.

CA Size The value of CA-percent affects the number of CA splits. Under ideal conditions, no CA splits should be allowed to occur. The CA-percent value may be determined by the procedure presented in Fig. 12.3.

12.1 FACTORS AFFECTING FREE SPACE

> 1. Subtract 10 from the data CISIZE.
> 2. Divide the result by the RECORDSIZE. Let the result be called N. Ignoring the fractional part, the integer part of N represents the total number of data records that can be contained in the data CI.
> 3. Determine the number of records worth of free space you intend to leave in each CI. It will depend upon the expected update activity. Call this value M. M is an integer and is less than N. The CI-percent figure is calculated as follows:
>
> $$\text{CI-percent} = \frac{M \times 100}{N}$$
>
> (Ignore the fractional part.)

Figure 12.2 A systematic procedure to determine the value of CI-percent.

The following example may help.

Example: A KSDS is defined on an IBM 3380 with the NOIMBED option. The CA size is one cylinder, and the CI size is 4096 bytes. We know from Appendix D that there are 150 data CIs per data CA. It was determined from the history of data set usage that one of every 15 data CIs is split before a reorganization may be scheduled. The LISTCAT command of AMS may be used to find the CI split value. In our case, there is a likelihood of 10 CI splits occurring for 150 data CIs per CA. Following step 3 of the procedure in Fig. 12.3, the CA-percent value will be

$$\text{CA-percent} = \frac{10}{150} \times 100 = 6.66, \text{ or } 7 \text{ percent}$$

Data Set Activity *If, after the initial load, a data set is used for read-only purposes, it is not necessary to leave any free space at all.* Data sets with delete activity and record update (without increase in record length) activity do not need any free space either. The only activities that may cause CI/CA splits and hence require free space are:

- New record adds
- Variable length record updates involving an increase in record size

1. Determine the number of data CIs per data CA. If the data CA size is one cylinder (the recommended size), use table 2 in Appendix D to find out the value. If the data CA size is less than one cylinder, interpolate according to the number of tracks per cylinder for the DASD. Let the value be called A.
2. Depending upon the update activity, determine the number of CI splits likely to occur in each data CA. Let it be called B.
3. Calculate CA-percent as follows:

$$\text{CA-percent} = \frac{B \times 100}{A}$$

(Round the fraction to the next higher value.)

Figure 12.3 Procedure for determining the value of CA-percent.

The greater the volume of such activities, the greater the free space required to minimize the splits.

Performance Free space allocation increases the DASD space requirements for KSDS and alternate index clusters but also reduces or eliminates the possibility of CI and CA splits. Increasing the space requirements results in increased DASD cost because of poor disk space utilization, while the elimination of splits reduces human costs resulting from better online system response time. Each environment will have its own priorities for giving preference to one aspect of performance over the other. In order to understand the impact of increased disk space requirement, note that the example discussed in Fig. 12.1 results in only 30% effective space utilization. Seventy percent of the disk space is allocated as CI and CA free space. Effective space utilization is calculated as follows:

$$\frac{(100 - \text{CI-percent}) \times (100 - \text{CA-percent})}{100}$$

12.2 FIXED FREE SPACE ALLOCATION

An excessive amount of free space allocation slows the sequential processing of a data set by increasing the physical distance that the read-write arm has to travel from one end of the data set to the other. Excessive free space also results in the retrieval of fewer records within a single seek location of the read-write arm. For these reasons, it is important to understand that under- as well as overallocation of free space may produce performance problems.

12.2 FIXED FREE SPACE ALLOCATION

Allocation of a fixed amount of free space throughout a data set is the most commonly used technique to reduce CI and CA splits. Each part of the data set acquires the same FREESPACE parameter values and, after the initial load, contains the same amount of CI free space and CA free space. Use your judgment to determine the initial values for the CI-percent and CA-percent. Monitor the data set regularly using the LISTCAT command of AMS. If it is subject to an excessive number of CI or CA splits, increase the value of CI-percent or CA-percent for the next data set allocation and reorganization. If it is subject to few CI or CA splits or none at all, you can reduce the value accordingly. This reevaluation should be continued until you achieve the desired results.

What determines an excessive number of CI or CA splits depends upon the application itself. For example, if you coded 20% as the CA-percent value, you are already expecting 20% of the CIs within each CA to split before causing a CA split. While you want to minimize CI splits you want to reduce the number of CA splits to zero.

Problem with Fixed Free Space Allocation Fixed free space allocation is based on the assumption that there will be uniform update activity throughout the data set. This may not always be the case. This feature is discussed in more detail in Section 12.3.

12.2.1 CI vs CA Free Space

We already know that the effective space utilization percentage for a data set is calculated as follows:

$$\frac{(100 - \text{CI-percent}) \times (100 - \text{CA-percent})}{100}$$

We can see that if we reduce the CI-percent figure, we can increase the CA-percent figure or vice versa and maintain the same effective space utilization value. For a predetermined effective space utilization, do you benefit more by increasing the CI-percent or by increasing the CA-percent? In the following example, there are four different combinations of

CI-percent and CA-percent values, but all yield the same disk utilization factor.

1. FREESPACE(40,60)

$$\text{Disk utilization} = \frac{(100 - 40) \times (100 - 60)}{100} = 24\%$$

2. FREESPACE(60,40)

$$\text{Disk utilization} = \frac{(100 - 60) \times (100 - 40)}{100} = 24\%$$

3. FREESPACE(20,70)

$$\text{Disk utilization} = \frac{(100 - 20) \times (100 - 70)}{100} = 24\%$$

4. FREESPACE(70,20)

$$\text{Disk utilization} = \frac{(100 - 70) \times (100 - 20)}{100} = 24\%$$

Which combination is optimal depends upon your application. If you have uniform record add/update activity, you are better off increasing CI-percent and reducing CA-percent. If a data set is subject to a low number of CI splits, it falls into that category. If the activity is nonuniform, it is advisable to leave less free space in each CI but more free CIs in a CA. This can be achieved by reducing the CI-percent and increasing the CA-percent. Although this approach will increase the number of CI splits, it greatly reduces the possibility of CA splits.

If you do not know which approach is the best, begin with a high CA-percent and a low CI-percent. Monitor the CI and CA splits with the LISTCAT command. Gradually reduce the CA-percent and increase the CI-percent, but always keep the effective DASD utilization the same. *The combination that gives you the minimum number of CI splits and no CA splits is the optimal value.* Figure 12.4 summarizes the discussion and the recommendations.

12.3 VARIABLE FREE SPACE ALLOCATION

Variable free space allocation provides for the allocation of different CI-percent and CA-percent values for different key ranges of a KSDS (don't confuse this with the KEYRANGES parameter). This technique is used if the system requirements determine that a KSDS will experience different record add/update activities in different parts of the data set. That part of the KSDS that experiences the most record adds will need the most free space. In the commonly used fixed free space allocation (Section

12.3 VARIABLE FREE SPACE ALLOCATION

> - Excessive CI-percent value at the cost of CA-percent value reduces the CI splits but increases the chances of CA splits.
> - Excessive CA-percent value at the cost of CI-percent value increases the CI splits but reduces the chances of CA splits.
> - Recommendation: Start with a high CA-percent and low CI-percent. Monitor CI and CA splits. Gradually reduce CA-percent value and increase CI-percent value but keep the disk utilization the same. Determine the combination that gives a minimum number of CI splits and no CA splits. That's the ideal value.

Figure 12.4 Factors influencing the distribution of free space between CI-percent value and CA-percent values, and a recommended procedure to determine their optimum values.

12.2) technique, we assume that record add activity is uniform throughout the data set, which is not true for all systems.

Example: We are asked to design a student admission system for the board of education of the city of Lincoln. The master file is a KSDS with Social Security Number as the prime key. Each time a student is admitted, a new record is added on-line to the master file. We are told that the social security numbers assigned to Lincoln were in the prefix range of 089 to 116. We conclude that most of the new admissions will have record adds in that particular prefix range, in which case we are likely to have more CI and/or CA splits in that key range value than in the rest of the data set. This means that we should leave more CI and CA free space from key value 089 to 116 than from 000 to 088 and 117 to 999.

For analysis purposes, we will treat this KSDS as three distinct entities:

Entity 1: Key range 000 to 088 has a low admission rate. Since social security numbers of new arrivals are unpredictable, we will leave no free space in the CIs and 5% free space in CAs. In other words, we use FREESPACE(0,5) for key values from 000 to 088.

Entity 2: Key range 089 to 116 has the highest admission rate. We decide to allocate 50% free space for both CI-percent and CA-percent. Therefore we use FREESPACE(50,50) for key values from 089 to 116.

Entity 3: Same as entity 1; we use FREESPACE(0,5) for key values from 117 to 999.

The procedure to implement the free space is:

1. Allocate the KSDS with FREESPACE(0,5).
2. REPRO the first batch of records into it using the FROMKEY(000) and TOKEY(088) parameters.
3. Use the ALTER command to change the free space to FREESPACE(50,50).
4. REPRO the next batch of records using the FROMKEY(089) and TOKEY(116) parameters.
5. Use ALTER again to change to FREESPACE(0,5).
6. REPRO the last batch of records using FROMKEY(117) and TOKEY(999).

These six steps should be performed in sequence and can be coded in a single job step.

Figure 12.5 gives the sample JCL. Note that the FREESPACE parameter of the ALTER command requires the name of the *data component,* not the cluster name. Also, make sure that the input data set in REPRO is a KSDS (or indexed sequential), because the FROMKEY and TOKEY parameters do not apply to other data set organizations. Since this technique is applied during the backup and reorganization of a KSDS, you should back up the master file to a KSDS (in this case STUDENTS.BACKUP.KSDS.CLUSTER) rather than to a physical sequential data set. The backup data set may be defined with FREESPACE(0,0).

It is evident that the variable free space technique requires detailed system analysis and extensive knowledge of the data set activity within the different key ranges. The intent is to move free space from places where little is required to places where it is required in greater amounts. In most cases, the savings in DASD space and the minimization of CI and CA splits more than compensates for the time spent in researching the application.

Nonuniform Update Activity Determination One way to determine nonuniform update activity in a data set is to do extensive system analysis. If you already have systems in the production environment, it may be quite cumbersome to reanalyze them to determine whether they are suit-

12.3 VARIABLE FREE SPACE ALLOCATION

```
//AMSJOB    JOB  (ACCTINFO),'JAY RANADE'
//ALTFSPC   EXEC PGM=IDCAMS,
//SYSPRINT  DD   SYSOUT=A
//SYSIN     DD   *
/*******************************************************/
/*****     BASE CLUSTER DEFINED WITH FREESPACE(0,5)  *******/
/*****         LOAD RECORDS UPTO KEY RANGE 088       *******/
/*******************************************************/
           REPRO                                      -
                IDS(STUDENTS.BACKUP.KSDS.CLUSTER)     -
                ODS(STUDENTS.KSDS.CLUSTER)            -
                FROMKEY(000)                          -
                TOKEY(088)
/*******************************************************/
/*****          CHANGE FREESPACE TO (50,50)          *******/
/*******************************************************/
           ALTER                                      -
                STUDENTS.KSDS.DATA                    -
                FREESPACE(50,50)
/*******************************************************/
/*****          LOAD RECORDS FROM 089 TO 116         *******/
/*******************************************************/
           REPRO                                      -
                IDS(STUDENTS.BACKUP.KSDS.CLUSTER)     -
                ODS(STUDENTS.KSDS.CLUSTER)            -
                FROMKEY(089)                          -
                TOKEY(116)
/*******************************************************/
/*****          CHANGE FREESPACE BACK TO (0,5)       *******/
/*******************************************************/
           ALTER                                      -
                STUDENTS.KSDS.DATA                    -
                FREESPACE(0,5)
/*******************************************************/
/******           LOAD REST OF THE RECORDS           *******/
/*******************************************************/
           REPRO                                      -
                IDS(STUDENTS.BACKUP.KSDS.CLUSTER)     -
                ODS(STUDENTS.KSDS.CLUSTER)            -
                FROMKEY(117)
/*
//
```

Figure 12.5 An example using the variable free space technique to allocate different amounts of CI and CA free space during the initial load of the data set.

able candidates for variable free space allocation. However, there is an easier way to narrow down the analysis to a few data sets. The technique is described in Fig. 12.6. In order to understand it better, let's use this technique in the following example:

Example: A KSDS is being used in a production environment, and at the time of analysis the LISTCAT-generated listing revealed that it has had two CA splits. Because it has undergone some CA splits, we can

1. Make sure that the KSDS being analyzed is in a live production environment and *has had at least a few CA splits*.
2. Execute the LISTCAT command on the data set to get the values of data CI splits, data CI size, HURBA for the data component, and CA-percent value for FREESPACE.
3. Calculate the CA free space utilization factor as follows:

$$\frac{(\text{CI splits}) \times (\text{data CI size}) \times 100}{(\text{High used RBA for data component}) \times (\text{CA-percent value for FREESPACE})}$$

The result should be a value between 0.01 and 1.00. If it is less than 0.5, it is a prime candidate for further analysis for variable free space allocation consideration.

Figure 12.6 Procedure to determine whether an in-production KSDS should be considered for variable free space allocation.

use the technique described in Fig. 12.6. The listing also gives the following values:

- Number of CI splits is 87.
- Data CI size is 4096 bytes.
- HURBA for data component is 6,144,000 bytes.
- CA-percent value for FREESPACE is 20.

Substituting these values into the expression given in step 3 of Fig. 12.6, we calculate the free space utilization factor:

$$\frac{87 \times 4096 \times 100}{6144000 \times 20} = 0.29$$

Since the result is less than 0.50, this particular data set should be investigated further to see if it can benefit from the variable free space allocation technique.

12.4 REORGANIZATION OF FILES

A KSDS that is being used for record adds and updates will sooner or later be subject to CI and CA splits. Although they cause poor performance during their occurrence, these splits *do not* affect random file requests later. However, they may cause slight performance problems for long sequential browses. Because CI and CA splits move the logical records around to different physical locations on the DASD, the data is said to be *physically disorganized*. Remember that logically the records are still organized in their prime key sequence due to the presence of the index component. The process of putting the logical records back into their proper physical sequence is called *reorganization*.

Why Reorganize? We already know that free space is allocated to reduce the possibility of CI and CA splits. But over a period of use, splits do occur, and after a sufficient number of them, the free space becomes either too low to be of any significance or too uneven to prevent further splits. Although the free space may still be there, it may not be located where it is needed the most. In reorganization, the disorganized KSDS is unloaded to a backup file, deleted, reallocated, and reloaded from the backup file. Reloading the records with appropriate free space values ensures that the records are again in physical sequence and that there is sufficient free space to minimize future CI and CA splits.

12.5 PREFORMATTING DATA SETS

Before we discuss preformatting, let's consider the following scenario. XYZ is a KSDS that is used as a data collection file for an application under CICS/VS. The prime key of the file is Social Security Number. When CICS is brought up, the file contains only one dummy record. The CI size for the file is 4096 bytes, and the record size is 1000 bytes. The DASD is an IBM 3380, the CA size is one cylinder, and therefore the number of CIs per CA is 150. As new records are added to the file, the first CI split occurs on the fifth record. After 149 CI splits have occurred, a CA split occurs and moves half the records to the second cylinder. If, at the end of the day, the file spans 10 cylinders, it has had 9 CA splits and about 750 to 1500 CI splits. If these figures alarm you, imagine a file being extended to 100 cylinders with 99 CA splits and 7500 to 15,000 CI splits. This is a universal problem associated with data collection files or transaction files.

The Preformatting Solution Now consider the same application using the same XYZ file. But before we bring up the file on-line under CICS/VS, we perform the following in batch mode:

1. Allocate XYZ using DEFINE CLUSTER with FREESPACE (100,100) as the free space parameter value.
2. Allocate a physical sequential file and load it with 10 records with the same record format as that of XYZ but with the following key values:
   100000000
   200000000
   300000000
   400000000
   500000000
   600000000
   700000000
   800000000
   900000000
   999999999
3. REPRO the records of the physical sequential file into the KSDS. FREESPACE(100,100) will ensure that each record of the input physical sequential file goes to a different CA. At the successful execution of REPRO, 10 records will have been loaded to 10 different cylinders of the KSDS.
4. Write a simple batch program that opens the KSDS as Input-Output, reads each record sequentially, *deletes them all from the KSDS,* and then closes the file. The file is ready to be allocated under CICS/VS.

The KSDS now has no records at all. However, VSAM has done internal preformatting of the file to our advantage. All future record adds will be directed to cylinders according to their key values. A record add with the key value 555555555 will go to the sixth CA, a record add with the key value 123456789 will go to the second CA, and so on. Because of the distributed record add facility, a number of CAs (cylinders in our case) are being used for different key ranges. This reduces the probability of CA splits.

How does it happen? Although the records have been deleted from the data component of the KSDS, the index component still points to the highest record keys of their respective CAs. So the index component, because of the preformatting, makes many CAs eligible for random record adds depending upon the key values. Figure 12.7 shows the layout of the KSDS after the records have been deleted from it. Note that the index component points to the data component CAs according to the key values they once had.

Although this technique reduces the possibility of CA splits, *it does not affect CI splits at all.* The CI splits will occur just as they did in an unpreformatted file.

You may customize this technique to suit your applications. Don't forget that each record will preformat only one CA. Select key values

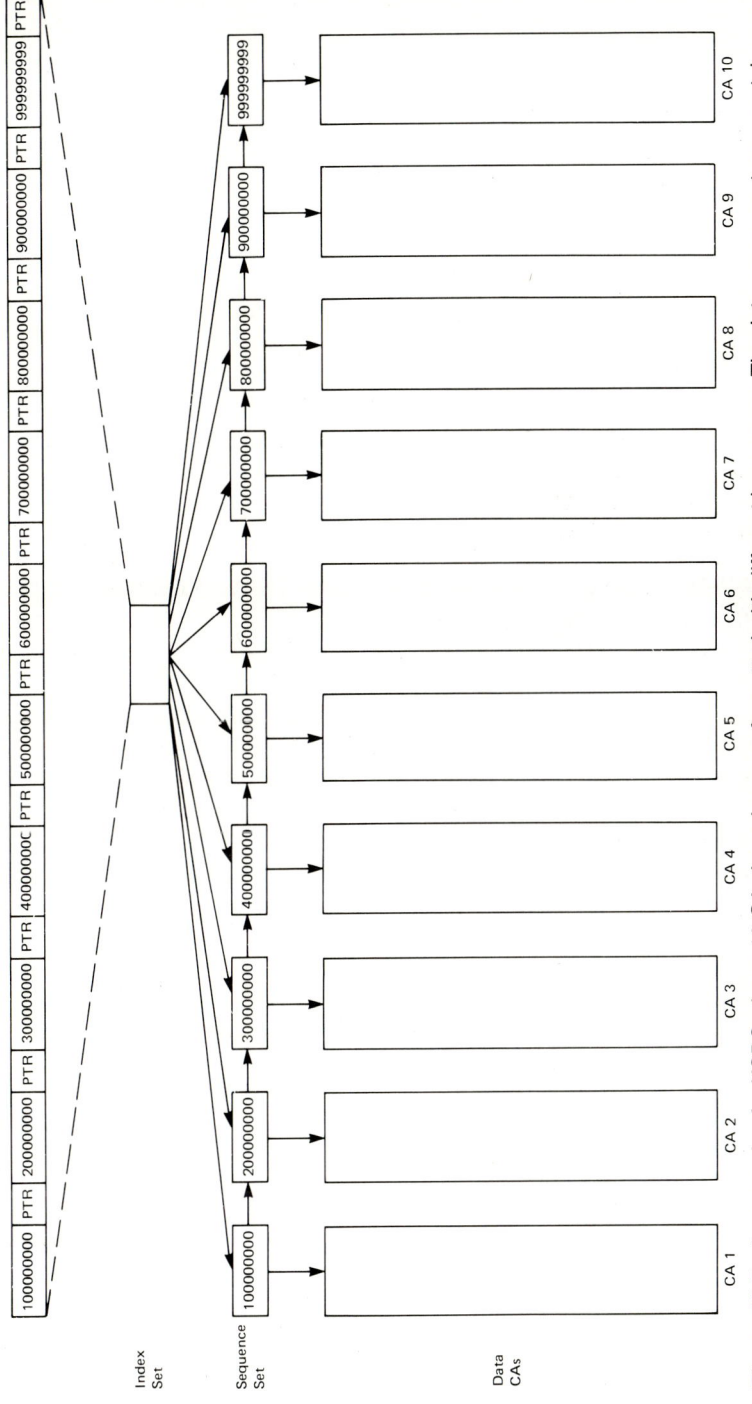

Figure 12.7 An example of a KSDS whose 10 CAs have been preformatted with different key ranges. The data component now contains no logical records, but the index component still points to it according to the key values it once had.

1. Allocate the KSDS with FREESPACE(100,100).
2. Allocate a physical sequential file with the same record length as the KSDS. Load it with as many records as the number of CAs you wish to format. Make sure the key values selected are such that their range should be able to contain approximately one CA's worth of data during the record collection process.
3. REPRO all the records from the physical sequential file to the KSDS.
4. Open the KSDS as Input-Output, and delete all the records it contains.

Figure 12.8 Procedure to preformat a KSDS to be used later as a data collection file in an on-line environment.

such that their range will be able to contain approximately one CA's worth of data during record add processing.

Figure 12.8 summarizes the preformatting technique described in this section. Note that you don't have to use REPRO to load records from the physical sequential file to the KSDS. You may write a program that carries out steps 2, 3, and 4 of Fig. 12.8. In Cobol, the program will function as follows:

1. OPEN the KSDS as OUTPUT and load it with records.
2. CLOSE the KSDS (very important).
3. OPEN the KSDS as Input-Output.
4. Delete all the records, and CLOSE the file again.

You may wonder whether deleting all the records in a KSDS will prevent CICS/VS from opening the file properly. You may have been led to believe that the KSDS must have at least one dummy record in it, but in fact, there is no such CICS/VS requirement. The only criterion is that the high used RBA (HURBA) must be nonzero. Once a file has had records, the HURBA becomes nonzero. Subsequent deletion of these records does not reduce that value.

Also be aware that deleting records in step 4 of Fig. 12.8 is not an essential process. If your application needs these records, you may skip step 4 and leave the records alone.

12.6 ALTERNATE INDEXES AND FREE SPACE

Since alternate indexes are KSDS in architecture, they are also subject to CI and CA splits. To minimize these splits, the FREESPACE parameter must be coded when an alternate index is allocated. The BLDINDEX command of AMS takes care of the free space when the alternate index is being loaded with the alternate key-pointer pair records. CI and CA splits should also be monitored on a regular basis. The values for the free space parameters may be increased or reduced on the basis of those split numbers.

An alternate index that has been defined with the NOUPGRADE option is not opened for update purposes, and therefore it does not need any free space. To conserve DASD space, you can allocate it with a FREESPACE(0,0) value.

chapter 13

Other Performance-Related Parameters

The commands and parameters that we will discuss in this chapter have no logical interrelationship or interdependence. They are grouped together because the simplicity of their use does not warrant a separate chapter for each one.

13.1 SPEED VS RECOVERY

SPEED and RECOVERY are mutually exlusive options of the DEFINE CLUSTER and DEFINE AIX commands. RECOVERY is the default option in both cases. These options are effective *only* during the sequential load or sequential resume load operations. For practical purposes, these operations are carried out as follows.

- In Cobol programs, a sequential load occurs when the file is OPENed as OUTPUT, while resume load is done when the file is OPENed as EXTEND.[1]
- Using AMS, the sequential load is performed using the REPRO command.

---

[1] For a detailed discussion on OUTPUT and EXTEND, refer to Ranade and Ranade (1986), *VSAM: Concepts, Programming, and Design.*

13.1 SPEED VS RECOVERY

SPEED, as the name suggests, expedites the load or resume load process. However, if the job fails before the file is closed, it is difficult to recover data. The target file must be deleted, reallocated, and reloaded from the beginning. Even if the job failure occurs as the last record is being loaded to the file, no recovery is possible.

On the other hand, RECOVERY gives you the ability to recover data up through the last-loaded record by using the VERIFY command followed by resume load. However, there is extra overhead in using this option, and it incurs more I/O's than the SPEED option.

These options are not applicable to random updates. Data is *always* recoverable if a system failure occurs during random updates to a file. It has been my experience that *although system designers frequently use the RECOVERY option, causing extra overhead, they do not make use of the recovery facilities provided by it.* One reason is the difficulty of implementing the recovery facilities. Let's find out how these options work internally.

How RECOVERY Works RECOVERY features come into play when VSAM determines that the data set being sequentially loaded was defined with the RECOVERY option. Before VSAM loads records into any CA, it formats all the CIs in the CA. Formatting CIs incurs extra I/O's. VSAM also writes a Software End of File (SEOF) marker in the next CA. A SEOF is written by moving binary zeros to the CIDF field of the first CI of the next CA; that also incurs an extra I/O. In Fig. 13.1, VSAM has already loaded CAs 1 and 2. It is about to load CA 3, so it formats all the CIs in that CA and writes an SEOF marker in the first CI of CA 4.

If the job is terminated at this point, we can resume data set load as follows:

1. Issue the VERIFY command of AMS to update the HURBA in the catalog and to facilitate proper opening of the file in the next step. In fact, VERIFY reads the first CI of every CA after the incorrect catalog HURBA control area and determines from the SEOF that the loading of the prior CA was in progress when the job terminated.
2. Determine which record was loaded last in the target data set.
3. Restart the load operation by reading records from the source file, skipping the records up to the last-loaded record of the target file as determined in step 2.

Although the approach appears to be straightforward, there is no simple procedure for carrying out steps 2 and 3. In step 2, you could read the file backwards to determine the last-loaded record; this process would require another program. In step 3, you could use the SKIP parameter of REPRO to bypass records if you knew the number of records to be skipped. You could also use the FROMKEY option of REPRO to skip

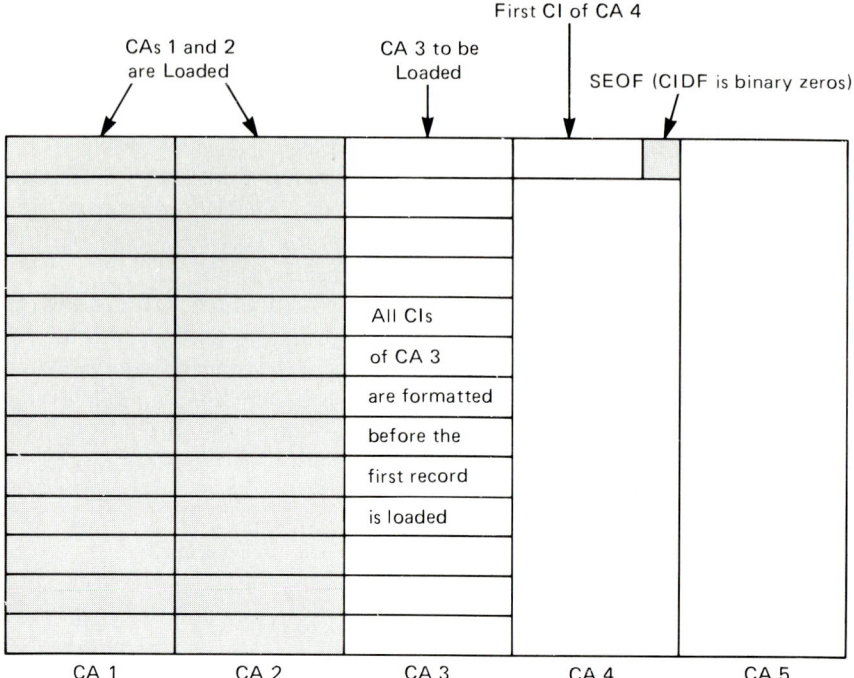

Figure 13.1 An example of the functioning of RECOVERY option during the loading of a data set. The data set has five CAs, and the third CA is about to be loaded with records.

those records if the source file was a KSDS (or indexed sequential). For practical purposes, determining the value of the records to be SKIPed is a nontrivial task unless you wish to read and count the records in the target file. But doing that will cause extra I/O's and defeat the whole purpose of resume load. Also, the use of FROMKEY requires that the source file be KSDS. There are not many cases where the source file in a load is key sequenced; usually it is a physical sequential file.

In addition to these technical issues, the execution of resume load and restart of the job requires the active intervention of a qualified person who knows AMS and VSAM well. Since data set loads are usually done at night, one cannot count on the presence of such a person in those shifts. Therefore, the recovery facilities provided by RECOVERY are seldom used. In summary, RECOVERY is a good concept but is difficult to implement for operational reasons. So the question arises, why cause additional I/O overhead if it is too difficult to implement this feature at all?

How SPEED Works VSAM neither preformats the CAs nor writes the SEOF markers for data sets defined with the SPEED option. Therefore the extra I/O overhead associated with these operations does not exist.

However, since VERIFY does not know about the SEOF, it cannot correct the HURBA in the catalog. The load process must be restarted from the beginning whenever there is a sequential load process failure.

Recommendations   As previously stated, most data sets are defined with RECOVERY, but the features provided by it are not used to resume a load after a sequential load termination. In that case, there is no point in creating the extra overhead. For example, if a 30-minute load job terminates only once a year, why incur 5 minutes of overhead every day? It makes more sense to be prepared for another 30 minutes of overhead once a year.

The only time you might want to use RECOVERY is for very large VSAM files where a complete restart could cause scheduling problems and an operations backlog. However, remember that you must provide your own recovery procedures, as explained earlier, and that a reasonably knowledgeable VSAM person should be available. You might also use your own check points as long as they do not cause excessive overhead.

Remember that the SPEED option must be hard-coded in the command, because RECOVERY, unfortunately, is the default.

13.2   ERASE VS NOERASE

The DELETE command of Access Method Services deletes the entry of the data set from the catalog and makes that space available for allocating other data sets. However, this command does not physically erase the contents of the data set. Sensitive information residing in a deleted file would not be accessible through the data set name, but it could be dumped to tape or to the printer using some simple utilities. This might pose a security risk.

The ERASE option of DEFINE CLUSTER or DEFINE AIX ensures that the DELETE command not only deletes the catalog entry but also physically overwrites the data component CIs with binary zeros. If it has not been specified at the time of data set allocation, the ERASE option can be coded at the time of the execution of DELETE command as follows:

```
DELETE    VSAM.FILE.NAME
     ERASE
```

Performance   Since the ERASE option results in the physical erasure of the data component, it increases the execution time of the deletion process. The larger the data set, the longer it will take to erase it. If the data component occupies an entire single-density IBM 3380, it may take anywhere from 15 to 20 minutes to delete it. Due to its potential impact on performance, this option should be used with great caution. *Only data* *sets with highly sensitive or confidential information should be considered for erasure.* Do not delete and reallocate such data sets immediately prior to the CICS startup process; this could severely delay bringing up CICS.

13.3 WRITECHECK VS NOWRITECHECK

The WRITECHECK option of DEFINE CLUSTER or DEFINE AIX is effective when a data set is opened for update purposes. Each time a record is written or rewritten to a data set, it is read back and compared with the contents of the buffer. A good return code is passed to the program only after VSAM has confirmed that the data is correctly written to the DASD. Clearly, the effective I/O activity for a particular file is increased, thus increasing the device busy percentage figure. Although it is still used by some designers to ensure complete data write integrity, modern DASDs are highly reliable and do not require this option. A data set opened for read-only purposes is not affected by this option.

13.4 SHAREOPTION 4

A shareoption of 4, whether used for cross-region or cross-system sharing, significantly increases the I/O's on the index component of a KSDS. This option specifies that the index records in buffers be ignored and that records be read directly from the DASD with each I/O request. The effect is the same as if the value of BUFNI (index buffers) were left at the default value. No look-aside is performed to read the index set records from the index buffers.

The only non-performance-related benefit of this particular shareoption is that it provides *some write integrity* when a file is open for update to various regions concurrently. Since write integrity cannot be ensured completely, any benefits realized are nullified by the increase in I/O activity. A large file with heavy update activity should not be considered for this shareoption.

13.5 SPANNED RECORDS

If a logical record does not fit in a single CI, it may span multiple CIs if the optional parameter SPANNED is coded at the time of data set allocation. Figure 13.2 gives an example of a SPANNED record. In this example, the record spans over three CIs. The performance implications of using this option are:

- A SPANNED record always starts on a CI boundary. Since the free space in the previous logical CI is not used, the disk space requirement is increased.

13.6 BUFFERSPACE

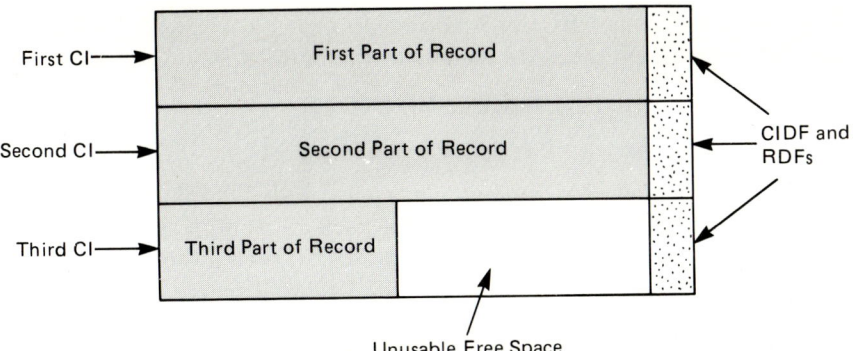

Figure 13.2 An example of a SPANNED record. It spans over three data CIs, leaving unusable free space in the third CI.

- Free space remaining at the end of the last CI cannot be used by any record (see Fig. 13.2). This feature also increases the disk space requirement.
- A SPANNED record requires as many I/O's as the number of CIs it spans. This is due to the fact that only the RDF of a CI indicates that the record is also extended over the next CI. Since each CI read is a separate random I/O, the I/O activity for a data set is increased.

SPANNED may be useful when there are only a few exceptionally large records in a variable-length record file. Under these circumstances, if spanned records are not used, you will have to increase the data CI size to accommodate the largest possible variable-length record. This will also increase the VSAM buffer requirements to accommodate the enlarged CI size. The use of the SPANNED feature is not recommended if the records are of almost uniform length.

CICS/VS 1.6.1 and prior releases did not support spanned records. However, with CICS/VS release 1.7, full support of these records is provided. Be aware that in addition to increased I/O activity, SPANNED also increases the data buffer requirements because each spanned record read requires multiple data buffers. For example, the record read in Fig. 13.2 will require three data buffers before the record can be processed.

13.6 BUFFERSPACE

This parameter may be optionally coded at the time of data set allocation. BUFFERSPACE value indicates to VSAM the amount of space to be allocated for the data and index buffers at the time the data set is opened. In Chaps. 15 and 16, we will talk about index and data buffer allocation using the BUFNI and BUFND parameters instead. Using the values of BUFNI and BUFND, VSAM calculates the buffer space as follows:

Buffer Space = (BUFNI × CISZ-OF-INDEX)
+ (BUFND × CISZ-OF-DATA)

If the BUFFERSPACE parameter is also coded, it may conflict with the value calculated by VSAM. Allocating separate buffer space for index and data components using BUFNI and BUFND is a more effective and desirable approach than using the BUFFERSPACE parameter.

Under most circumstances, this parameter should not be coded. The only exception to this recommendation is when a VSAM file is dynamically allocated and you do not have the opportunity to code BUFNI and BUFND values. The following are a few examples of dynamic allocation:

- Records are copied into a KSDS using the REPRO command with the OUTDATASET (rather than OUTFILE) parameter. The file will be dynamically allocated because there is no DD statement associated with the OUTDATASET parameter. Since a DD statement of JCL is not coded, you cannot code the BUFNI and BUFND values. The only way to override the default values for buffer allocation is to use the BUFFERSPACE parameter.
- A VSAM file is opened using the path name for an alternate index cluster as follows:

```
//PATH1   DD  DSN=EMPLOYEE.KSDS.CLUSTER.PATH1,
//              DISP=SHR,AMP=('BUFNI=3','BUFND=7')
```

The values of BUFNI and BUFND coded on the DD statement will be used for the alternate index to which that path belongs. Since there is no DD statement for the base cluster, it will be allocated dynamically, thus depriving you of the opportunity to code its BUFNI and BUFND parameters. In such a case, you should use the BUFFERSPACE parameter in DEFINE CLUSTER to allocate the desired number of buffers.

With the exception of dynamic allocation, use of the BUFFERSPACE parameter is not recommended. If a file can be allocated dynamically sometimes and allocated through the explicit DD statements of JCL at other times, you may use the ALTER command of Access Method Services to modify the BUFFERSPACE value.

For example, let's say that we open a base cluster dynamically using the path name. The DD statement for path is coded as in the example above. The values of BUFNI and BUFND will apply to the alternate index cluster associated with that path. Let's also say that if we were

13.7 GDGs AND VSAM CATALOGS (MVS ONLY)

given the opportunity, we could have coded the DD statement for the base cluster as follows:

```
//BASECL    DD   DSN=EMPLOYEE.KSDS.CLUSTER,
//                DISP=SHR,AMP=('BUFNI=5','BUFND=10')
```

Since we cannot do that, we can calculate the buffer space value as follows:

BUFFERSPACE = (5 × CISZ-OF-INDEX)
+ (10 × CISZ-OF-DATA)

If CISZ-OF-INDEX = 2048 and CISZ-OF-DATA = 4096, then

BUFFERSPACE = 5 × 2048 + 10 × 4096 = 51,200 bytes

We alter the BUFFERSPACE value in the data set as follows:

```
ALTER    EMPLOYEE.KSDS.CLUSTER
   BUFFERSPACE(51200)
```

Now, if we open the base cluster dynamically through the path, it will automatically allocate 51,200 bytes of storage for its index and data buffers.

When we are done with that job step, we can alter the buffer space values back to the default values of AMS: one index buffer and two data buffers. The default value will be

BUFFERSPACE = 1 × 2048 + 2 × 4096 = 10,240 bytes

We alter the value back to the default as follows:

```
ALTER    EMPLOYEE.KSDS.CLUSTER
   BUFFERSPACE(10240)
```

In the future, if this data set is opened through the explicit use of a DD statement of JCL, the hard-coded values of BUFNI and BUFND will override the default allocation.

If the BUFFERSPACE value in the catalog entry (through DEFINE CLUSTER or ALTER) is greater than the value calculated by VSAM from the BUFNI and BUFND values, the catalog entry overrides the other value.

13.7 GDGs AND VSAM CATALOGS (MVS ONLY)

You may be aware that the index for generation data groups (GDGs) can be allocated not only by using IEHPROGM but also through the use of an AMS command called DEFINE GDG. The entry for GDGs may occur in a VSAM catalog or an ICF catalog. If a VSAM catalog is used, there are some catalog-space-related performance problems associated with it. As the old entries of a generation data set are removed from the catalog (on the basis of the LIMIT parameter), the space they used in the catalog is not reclaimed. The net effect is that the catalog keeps on growing in size. However, this problem does not exist with ICF catalogs. It is, therefore, recommended that GDG index entries be defined only in OS catalogs (CVOL) or ICF catalogs.

13.8 REUSE

The REUSE parameter is not directly performance-related. It may, however, be used in association with performance-related techniques where it is required to fix the physical location of the data set on the DASD.

If cache DASD controllers are being used to put the index component tracks in cache (using the BINDDATA command), it may be appropriate to ensure that the physical address of the index component on the DASD does not change. This can be done by defining the data set with the REUSE parameter. Then there will never be a need to delete or reallocate that cluster for reorganization purposes. Whenever the data set is opened as OUTPUT (in Cobol) or REPROed with the REUSE option, all its old records will be logically deleted by having the high used RBA (HURBA) in the catalog automatically set to zero. It will look like the file was newly allocated. However, the physical location of the index and data components on the DASD will not have changed.

The HURBA is reset to zero *only when the data set is opened in the load mode*. Later, if random updates are done by opening the file as INPUT-OUTPUT (Cobol), the REUSE parameter will be ignored and will have no effect.

13.9 BLDINDEX

The BLDINDEX command is used to build alternate indexes from the base cluster. You can build a multiple number of alternate indexes in a single execution of the command. Let's take an example.

Example: We have a base cluster named EMPLOYEE.KSDS.CLUSTER that has two associated alternate indexes:

    EMPLOYEE.KSDS.AIX1.CLUSTER
    EMPLOYEE.KSDS.AIX2.CLUSTER

To build these alternate indexes in a single pass, we execute the following command:

13.9 BLDINDEX

```
BLDINDEX                            -
    INFILE(BASE)                    -
    OUTFILE(AIX1 AIX2)              -
    CATALOG(VSAM.USER.CATALOG)
```

BASE points to the DD name of the base cluster, and AIX1 and AIX2 refer to the DD names of the alternate index cluster's JCL statements. When this command is executed, three distinct functions will be executed in the following order:

1. *Read:* Records of the base cluster are read sequentially, and for each record read two key-pointer pairs are extracted, one for each alternate index.
2. *Sort:* Key-pointer pairs of individual alternate indexes are sorted into ascending order on the alternate key field. The sort routine is a built-in function of AMS. If the number of records is small and enough virtual storage is available, the sort is done in core (internal sort). Otherwise, two sort work files will be used for an external sort.
3. *Load:* After a successful sort, records are loaded sequentially into each of the two alternate index clusters.

Pros and Cons of Multiple Loads In the above example, steps 2 and 3 will be executed for each alternate index separately. By concurrently building a multiple number of alternate indexes, we are saving on the I/O's and the execution time of step 1. By building one index at a time, step 1 will be executed as many times as there are alternate indexes. In building multiple indexes, this procedure extracts key-pointer pairs for step 2 in a single pass. This could be a considerable saving in I/O's and therefore expedite the execution process.

However, this approach increases the DASD space requirement for its work files. Since key-pointer pair records extracted in step 1 must be stored in a file, you need more space if a number of such files are being created. Usually, the small price paid for temporarily using some additional DASD space is worth it.

Buffer Allocation I/O's in step 1 can be made faster through the proper allocation of data buffers for the base cluster. Ideally, the number of data buffers should equal the number of data CIs per DASD track plus 1. As an example, if our data CI size is 4096 bytes and the DASD is an IBM 3380, there will be 10 CIs per track. The value of BUFND should be 11, so the DD statement will be coded as follows:

```
//BASE     DD   DSN=EMPLOYEE.KSDS.CLUSTER,
//              DISP=OLD,AMP=('BUFND=11')
```

```
//AMSJOB    JOB  (ACCTINFO),'JAY RANADE',
//KSDSBLDI  EXEC PGM=IDCAMS
//SYSPRINT  DD   SYSOUT=A
//BASE      DD   DSN=EMPLOYEE.KSDS.CLUSTER,
//               DISP=OLD,AMP=('BUFND=11')
//AIX1      DD   DSN=EMPLOYEE.KSDS.AIX1.CLUSTER,
//               DISP=OLD,AMP=('BUFND=33')
//AIX2      DD   DSN=EMPLOYEE.KSDS.AIX2.CLUSTER,
//               DISP=OLD,AMP=('BUFND=20')
//IDCUT1    DD   DSN=SORT.WORK.FILE.ONE,DISP=OLD,
//               AMP='AMORG',VOL=SER=WORK01,UNIT=3380
//IDCUT2    DD   DSN=SORT.WORK.FILE.TWO,DISP=OLD,
//               AMP='AMORG',VOL=SER=WORK02,UNIT=3380
//SYSIN     DD   *
                 BLDINDEX                              -
                    INFILE(BASE)                       -
                    OUTFILE(AIX1 AIX2)                 -
                    CATALOG(VSAM.USER.CATALOG)
/*
//
```

Figure 13.3 An example of complete JCL coding for building a multiple number of alternate indexes concurrently as discussed in Section 13.9.

The value of BUFND should be adjusted if the CI size or the type of DASD is different.

The I/O's in step 3 can also be made faster through the proper allocation of data buffers for each of the alternate indexes. The number of data buffers should be the number of data CIs per DASD track plus 2. For example, if the data CI sizes for AIX1 and AIX2 are 1024 and 2048 bytes, respectively, and the DASD is an IBM 3380, there will be 31 and 18 CIs per track, respectively. The value of BUFND should be 33 for AIX1 and 20 for AIX2. Their DD statements can be coded as follows:

```
//AIX1    DD   DSN=EMPLOYEE.KSDS.AIX1.CLUSTER,
//             DISP=OLD,AMP=('BUFND=33')
//AIX2    DD   DSN=EMPLOYEE.KSDS.AIX2.CLUSTER,
//             DISP=OLD,AMP=('BUFND=20')
```

CATALOG Parameter It should be noted that the CATALOG parameter of BLDINDEX is not necessarily the catalog in which the base cluster and alternate indexes are defined. It refers to the catalog where the sort work files will be temporarily allocated. Such work files are usually coded on the DD statements of IDCUT1 and IDCUT2.

Figure 13.3 gives the complete JCL coding for the example discussed in this section.

Make sure that if VSAM.USER.CATALOG is a VSAM catalog there is enough suballocated VSAM space on WORK01 and WORK02 to allocate temporary work files. If it is an ICF catalog, then both of those packs must be eligible for allocating VSAM data sets; that is, they must have

VSAM Volume Data Sets (VVDSs) defined on them. The work files are ESDS in architecture and are used only for the duration of the job step. VSAM cannot use non-ESDS files as work files. The reason for using two separate work packs, WORK01 and WORK02, is to improve performance by using the read-write arms of two separate DASDs. If the BLDINDEX step fails in the middle, *the ESDS work files are not always deleted by AMS*. You will have to delete these files manually. If the DASD space on these work packs is mysteriously disappearing, one reason could be the allocation of superfluous VSAM work files that were not deleted after a BLDINDEX failure.

Other Uses of BLDINDEX The building of alternate indexes for the first time is not the only reason for using the BLDINDEX command. It can also be used for the following purposes:

- Members of the upgrade set (alternate indexes) may have been subject to heavy update activity due to a large number of record adds and/or updates in the base cluster. If the alternate indexes have had a lot of CI and CA splits, they should be reorganized. BLDINDEX can be used to do this.
- If some of the alternate indexes are not members of the upgrade set, they are not automatically kept in synchronization when a base cluster record is updated. One way to bring them to the same level as the records of the base cluster is to execute BLDINDEX to rebuild the alternate indexes.

13.10 UPGRADE VS NOUPGRADE

All of the alternate indexes defined with the UPGRADE (the default) option become members of the *upgrade set* of the base cluster. When the base cluster is opened for update purposes, all of the associated members of its upgrade set are automatically opened. It is then VSAM's responsibility to maintain all the changes to the base cluster in the members of the upgrade set as well. An upgrade set places considerable overhead on the system. For example, if a base cluster has six members in the upgrade set, the addition of a single record to it results in seven record adds in all. Each member of the upgrade set causes the same update overhead as any other KSDS under normal circumstances.

Whether an alternate index should be made a member of the upgrade set is an application decision. But the *need* must be weighed against the corresponding sacrifice in *speed*. For alternate indexes that must be kept in synchronization with the base cluster, there is no choice but to bear this overhead. You can improve the performance by properly allocating index buffers for the alternate indexes as well as for the base cluster. Further details on buffer allocation are given in Chaps. 15 through 17.

chapter 14

Space Estimation for Data Sets

Space estimation for VSAM files does not directly influence performance and fine tuning. It is too often done by programmers using guesswork rather than scientific methodology. To correct this situation, this chapter provides a step-by-step procedure for each of the three VSAM data set organizations.

Incorrect space estimates can have minor effects on performance. For example:

- Overallocation wastes an expensive resource, the DASD.
- Overallocation results in an increase in the seek time delay by increasing the range of distance the read-write arm has to traverse.
- Underallocation results in multiple secondary allocations of the data set, causing such problems as EDB overhead and the fragmentation and physical dispersal of data set extents.

Thus it is important that we spend some time in determining the correct values of the space requirements for our applications. In the preceding chapters, we discussed the parameters of data set allocation in great detail. These parameters influence the space requirements and must be known beforehand. Some of the parameters and characteristics you should know in order to calculate the space requirements are:

14.1 ESTIMATING FOR A KSDS

- Data CI size (Chap. 9)
- Record size (Chap. 9)
- Data CA size (Chap. 10)
- Values of the FREESPACE parameter (Chap. 12)
- Use of IMBED (Chap. 11)
- Type of DASD (Chap. 6)

Once these are known, you are ready to proceed.

14.1 ESTIMATING FOR A KSDS

Estimating space requirements for a KSDS is a five-step procedure. We will use an ongoing case study to apply the procedure to a real-life environment. To simplify matters we first deal with fixed-length records.

14.1.1 Estimating Space for Fixed-Length Records

Step 1: Determine the Number of Records per CI The first step involves calculating the number of records that will fit in a data CI. This will depend upon the data CI size, the record size, and the first value of the FREESPACE parameter (CI-percent value). Substitute the values in the following formula:

$$\text{Records per CI} = \frac{\text{DCISZ} - 10}{\text{RECSZ}} \times \frac{100 - \text{CIPERCENT}}{100}$$

where DCISZ is the data component CI size, RECSZ is the data record size, and CIPERCENT is the CI-percent value of FREESPACE. Ignore the fractional part of the result, and note the integer value for further use.

This formula is valid for most values of the variables included in it. There are, however, some exceptions to the rule. If we know that only one data record will fit into the data CI, we don't have to go through this procedure. The largest single record that can fit into a single data CI is the CI size minus 7 bytes. Also, the FREESPACE parameter value of CI-percent will ensure that there is free space worth at least one data record in the CI. If your coded value is less than that, VSAM will put at least one record's worth of free space into the CI at the time of initial load. Keeping these considerations in mind, determine the number of whole records that the data CI is capable of holding after providing for the initial CI free space value.

Case Study 1: Let's suppose that the data CI size is 4096 bytes, the record size is 200 bytes, and the free space is coded as FREE-

CI sizes	Index option	CI's per cylinder for different devices					
		3330	3350	3380	3370*	9332*	9335*
512	IMBED	360	783	644	682	222	355
	NOIMBED	380	810	690	744	296	426
1,024	IMBED	198	435	434	341	111	177
	NOIMBED	209	450	465	372	148	213
2,048	IMBED	108	232	252	170	55	88
	NOIMBED	114	240	270	186	74	106
4,096	IMBED	54	116	140	85	27	44
	NOIMBED	57	120	150	93	37	53
6,144	IMBED	36	77	84	56	18	29
	NOIMBED	38	80	90	62	24	35
8,192	IMBED	27	58	70	42	13	22
	NOIMBED	28	60	75	46	18	26
12,288	IMBED	18	38	46	28	9	14
	NOIMBED	19	40	50	31	12	17
16,384	IMBED	13	29	35	21	6	11
	NOIMBED	14	30	37	23	9	13
32,768	IMBED	6	14	17	10	3	5
	NOIMBED	7	15	18	11	4	6

*IBM 3370 is an FBA device used with DOS/VSE.

IBM 9332 and IBM 9335 are FBA devices used with 9370 series of computers and DOS/VSE system. Although FBA devices have no concept of a cylinder, use the recommendations in Chap. 10 to allocate space on such devices in whole cylinders.

Figure 14.1 Table giving relationship between different CI sizes, types of DASD. Use of IMBED/NOIMBED and the number of data CI's per CA.

SPACE(30,40). The number of records that a single data CI can contain is

$$\text{Records per CI} = \frac{4096 - 10}{200} \times \frac{100 - 30}{100}$$

$$= \frac{4086}{200} \times \frac{70}{100} = 14.301, \text{ or } 14 \text{ records}$$

Step 2: Determine the Number of CIs per CA The number of CIs that a CA can contain depends upon two factors: (1) The type of DASD and (2) the number of tracks per CA. Different types of DASDs have different storage characteristics. While a single track of an IBM 3380 can contain 10 CIs of 4096 bytes each, a single track of an IBM 3330 can contain only three CIs of that size. The number of tracks per CA is governed by the

14.1 ESTIMATING FOR A KSDS

IBM device	Tracks per cylinder
3330	19
3350	30
3375	12
3380	15
3370*	12
9332*	4
9335*	6

*FBA device.

Figure 14.2 Track capacities of some IBM DASDs.

values of the space allocation parameter. The recommendation in Chap. 10 was to allocate space by cylinders, thereby making a data CA one cylinder in size. The tabulation in Fig. 14.1 shows a relationship between type of DASD, CI size, and number of CIs that can be contained in a cylinder with or without the use of IMBED. If the CA size is less than a cylinder, use the information in Fig. 14.2 to determine the number of tracks per cylinder, and calculate the number of CIs per track to determine the number of CIs per CA. In this chapter we will concentrate on CAs that are one cylinder in size. Also, recall from Chap. 11 that the IMBEDed sequence set uses the first track of a CA. Therefore, if IMBED is being used, be sure to get the figures from an IMBED row in Fig. 14.1.

Case Study 1: Let's suppose that in our example the space allocation was done in cylinders and therefore the CA size is one cylinder. The device type is an IBM 3380, and IMBED was used for the allocation. Referring to Fig. 14.1, we find that a CA size of one cylinder with an IMBEDed sequence set on an IBM 3380 will contain 140 CIs that are each 4096 bytes long. Therefore, in this case there are 140 CIs per CA.

Step 3: Determine the Number of Effective CIs per CA The number of effective CIs in a CA depends upon the CA-percent value of the FREESPACE parameter. The value is determined as follows:

$$\text{Effective CIs per CA} = \text{TOTCI} \times \frac{100 - \text{CAPERCENT}}{100}$$

where TOTCI is the total number of CIs per CA as determined in step 2, and CAPERCENT is the second value (CA-percent) of the FREESPACE parameter.

Case Study 1: In our example, the FREESPACE parameter was coded as FREESPACE(30,40), so the value of CAPERCENT is 40. In step

2, we determined that there are 140 CIs per CA. The effective number of CIs per CA is calculated as follows:

$$\text{Effective CIs per CA} = 140 \times \frac{100 - 40}{100}$$

$$= 140 \times \frac{60}{100} = 84$$

Only 84 CIs out of 140 will contain records at the time of the initial load. The other CIs will contain records only if they are used during CI splits.

Step 4: Determine the Number of Records per CA Multiplying the results in steps 1 and 3 gives the total number of records per CA:

Records per CA = (records per CI) × (effective CIs per CA)

Case Study 1: In our example there are 14 records per CI and 84 effective CIs per CA (one cylinder of 3380 in our case). Therefore,

$$\text{Records per CA} = 14 \times 84 = 1176$$

At the time of initial load, our example KSDS will accommodate 1176 records on each DASD cylinder.

Step 5: Determine Primary and Secondary Space Requirements We must determine the number of records that the KSDS is expected to contain at the time of the initial load. By dividing this number by the result in step 4, you will get the number of CAs that it will take to hold those records initially. If this is a read-only data set, you can simply allocate this value as the primary space allocation figure. If the data set also has new record adds, updates, and/or deletes, you have to keep a certain percentage of the CAs free to accommodate CA splits without performing a secondary space allocation.

Primary space allocation is calculated as follows:

$$\text{Primary space value} = \frac{\text{EXPRECS}}{\text{RECSCA}} \times \frac{100 + \text{GRFACT}}{100}$$

where EXPRECS is the expected number of records at the time of initial load, RECSCA is the number of records per CA calculated in step 4, and GRFACT is the growth factor given as a percentage of CAs to accommodate CA splits before getting a secondary allocation. This value will be zero for read-only files.

Once you have calculated the primary space allocation figure, you must determine the secondary allocation value. For read-only data sets, this value will be zero. For other data sets, the judgment must be made

14.2 ESTIMATING FOR AN ALTERNATE INDEX

on the basis of the nature of the applications. Usually, 10% of the primary allocation is sufficient to support secondary allocations.

Case Study 1: In our example, we expect to have 200,000 records in the KSDS at the time of initial load. We also keep a margin of 5% of the CAs for future splits without increasing the secondary allocation of the data set:

$$\text{Primary space value} = \frac{200,000}{1176} \times \frac{100 + 5}{100} = 178.5 \text{ cylinders}$$

We can round this value up to 180 cylinders. Be aware that *5% of the cylinders in this figure will not be used for initial load;* they will contain records only after the other CAs split. We also decided to have 10% of the 180 cylinders, i.e., 18, as the secondary space allocation value. The space parameter for our example will be coded as

CYLINDERS(180,18)

14.1.2 Estimating Space for Variable-Length Records

So far we have assumed that the KSDS has fixed-length records only. The calculations must be varied slightly if the records are of variable length. It is difficult to predict the average record length in such a file. Also, there might be more than two 3-byte RDF fields in the CIs of a variable-length record file.

Without getting into further complications, determine the average record length based on your judgment of the facts and follow the steps outlined for fixed-length records in Section 14.1.1. Add a safety factor of 5% to the value calculated in step 5, and use it as the primary space allocation figure.

14.2 ESTIMATING FOR AN ALTERNATE INDEX

For all practical purposes, an alternate index is a KSDS; therefore, the space for an alternate index cluster is estimated in the same way as for that of a KSDS. A unique key alternate index is comparable to a fixed-length record KSDS, while a nonunique key alternate index is similar to a variable-length record KSDS. There are slight variations in the estimations if the alternate index is on an ESDS. But in this section we will discuss only the technique that is universally applicable to all possibilities.

Since an alternate index is a KSDS, we will need the following values (as discussed in Section 14.1) before we can estimate space requirements:

- Alternate index data CI size
- Alternate index data CA size

- Values of FREESPACE parameter
- Use of IMBED
- Type of DASD
- Alternate index record size

Bear in mind that these figures refer to the alternate index cluster and not to the base cluster. The values of the first five items are available as before. The alternate index record size can be calculated as follows:

$$\text{Alternate index record size} = 5 + AKL + (N \times PTRLEN)$$

where AKL is the length of the alternate key and N is the average number of occurrences of the pointer. For a unique key alternate index, the value of N is always 1. For a nonunique key alternate index, N is the average number of occurrences of a base cluster pointer for each alternate key value.

PTRLEN is the length of the base cluster pointer. If the base cluster is a KSDS, the value of PTRLEN is the length of the prime key; if the base cluster is an ESDS, its value is always 4.

After you have calculated the alternate index record size, you can use steps 1 to 5 in Section 14.1.1 to calculate the primary and secondary space requirements.

Case Study 2—Unique key alternate index on a KSDS: Let's allocate a unique key alternate index on a KSDS. The DASD is an IBM 3380, and the CI size of the alternate index cluster is determined to be 2048 bytes. Since the space allocation will be done in cylinders, the CA size will be one cylinder. IMBED will be used for the sequence set of the alternate index. Based on activity in the base cluster, the free space values for the alternate index cluster will be coded as FREESPACE(10,20). The record size of the alternate index can be calculated as follows:

$$\text{Record size} = 5 + AKL + (N \times PTRLEN)$$

where AKL is the length of the alternate key, i.e., the employee number, which is 4 bytes long; $N = 1$, since this is a unique key alternate index; and PTRLEN is the length of the social security number field, i.e., the prime key, which is 9 bytes long. By substituting the values into the formula, we obtain

$$\text{Record length} = 5 + 4 + 1 \times 9 = 18 \text{ bytes}$$

Now we can follow all five steps in Section 14.1.1 to calculate the space requirements.

14.2 ESTIMATING FOR AN ALTERNATE INDEX

Step 1: Determine the number of records per CI.

$$\text{Records per CI} = \frac{\text{DCISZ} - 10}{\text{RECSZ}} \times \frac{100 - \text{CIPERCENT}}{100}$$

$$= \frac{2048 - 10}{18} \times \frac{100 - 10}{100}$$

$$= \frac{2038}{18} \times \frac{90}{100}$$

$$= 101.9, \text{ or } 101 \text{ records}$$

Step 2: Determine the number of CIs per CA. Referring to Fig. 14.1, we find that an IBM 3380 cylinder will have 252 CIs of 2048 bytes each with the use of IMBED option.

Step 3: Determine the number of effective CIs per CA:

$$\text{Effective CIs per CA} = \text{TOTCI} \times \frac{100 - \text{CAPERCENT}}{100}$$

$$= 252 \times \frac{100 - 20}{100}$$

$$= 252 \times \frac{80}{100} = 201.6, \text{ or } 201 \text{ CIs}$$

Step 4: Determine the number of records per CA:

$$\text{Records per CA} = (\text{records per CI}) \times (\text{effective CIs per CA})$$

$$= 101 \times 201 = 20{,}301$$

Step 5: Determine the primary and secondary space required. We will assume that there are 200,000 records in the base cluster. Since it is a unique key alternate index, there will be 200,000 records in it as well. We will allow for a growth factor of 10% to accommodate CA splits in the alternate index cluster before resorting to the first secondary allocation:

$$\text{Primary space value} = \frac{\text{EXPRECS}}{\text{RECSCA}} \times \frac{100 + \text{GRFACT}}{100}$$

$$= \frac{200{,}000}{20{,}301} \times \frac{100 + 10}{100}$$

$$= \frac{200{,}000}{20{,}301} \times \frac{110}{100} = 10.8, \text{ or } 11 \text{ cylinders}$$

$$\text{Secondary space value} = \frac{11 \times 10}{100} = 1.1, \text{ or } 1 \text{ cylinder}$$

The space allocation parameter for the alternate index cluster will be coded as

CYLINDERS(11,1)

Case Study 3—Nonunique key alternate index on an ESDS: The base cluster is an ESDS with approximately 300,000 records. Its nonunique key alternate index is to be allocated on an IBM 3380, and its CI size is determined to be 1024 bytes. Since the space allocation is to be done in cylinders, the CA size will be one cylinder. NOIMBED will be used, and, based on update activity in the base cluster, the free space values for the alternate index cluster will be FREESPACE(20,25).

The alternate key is the employee name which is 15 bytes long. Since there can be many employees in the ESDS with the same name, we have defined the alternate index with the nonunique key option. It has been estimated that on an average there can be up to three employees with a similar name. The record size of an alternate index is calculated as follows:

$$\text{Record size} = 5 + AKL + N \times PTRLEN$$
$$= 5 + 15 + 3 \times 4 = 32 \text{ bytes}$$

Note that the pointer length (PTRLEN) for an ESDS is 4 bytes. Now we can follow all the steps in Section 14.1.1 to calculate the space requirements.

Step 1:

$$\text{Records per CI} = \frac{DCISZ - 10}{RECSZ} \times \frac{100 - CIPERCENT}{100}$$

$$= \frac{1024 - 10}{32} \times \frac{100 - 20}{100}$$

$$= \frac{1014}{32} \times \frac{80}{100} = 25.35, \text{ or } 25 \text{ records}$$

Step 2: From Fig. 14.1, we know that an IBM 3380 cylinder will have 465 CIs of 1024 bytes each with the use of NOIMBED option.

Step 3:

$$\text{Effective CIs per CA} = TOTCI \times \frac{100 - CAPERCENT}{100}$$

$$= 465 \times \frac{100 - 25}{100}$$

$$= 465 \times \frac{75}{100} = 348.75, \text{ or } 348 \text{ CIs}$$

14.3 ESTIMATING FOR AN ESDS

Step 4:

Records per CA = (records per CI) × (effective CIs per CA)
= 25 × 348 = 8700

Step 5: We already know that there are 300,000 records in the base cluster. Since the average occurrence of the alternate key has been estimated to be 3, there will be only 100,000 records in the alternate index cluster. We will allow for a growth factor of 10% to accommodate CA splits in the alternate index cluster before expecting the first secondary space allocation.

$$\text{Primary space value} = \frac{\text{EXPRECS}}{\text{RECSCA}} \times \frac{100 + \text{GRFACT}}{100}$$

$$= \frac{100{,}000}{87{,}00} \times \frac{100 + 10}{100}$$

$$= 12.6, \text{ or } 13 \text{ cylinders}$$

$$\text{Secondary space value} = 13 \times \frac{10}{100} = 1.3, \text{ or } 1 \text{ cylinder}$$

The space allocation parameter for this alternate index cluster will be coded as

CYLINDERS(13,1)

14.3 ESTIMATING FOR AN ESDS

Space estimation for an ESDS is the same as for a KSDS. Consider an ESDS as a KSDS with NOIMBED and FREESPACE(0,0). With these two things in mind, you may use the same five steps as in Section 14.1.1 to calculate the space requirements for ESDS files.

Case Study 4—Space estimation for an ESDS: The base cluster is an ESDS with approximately 500,000 records. It has fixed-length records of 300 bytes each, the CI size is 4096 bytes, and the DASD is an IBM 3380. The space allocation will be done in cylinders, so the CA size is one cylinder.

Step 1:

$$\text{Records per CI} = \frac{\text{DCISZ} - 10}{\text{RECSZ}} \times \frac{100 - \text{CIPERCENT}}{100}$$

$$= \frac{4096 - 10}{300} \times \frac{100 - 0}{100}$$

$$= \frac{4086}{300} = 13.6, \text{ or } 13 \text{ records}$$

Steps 2 and 3: Since an ESDS has no CA-percent free space, step 3 will yield the same results as step 2. According to Fig. 14.1, an IBM 3380 cylinder will have 150 CIs of 4096 bytes each (consider only the row with the NOIMBED option).

Step 4:

Records per CA = (records per CI) × (effective CIs per CA)
= 13 × 150 = 1950 records

Step 5: Since an ESDS is not subject to CA splits, the growth factor (GRFACT) may be considered zero. If the ESDS is ever opened for loading additional records at the end of the file, a growth factor percentage may be considered separately. In our case, we assume no growth in the data set:

$$\text{Primary space value} = \frac{\text{EXPRECS}}{\text{RECSCA}} \times \frac{100 + \text{GRFACT}}{100}$$

$$= \frac{500{,}000}{1950} \times \frac{100 + 0}{100}$$

$$= 256.4, \text{ or } 260 \text{ cylinders}$$

The space allocation parameter for this ESDS will be coded as

CYLINDERS(260,0)

14.4 ESTIMATING FOR AN RRDS

The space requirement for an RRDS depends upon the highest relative record number (RRN) that the file is required to contain. There is no concept of free space in an RRDS. *Each* record in an RRDS has an associated 3-byte-long RDF in the control interval. Therefore, 3 bytes must be added to the record length when you do the space estimates. Since an RRDS supports only fixed-length records, there is no consideration for space estimates for variable-length records. The following information must be known before attempting to calculate the space requirements:

- Type of DASD
- CI size
- CA size
- Record size
- Highest RRN supported

As before, we will take a step-by-step methodical approach.

Step 1: Calculate the Number of Records per CI The total number of records an RRDS CI can contain is calculated as follows:

14.4 ESTIMATING FOR AN RRDS

$$\text{RECSPERCI} = \frac{\text{CISZ} - 4}{\text{RECLEN} + 3}$$

where RECSPERCI is the number of records per CI, CISZ is the control interval size, and RECLEN is the record length.

Step 2: Calculate the Number of Records per CA We will assume that the CA size in our case is always one DASD cylinder. Refer to Fig. 14.1 to find how many CIs a DASD cylinder can have. Refer to the values with the NOIMBED option even though this parameter is not applicable to an RRDS.

$$\text{RECSPERCYL} = \text{CISPERCYL} \times \text{RECSPERCI}$$

where RECSPERCYL is the number of records per cylinder, CISPERCYL is the number of CIs per cylinder (Fig. 14.1), and RECSPERCI is the number of records per CI determined in step 1.

Step 3: Determine Space Requirements At this point, you need to know the highest RRN that you can expect to store in the data set. The space required to support this RRN will be as follows:

$$\text{Space requirement (cylinders)} = \frac{\text{HRRN}}{\text{RECSPERCYL}}$$

where HRRN is the highest RRN supported and RECSPERCYL is the number of records per cylinder from step 2.

Be sure to round up the fractional part of the result to a whole number of cylinders.

Note that the space requirement in an RRDS depends only upon the highest RRN supported by the data set. Even though the data set may contain only one record with the highest possible RRN and the rest of the slots are empty, the space requirements will stay the same.

Case Study 5—Space Estimation for an RRDS: In our example, the RRDS is to be allocated on an IBM 3380. Its record length is 100 bytes, and the CI size is 4096 bytes. The highest RRN that has to be supported is 366,000. To calculate the space requirement, follow these steps:

   Step 1: Calculate the number of records per CI.

$$\text{RECSPERCI} = \frac{\text{CISZ} - 4}{\text{RECLEN} + 3}$$

$$= \frac{4096 - 4}{100 + 3} = 39.7, \text{ or 39 records}$$

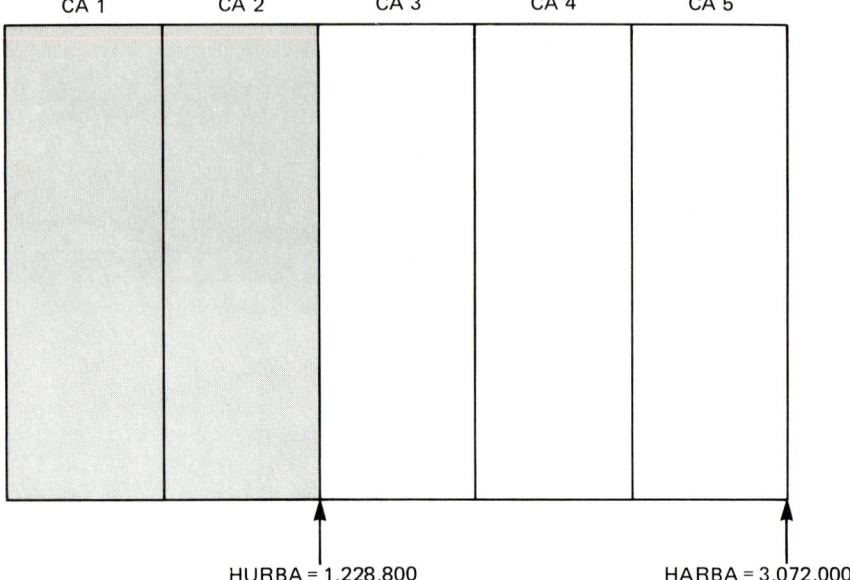

Figure 14.3 An example of HURBA and HARBA. The data set consists of five CAs (five cylinders, in this case). CAs 1 and 2 have records, and CAs 3 through 5 do not have records. HURBA indicates two cylinders are in use. HARBA indicates that total space allocation is five cylinders.

Step 2: Calculate the number of records per CA (cylinder).

$$\text{RECSPERCYL} = \text{CISPERCYL} \times \text{RECSPERCI}$$
$$= 150 \times 39 = 5850 \text{ records}$$

The value of 150 for the number of CIs per cylinder is taken from Fig. 14.1, for an IBM 3380 and a CI size of 4096 bytes.

Step 3: Determine space requirements.

$$\text{Space required (cylinders)} = \frac{\text{HRRN}}{\text{RECSPERCYL}}$$
$$= \frac{366{,}000}{5850} = 62.5 \text{ cylinders}$$

Rounding the figure up to the next highest integer, the value will be 63 cylinders. The space parameter will be coded as

CYLINDERS(63,0)

14.5 HURBA AND HARBA

The high used RBA (HURBA) and high allocated RBA (HARBA) of a data set can be obtained from the LISTCAT-produced listing of a data set.

14.5 HURBA AND HARBA

HURBA denotes the relative byte address up to which the data set has been used. In a KSDS, it is always on a CA boundary. HURBA reflects the last CA address that contains or once contained records.

HARBA refers to the relative byte address of the highest allocated CA. It is always equal to or greater than HURBA. If HURBA and HARBA are equal, there are no free CAs remaining in the data set.

Figure 14.3 gives an example of HURBA and HARBA. The number of VSAM-addressable bytes in a cylinder is not the same as the number of storage bytes in that cylinder. Although an IBM 3380 contains 719,520 bytes, the number of VSAM-addressable bytes is less than that. This value depends primarily on the CI size and can be calculated as follows:

VSAM-addressable bytes in a cylinder

$$= (CI\ size) \times (number\ of\ CIs\ per\ cylinder)$$

In Fig. 14.3 we assume that the device is an IBM 3380 and the CI size is 4096 bytes. According to Fig. 14.1, there are 150 CIs of 4096 bytes in one cylinder of an IBM 3380. Substituting these values into the above equation yields

$$\text{VSAM-addressable bytes per cylinder} = 4096 \times 150$$
$$= 614{,}400\ \text{bytes}$$

You will find that the HURBA and HARBA of our KSDS are *exact* multiples of this number. In Fig. 14.3, if we divide the HURBA and HARBA by 614,400, the results are 2 and 5 cylinders, respectively, the number of cylinders used and allocated for our data set.

HURBA and HARBA come in handy in determining whether a data set is overallocated. The utilization of the data set space as a percentage of total allocated space may be calculated as follows:

$$\text{Utilization percentage} = \frac{\text{HURBA}}{\text{HARBA}} \times 100$$

It is good practice to scan production data sets for space utilization on a regular basis.

four
BUFFER MANAGEMENT

Buffer management is the most effective way to reduce I/O's. It is not unusual to cut I/O's by half or more with the proper use of buffers. Chapter 15 discusses batch jobs, including alternate index considerations and backup, recovery, and reorganization of data sets. Chapter 16 concentrates on the NSR buffers, and Chap. 17 deals with LSR buffer management in a CICS environment.

Don't be surprised if your batch jobs run in one-half or one-quarter of the time when you use the techniques discussed here. You can also look forward to experiencing a significant reduction in CICS I/O's and an improvement in response time.

chapter 15

Batch Environment

In addition to the performance techniques discussed so far, buffer management plays the most significant role in the fine tuning of a VSAM-based system. With proper buffer allocation, a batch job can be executed in one-half to one-fourth of the usual run time. Unfortunately, the default buffer allocation used in most systems is also the most inefficient way to manage I/O's. For this reason the recommendations discussed here are very important for performance management.

15.1 WHAT ARE BUFFERS?

Before an application can perform any processing on a logical record, the record must be transferred from the DASD to the main memory of the computer. When a command is issued to write a record, it is transferred from main memory to the DASD. *The portions of the main memory that are reserved as temporary work spaces for transferring data to and from the DASD are called the buffers* (Fig. 15.1). In VSAM, the smallest unit of data storage that is transferred between the buffers and the DASD is a CI. Since a KSDS or an alternate index have both data and index components, separate buffers are needed to process them individually. An ESDS or an RRDS need buffers for the data component only. Each transfer of data between the buffers and the DASD is called an I/O.

You cannot specify buffers indiscriminately. In a non-MVS/XA en-

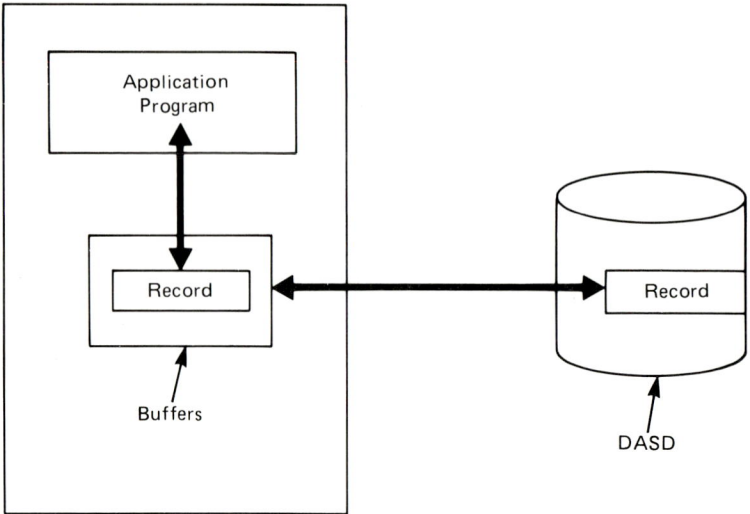

Figure 15.1 Buffers in a processing environment.

vironment, there are virtual storage constraints caused by the 24-bit addressability limitation. Your program and the buffers are limited by the REGION parameter of JCL, which itself is limited by the size of the private area in the system.[1] Because of these limitations, you must make prudent use of storage for buffer allocation. Each buffer is the size of a CI. You may allocate a multiple number of buffers for the data as well as the index component. As we will see later, this helps to reduce I/O's.

If you do not explicitly specify the number of buffers, VSAM resorts to the default buffer allocation. *The default allocation is one index buffer and two data buffers for a KSDS.* In the majority of cases, this is the worst allocation from an I/O performance point of view. Unless the data set is used infrequently, you should specify the buffers as required by the application.

15.2 HOW TO SPECIFY BUFFERS

In a batch environment, the index (BUFNI) and the data buffers (BUFND) may be allocated using the following techniques.

Data Set Allocation Time You can code the optional BUFFERSPACE parameter of DEFINE CLUSTER or DEFINE AIX at the time of data set allocation. This value specifies the size of the buffer area for both the

---

[1]The *private area* is the area left for applications to run after a major part of the system is used by systems software and areas like SQA, CSA, PLPA, and MVS NUCLEUS.

15.2 HOW TO SPECIFY BUFFERS

data and index components. When the file is opened, VSAM determines how much of that space should be allocated to the index and data buffers. Again, the default parameter value for a KSDS is the buffer space for one index CI and two data CIs. The value of the BUFFERSPACE parameter can also be changed using the ALTER command of AMS.

Since you have no control over specifying the index and data buffers separately, the use of this parameter is not recommended in most cases. The only circumstances justifying its use are for files that are opened *dynamically* without the coding of DD statements in the JCL, for example when you have used the INDATASET and OUTDATASET parameters of REPRO instead of the IFILE and OFILE parameters. A VSAM file also goes through a dynamic open when the data set is opened via the alternate index path. Use of the BUFFERSPACE parameter is justified in these few cases and is explained in Section 15.5.1.

ACB Macro The values of the number of index buffers (BUFNI) and data buffers (BUFND) may be specified in the ACB macro of an assembler program as follows.

```
Label     ACB     AM=VSAM,
                  BUFND=11,
                  BUFNI=5,
                  DDNAME=VSAMFILE,
                    :
                    :
                  STRNO=1
```

Since the Cobol language does not provide any means to specify this macro, it cannot be used for such programs. Every time you wish to change the values of the buffers, you must reassemble and relinkedit the program. Therefore, this technique is *not recommended* either.

AMP Parameter The Access Method Parameter (AMP) of JCL can be used to specify the VSAM strings, index buffers, data buffers, and buffer space values. A coding example of this parameter is:

```
//VSAMFILE  DD   DSN=EMPLOYEE.KSDS.CLUSTER,
//                DISP=SHR,
//                AMP=('STRNO=1','BUFNI=5','BUFND=11')
```

Usually, the number of string requirements (STRNO) for a batch job is 1. Since this value is also the default parameter, it need not be coded. The values of the index buffers (BUFNI) and the data buffers (BUFND) are the subject of the remainder of this chapter. The bufferspace (BUFSP) value can be determined by VSAM from the BUFNI and BUFND values, so it need not be coded either. In summary, VSAM buffer allocation in a batch job involves proper BUFNI and BUFND values. *The use of the AMP parameter is the only recommended technique for files that are not opened dynamically in a batch environment.*

15.3 INDEX BUFFERS

Index buffers are specified by assigning a value to BUFNI in either the ACB macro of an assembler program or the AMP parameter of the JCL. From previous chapters, we are already familiar with the two parts of an index component, the index set and the sequence set. We will make use of buffering techniques to cut down on I/O's on each component.

15.3.1 Random Access

In random access, the most frequently retrieved records in an index component are the index set records. Index set records consist of all the index CIs above the sequence set records. The ideal technique keeps all the index set records in the buffers, thus reducing their I/O's to zero. Additionally, one sequence set buffer is required for each additional string of VSAM. Under most circumstances, a batch job requires only one string for processing. Therefore, *fine tuning the index buffers involves allocating enough buffers to keep all the index set CIs in core, plus one additional buffer for the sequence set reads.*

To determine the number of buffers you need, first produce a listing of the data set. It contains all the values you will be using to calculate the value of BUFNI. The formulas used to calculate the value of BUFNI differ with the use of the IMBED and REPLICATE parameters of data set allocation.

IMBED and NOREPLICATE The value of BUFNI will be

$$\text{BUFNI} = \frac{\text{HURBAI}}{\text{CISZI}} + 1$$

where   HURBAI = high used RBA for the index set of the index component. There will be more than one value of HURBA in the index listing. Take the value shown by EXTENT-TYPE X'00'. The other values of HURBA will have a number significantly higher than that. Ignore them.

CISZI = CI size for the index component. The calculated result should be an integer number. If the result contains a fraction, you probably picked up the wrong values in the listing. Find the correct values. Also, the result you get should fall in the

15.3 INDEX BUFFERS

range between 1 and 20. If it turns out to be a significantly larger number, you probably did not pick up the high used RBA value from the EXTENT-TYPE '00'.

NOIMBED and NOREPLICATE

$$\text{BUFNI} = \frac{\text{HURBAI}}{\text{CISZI}} - \frac{\text{HURBAD}}{\text{CISZD} \times (\text{CI/CA})} + 1$$

where HURBAI = High used RBA of the index component;
CISZI = CI size of the index component;
HURBAD = High used RBA of the data component;
CISZD = CI size of the data component; and
CI/CA = Number of data CIs within each data CA.

The values of each of the variables in the formula are provided in the listing itself. Again, the result should be an integer between 1 and 20.

IMBED and REPLICATE

$$\text{BUFNI} = \frac{\text{HURBAI}}{\text{CISZI} \times (\text{PHYRECS/TRK})} + 1$$

where HURBAI = High used RBA for the index component as given in the EXTENT-TYPE X'00';
CISZI = CI size for the index component;
PHYRECS/TRK = Physical records per track for the index component as given by LISTCAT. This value is also the number of index CIs per DASD track. For the index component, a CI is a physical record.

Again, the result should be an integer value between 1 and 20.

NOIMBED and REPLICATE

$$\text{BUFNI} = \frac{\text{HURBAI}}{\text{CISZI} \times (\text{PHYRECS/TRK})} - \frac{\text{HURBAD}}{\text{CISZD} \times (\text{CI/CA})} + 1$$

where HURBAI = High Used RBA for the index component;
CISZI = CI size for the index component;
PHYRECS/TRK = Number of physical records per DASD track for the index component;
HURBAD = High Used RBA for the data component;
CISZD = CI size for the data component; and
CI/CA = Number of data CIs per data CA.

In this case too, the value of BUFNI should be an integer and fall between 1 and 20.

Considerations for KEYRANGES If we had used the KEYRANGES parameter, the data set listing would not give you the correct value of the high used RBA of the data component (HURBAD) directly. This value must be calculated. First determine the number of key range groups for the data set. This value can also be determined from the command syntax of the DEFINE CLUSTER or DEFINE AIX parameters. Expect to find as many sets of space allocation values in the listing as the number of key range groups. In the space allocation value of *each group,* subtract the value of the *low* allocated RBA from the high used RBA. Adding all the values determined from each group together will give you the value of HURBAD to use in the formulas above.

Additional Strings So far, we have assumed that the batch jobs require only one VSAM string (STRNO = 1) for processing. There are some circumstances in which you may need more than one string. Each string ensures one positioning within the data set. If you maintain multiple positions within the data set, you will require a multiple number of strings. If you are an Assembler programmer, you know that a position is defined by a request parameter list (RPL) or a chain of RPLs. As a programmer, you have to know how many positions you are going to maintain within the data set. In these circumstances, replace the value of 1 in the preceding formulas with a value equal to the number of positions. This value of BUFNI should be used in the AMP parameter.

Index Levels and BUFNI Determine the number of index levels from the data set listing. If the number of levels is 1, the value of BUFNI will be 1. If the number of levels is 2, the value of BUFNI will be 2. If the number of levels is 3, the value of BUFNI will be between 4 and 20. For very large data sets and a multiple-string environment, the value of BUFNI may exceed 20 but by a very small number.

Thus we see that you don't have to use the formulas for a one- or two-level index because the value of BUFNI for them will be 1 and 2, respectively.

Minimum Buffer Allocation All the formulas we have discussed so far give us a value for BUFNI that will generate the fewest possible I/O's for a randomly accessed data set. If, due to virtual storage constraint problems, you cannot allocate such a large number of buffers, the next best thing to do is to allocate as many index buffers as there are index levels. So the value of BUFNI will be 1, 2, or 3, depending on whether the data set has a one-, two-, or three-level index. This value will ensure that there are no I/O's in the highest level of index. I/O's will be necessary only on the lower levels. Although this may not be an ideal solution, it will still significantly reduce I/O's.

15.4 DATA BUFFERS

Example: Let's suppose we have a KSDS defined with the IMBED and NOREPLICATE options. From the data set listing, we determine that the value of the HURBA for the index set (EXTENT-TYPE X'00') is 16,384 bytes and that the index CI size is 2048 bytes. The value of BUFNI (considering a string value of 1) will be calculated as follows:

$$\text{BUFNI} = \frac{\text{HURBAI}}{\text{CISZI}} + 1$$

$$= \frac{16{,}384}{2048} + 1 = 8 + 1, \text{ or } 9$$

The AMP parameter will then be coded as

```
//VSAMFILE    DD  DSN=VSAM.FILE,DISP=SHR,
//                AMP=('BUFNI=9',........
```

15.3.2 Sequential Access

A data set is said to be accessed sequentially if, after open, it is read starting from the beginning and continuing on to the end. In Cobol programs, it is specified by ACCESS MODE IS SEQUENTIAL in the SELECT statement. *Index buffers do not play any significant role in such processing.* Once VSAM has access to the first sequence set CI, it follows horizontal pointers to the next sequence set CI without ever going to the index set again. *So, for sequential access, the coding of BUFNI can be omitted and left at the default value of 1.*

15.3.3 Mixed Mode Access

A data set is said to have mixed mode access if it is used for both random and sequential access in the same program. In Cobol programs, it is specified by ACCESS MODE IS DYNAMIC in the SELECT statement. Since random access is part of the mixed mode access, the index buffer rules to be followed are those for random access. *Calculate the value of BUFNI as if the data set were used for random access only, and use that value for the AMP parameter.*

15.4 DATA BUFFERS

Data buffers are specified by assigning a value to BUFND in either the ACB macro of an Assembler program or the AMP parameter of JCL. As with BUFNI, it is recommended that BUFND be specified in the JCL so that any change in its value does not require reassembly and relinkedit of the program.

15.4.1 Random Access

Random access of records in a data set does not require more than one data buffer per VSAM string. For all practical purposes, we can *let the value of BUFND default in such cases*. No coding of BUFND will be necessary in the AMP parameter.

15.4.2 Sequential Access

Data buffers play a significant role in the fine tuning of a system if the data is accessed sequentially. The default value of data buffers for a KSDS in a batch job is 2. One of these two buffers is reserved for splits, while the other is used for I/O's. Thus, a sequential read of the entire file will cause as many I/O's on the data component as the number of data CI's that contain records. If we provide more data buffers, VSAM will schedule a read-ahead of the data CIs in a single I/O operation. The CIs read in advance will be processed without any physical movement of the read-write arm of the DASD. This can dramatically reduce the number of I/O's. The number of data buffers depends upon whether the file is being read for input or is being created for output. Both are discussed here.

Data Buffers for Input Data Set The best performance results are achieved when the data component is read in full DASD tracks. Therefore, the number of buffers depends on the DASD type and the CI size of the data component. The number of data CIs per DASD track can be calculated as follows:

$$\text{CIs per track} = \frac{(\text{PHYRECS/TRK}) \times (\text{PHYREC-SIZE})}{\text{CISZD}}$$

where   PHYRECS/TRK = Physical records per track given by the data set listing;
   PHYREC-SIZE = Physical record size given by the data set listing; and
   CISZD = Data CI size.

The value of BUFND will be

$$\text{BUFND} = \text{CIs per track} + 1$$

One of the buffers provided is set aside by VSAM for splits. Note that VSAM requires this extra buffer even for read-only data sets, which may never be subject to CI or CA splits.

Example: A KSDS is allocated on an IBM 3380. A LISTCAT of it produces the following values:

15.4 DATA BUFFERS

$$CISIZE = 2048 \text{ bytes}$$
$$PHYREC\text{-}SIZE = 2048 \text{ bytes}$$
$$PHYRECS/TRK = 18$$

The number of CIs per track will be

$$\text{CIs per track} = \frac{18 \times 2048}{2048} = 18$$

Thus the value of BUFND for read-only access will be

$$BUFND = 18 + 1 = 19$$

The AMP parameter will be coded as follows:

```
//VSAMFILE    DD   DSN=VSAM.FILE,DISP=SHR,
//                 AMP=('BUFND=19',........
```

Data Buffers for Output Data Set A data set is opened as output if it is to be loaded with records in the create mode. In Cobol programs, the data set is coded with ACCESS MODE IS SEQUENTIAL and is OPENed as OUTPUT. We will get the best performance when the data is written in complete tracks. We can determine the number of data CIs per track by using the formulas in the example above. We add 2 to this value to allocate one buffer that VSAM sets aside for splits and one to take care of overlap processing. The overlap processing buffer takes care of concurrent movement of data to the output buffers while the data is being written to the track. It provides some additional performance benefits. The value of BUFND will be:

$$BUFND = \frac{(PHYRECS/TRK) \times (PHYREC\text{-}SIZE)}{CISZD} + 2$$

The values of the variables can be found in the data set listing as explained before.

15.4.3 Mixed Mode Access

In mixed mode access, a data set has random and sequential access capabilities in the same program. In Cobol programs, the position is set by the START verb and the records are read sequentially using the READ NEXT statement. *Since sequential access is a part of this mode, the value of BUFND is the same as if the data set were being used for sequential access only.*

15.5 ALTERNATE INDEX CONSIDERATIONS

An alternate index, whether it is defined over a KSDS or an ESDS, is itself a KSDS in architecture. All the buffer management techniques discussed for a KSDS also apply to the alternate index. Since an alternate index KSDS can also be defined with the IMBED and REPLICATE parameters, be sure to use the appropriate formula when you calculate the values of BUFNI and BUFND for the alternate index.

The data and index buffers pertaining to an alternate index *do not* apply to the base cluster. The base cluster is expected to have its own set of data and index buffers. For example, let's say we have a base cluster and its two alternate indexes as follows:

```
EMPLOYEE.KSDS.CLUSTER
EMPLOYEE.KSDS.AIX1.CLUSTER
EMPLOYEE.KSDS.AIX2.CLUSTER
```

Let the paths to the two alternate indexes have the names

```
EMPLOYEE.KSDS.PATH1
EMPLOYEE.KSDS.PATH2
```

An example of the coding of the DD statements and the associated AMP parameters might be:

```
//BASECL   DD  DSN=EMPLOYEE.KSDS.CLUSTER,DISP=SHR,
//             AMP=('BUFNI=5','BUFND=11')
//BASECL1  DD  DSN=EMPLOYEE.KSDS.PATH1,DISP=SHR,
//             AMP=('BUFNI=2','BUFND=5')
//BASECL2  DD  DSN=EMPLOYEE.KSDS.PATH2,DISP=SHR,
//             AMP=('BUFNI=2','BUFND=5')
```

The values of BUFNI and BUFND have been determined using the formulas in this chapter. Remember that these values have been calculated separately for the base cluster and each of its associated alternate indexes.

15.5.1 Dynamic Open via Path

When a base cluster is opened by using its alternate index path name, you need to code the DD statement only for the path itself. Since the base cluster is dynamically opened, you may not code the DD statement for the base cluster. An example of the JCL coding for a open via path is as follows:

15.5 ALTERNATE INDEX CONSIDERATIONS

```
//PATH1    DD  DSN=EMPLOYEE.KSDS.PATH1,DISP=SHR,
//             AMP=('BUFNI=2','BUFND=5')
```

As a result, the base cluster associated with this path's alternate index is opened by VSAM dynamically (SVC 99). Since there is no DD statement for the base cluster, we have to find an alternative way to allow for index and data buffers. This is where the BUFFERSPACE parameter of DEFINE CLUSTER comes in handy. The procedure works as follows:

1. Determine the values of BUFNI and BUFND for the base cluster as usual with the techniques discussed in this chapter.
2. Calculate the value of buffer space required:

   BUFFERSPACE = (CISZI × BUFNI) + (CISZD × BUFND)

   where CISZI = Index CI size,
          CISZD = Data CI size,
          BUFNI = Number of index buffers, and
          BUFND = Number of data buffers.

3. Use the ALTER command of AMS to change the value of BUFFERSPACE as calculated in step 2.

Let's consider an example.

Example: A base cluster is dynamically opened via its path. Since we cannot code the values of BUFNI and BUFND for the AMP parameter, we use the ALTER command to change its BUFFERSPACE value. The value of BUFNI and BUFND are determined to be 4 and 2, respectively. The CI sizes for the index and data components are 2048 and 4096 bytes, respectively. The buffer space is calculated as follows:

$$\text{BUFFERSPACE} = (4 \times 2048) + (2 \times 4096)$$
$$= 16,384$$

We execute the ALTER command to change the value of the buffer space in the catalog:

```
ALTER    EMPLOYEE.KSDS.CLUSTER
   BUFFERSPACE(16384)
```

After the execution of the command, when the KSDS is dynamically opened via its path, 16,384 bytes worth of buffer space is allocated for its index and data components.

Warning It is advisable that you ALTER the value of BUFFERSPACE back to its original value after the job that needs it is finished. The reason for this is that the next time you open the base cluster directly (rather than via its path), the value of BUFFERSPACE may interfere with the values of BUFNI and BUFND coded in its AMP parameter. Usually it is recommended that you change back the value of buffer space with the ALTER command with a value calculated as follows:

$$\text{BUFFERSPACE} = (\text{CISZD} \times 2) + \text{CISZI}$$

This value is also the default value when the data set is defined.

Base Processing via Path Whenever a base cluster is opened for processing via an alternate index path, all its file requests are random. This is true irrespective of whether the alternate index is being read sequentially or randomly. *Therefore, when calculating the value of BUFNI for the base cluster, apply the same principles as you would for a randomly accessed file.*

15.6 DOS/VSE CONSIDERATIONS

DOS/VSE JCL does not provide for any facility to code the values of BUFNI and BUFND for its DLBL statement. However, it does provide a parameter called BUFSP, which has the same meaning as BUFFERSPACE in AMS commands. For DOS/VSE systems, calculate the value of BUFSP as follows:

$$\text{BUFSP} = (\text{BUFNI} \times \text{CISZI}) + (\text{BUFND} \times \text{CISZD})$$

Place the value of BUFSP in the DLBL statement. An example of coding such a DLBL statement is:

```
//DLBL    BASECL,'EMPLOYEE.KSDS.CLUSTER',,
          VSAM,BUFSP=16384
```

15.7 BACKUP AND REORGANIZATION

A VSAM data set is backed up, usually, by offloading it to a physical sequential file. It is reorganized by deleting the VSAM file, reallocating it, and loading it back from the backup data set. There is no difference between a backup and the sequential reading of a VSAM file for input only. Also, the restore function is the same as the sequential processing of a VSAM file as output.

Therefore, all the techniques for calculating the value of BUFND discussed in Section 15.4.2 also apply to the backup, restore, recovery, and reorganization functions of VSAM data sets. In a nutshell: All these functions should be performed by doing full DASD track reads or writes. *Physical sequential files used during backup/restore function should also be doing full track I/O's for optimum performance.*

chapter 16

CICS Environment—NSR

The most prevalent cause of poor response time in a CICS environment is an excessive number of I/O's. Proper buffer management can cut CICS I/O's by half or more. There are two ways you can allocate your VSAM buffers under CICS: by using the NonShared Resource (NSR) technique and by using the Local Shared Resource (LSR) buffer pool technique. The concept of NSR and LSR buffer pools has been introduced in Chap. 4. We will discuss the NSR technique in this chapter and the LSR technique in Chap. 17. If you are not already familiar with them, review Sections 4.1.6 and 4.1.7.

In NSR buffer pools, every VSAM data set has its own set of buffers, which it *does not* share with any other data set. In the case of a KSDS, the index and data components have separate buffers. The buffer allocation may be determined by using the following techniques.

Data Set Allocation Time   You can code the optional BUFFERSPACE parameter of DEFINE CLUSTER or DEFINE AIX at the time of data set allocation. The value specifies the size of the buffer area for both the data and index components. Later, when the file is opened, VSAM determines how much of that space should be allocated to the index buffers and how much to the data buffers. The default parameter value for a KSDS is the buffer space for one index CI and two data CIs. The value of BUFFERSPACE can also be changed using the ALTER command of

213

AMS. *Since you have no control over specifying the index and data buffers separately, the use of this parameter is not recommended in CICS.*

File Control Table Various parameters influencing VSAM performance can be specified in the File Control Table (FCT) of CICS. These parameters include string numbers (STRNO), index buffers (BUFNI), data buffers (BUFND), etc. Each data set and its buffering parameters are specified through the DFHFCT macro. The table is assembled and linkedited and becomes a CICS load module with a name DFHFCTxx, where xx is the suffix for the library member. *This is the only recommended technique for a CICS environment.* This technique is discussed in detail in Section 16.2.

16.1 WHERE DO THE BUFFERS RESIDE?

If unlimited virtual storage were available, one could allocate a sufficient number of index and data buffers and reduce the VSAM I/O's. Under most circumstances, this kind of luxury is not available. In a non-MVS/XA environment, you have to run the CICS system within the constraints set by the 24-bit addressability limitation. For all practical purposes, the size of the private area is somewhere between 6 and 8 megabytes. The CICS management modules, the dynamic storage area (DSA) of CICS, and the VSAM buffers all have to reside within this available virtual storage. In DOS/VSE, the partition size limits the amount of available addressability.

MVS/XA In an MVS/XA environment, and with an appropriate release of CICS/VS, VSAM buffers can be allocated beyond the 24-bit address space. The size of the addressability in MVS/XA is 31 bits, which can have virtual storage of 2048 megabytes. With CICS/VS release 1.6.1, the VSAM buffers reside above the 16-MB line. Therefore you have a smaller problem with buffer allocations. However, if the underlying file structure for an IMS data base under CICS is VSAM, the buffers will still exist in the 16-MB zone and will still be subject to virtual storage constraints. Figure 16.1 summarizes our discussion on the VSAM buffers and operating system addressability restrictions.

16.2 FILE CONTROL TABLE AND THE LSRPOOL OPERAND

All the VSAM data set related options, including the performance parameters, are coded in the File Control Table. A single VSAM file requires the coding of one DFHFCT macro in the table. Some of the VSAM-related operands of the macro are given in Figure 16.2. The shaded operands affect the VSAM/CICS I/O performance in an NSR environment. The BASE operand logically connects the base cluster and alternate in-

16.2 FILE CONTROL TABLE AND THE LSRPOOL OPERAND

- In a non-MVS/XA environment, native VSAM and IMS/DB VSAM buffers reside below the 16 megabyte line.
- In a DOS/VSE environment, the partition size determines the available addressability.
- In an MVS/XA environment with CICS/VS 1.6.1 or higher release, the native VSAM buffers reside above the 16-megabyte line but IMS/DB VSAM buffers reside below the 16-megabyte line.
- You have more freedom in allocating VSAM buffers if they reside in a virtual storage constraint-free zone which is above the 16-megabyte line.

Figure 16.1 VSAM buffers and virtual storage constraints in a CICS environment.

```
DFHFCT    TYPE=DATASET,
          DATASET=ddname,
          ACCMETH=VSAM,
          DISP={OLD or SHR},
          DSNAME=data set name,
          FILSTAT=({ENABLED or DISABLED},
                   {OPENED or CLOSED}),
          BASE=name,
          STRNO={1 or number},
          BUFNI= number,
          BUFND= number,
          LSRPOOL={1 or number or NONE},
          DSNSHR={ALL or UPDATE}
                      .
                      .
                      .
                      .
                      .
```

Figure 16.2 Some of the important operands of the DFHFCT TYPE = DATASET macro of CICS used for a VSAM data set. The shaded operands affect performance.

dex paths in an NSR environment. If not coded, performance may degrade. STRNO specifies the number of VSAM strings to be allocated for this file. BUFNI and BUFND specify the number of index and data buffers, respectively, for the data set.

All of these operands will be discussed in detail in subsequent sections. Note that they have the same names as the AMP parameters of JCL discussed in Chap. 15.

LSRPOOL Operand   Until release 1.6.1 of CICS/VS, the default buffer allocation for a VSAM data set was the NSR buffers. The only way you could make the data set eligible for the LSR buffer pool was by coding an operand of DFHFCT as follows:

SERVREQ = (SHARE, ...)

However, with CICS/VS release 1.7, the default places a VSAM data set in the LSR buffer pool. You can override the default and make the data set eligible for NSR with the statement

LSRPOOL = NONE

The LSRPOOL operand did not exist in CICS/VS 1.6.1. Since this chapter deals with buffer allocation and performance management for NSR pool eligible VSAM files, be sure you are aware of the changes in the macro operands when moving from CICS/VS 1.6.1 to the later releases. *Be sure to code LSRPOOL=NONE in the DFHFCT TYPE=DATASET entry of a VSAM file when you intend to use NSR buffers.*

16.3   VSAM STRINGS (STRNO) ALLOCATION

16.3.1   How Many Strings Are Needed?

In a batch environment, unless the program is coded to keep multiple positions in the data set, you require only one VSAM string. Therefore, it was recommended that STRNO not be coded in the AMP parameter in a batch environment because the default value for STRNO is 1.

In a CICS environment, you have multiple terminals executing many transactions at the same time. A string value of 1, which is also the default in CICS/VS, will serialize all file requests for a particular VSAM data set, which can seriously degrade transaction response time in an on-line environment. Depending upon the file activity, *you will probably need more than one VSAM string for most VSAM files.* The number of strings determines the number of concurrent file requests that CICS can issue against a file. If at any time there are more pending file requests than the

16.3 VSAM STRINGS (STRNO) ALLOCATION

number of VSAM file strings, they are queued up by CICS until a string is freed by a completed file request. The number of strings is specified as follows:

   STRNO = number

The default value is 1 and the maximum value is 255.

STRNO and String Waits The number of strings to specify depends on the amount of I/O activity against that particular VSAM file. A very active file will need more strings than a less frequently accessed file. You have to start with an intelligent guess or perhaps start with a string number of 1. Then print the CICS shutdown statistics after CICS is brought down. These statistics will give you the VSAM file string waits for each data set. If there are no string waits, you have probably allocated too many strings and are wasting CICS resources. If there are excessive string waits, the value should be increased. To determine the optimum value for the STRNO operand, you have to adjust its value until the number of waits is insignificant.

It should be emphasized that a reasonable number of string waits is expected and indicates optimum resource allocation. If the string waits are between 1% and 5% of the total number of file requests, they should be considered reasonable. CICS shutdown statistics also give you the total number of file requests issued for a particular VSAM data set. The string wait percentage is calculated as follows:

$$\text{String wait percentage} = \frac{\text{total string waits}}{\text{total file requests}} \times 100$$

If the statistics show that most of the requests are file browse requests (READ NEXT or READ PREV), the allowable wait should be close to 1%. If most of the activity is random reads, adds, deletes or rewrites, the wait can be up to 5% without any serious effect on performance.

Strings and Buffers The number of strings directly affects the index and data buffers. The default value in CICS is:

   BUFNI = STRNO
   BUFND = STRNO + 1

We will see in the next section on index buffers that we usually do not let the value of BUFNI default to the string value. Usually it is allocated as

   BUFNI = STRNO + number of index set records

Therefore, *the greater number of strings, the more buffer space you need for the data set.*

16.3.2 Duration of a String

Since the number of strings directly affects the index and data buffer requirements, it is important to know which particular operations increase the string requirements. VSAM gets hold of a string when a file request is issued. It releases the VSAM string when the file request is implicitly ended or an explicit request is made to release the string. *If we can find a way to expedite the file requests, the VSAM strings will be held for a shorter period of time, and the string requirements will be reduced. As a result, the buffer requirements will be reduced.* A number of factors affect the duration of the string.

READ   A KSDS read involves reading the index set records, the sequence set record, and the data component CI. A single string is acquired and held for all these operations. If the CICS read is performed in the *move mode,* the string is released as soon as the logical record is moved to the working area. If the read is done in the *locate mode,* the string is released at the end of the CICS task. There are two techniques to reduce the string requirements for read requests:

- Keep the index set records in buffers.
- Use move mode only.

READ for Update and REWRITE   The string is held for the duration of the reading of the index set records, the sequence set record, and the data CI, and then for rewriting the data CI after the record update. The string requirement may be reduced by keeping the index set records in buffers.

DELETE   The string is held for the duration of the reading of index set records, the sequence set record, and the data CI and for rewriting the data CI after the record deletion. The string requirements may be reduced by keeping the index set records in buffers.

Browse Operation   The VSAM string is held for the entire duration of the browse. The duration of the browse includes STARTBR, READ NEXTs, and ENDBR requests. If ENDBR is not issued, the string is released at the end of the CICS task. If a browse operation involves multiple READ NEXT requests spanning multiple data CIs, the string will be held by the task for a long time. Long browses are often the cause of excessive string waits. The string requirements may be reduced by keeping the following things in mind:

- Keep browses as short as possible.
- Issue an ENDBR to release the string rather than waiting for the task to end.

16.4 INDEX BUFFERS (BUFNI)

> - A string is held for the duration of the execution of all of the I/O's involved in a file request. If the I/O's can be reduced *by keeping the index set records in buffers,* the string requirements will also be reduced.
> - Don't wait for CICS to release a string at the end of the task. Issue an ENDBR at the end of a browse or UNLOCK for an unexecuted REWRITE or DELETE to release the string.
> - Don't use the locate mode for read-only file requests.
> - Use other performance features such as IMBED and REPLICATE to expedite I/O's and thus use a string for a shorter duration.

Figure 16.3 Guidelines for reducing VSAM string requirements.

Incomplete Updates   There may be an application decision not to issue a DELETE or a REWRITE after a successful READ for update. Under these circumstances it is advisable to issue an UNLOCK to release the string right away. Failure to do so will keep the string tied up for the duration of the task.

WRITE   The string is held for the duration of the reading of the index set records, the sequence set record, and the data CI and then for the rewriting of the data CI with the new record. String requirements may be reduced by keeping the index set records in buffers.

Summary   The discussion regarding string requirements and file requests is summarized in Fig. 16.3.

16.4   INDEX BUFFERS (BUFNI)

In a CICS environment, the number of index buffers for a VSAM file may be specified in the BUFNI operand of the DFHFCT macro. An example of its coding is:

```
DFHFCT    TYPE=DATASET,
          DATASET=EMPLOYEE,
             ⋮
          STRNO=3
          BUFNI=6
             ⋮
```

The following characteristics of VSAM should be reviewed to understand the significance of the value of the BUFNI operand:

- VSAM always looks for the index set records in buffers and attempts a physical I/O only if it does not find them there. *Therefore, you can cut down on I/O's if you can keep the index set records in core at all times.*
- VSAM will not look for the sequence set record in the buffers unless the I/O request is within the same string. Thus a browse request looks for the sequence set record in the buffers before attempting a physical I/O. Different CICS tasks may have different copies of the same sequence set record and will not share its use in an NSR environment. *Therefore, it does not pay to keep the sequence set records in core in NSR, because VSAM will do a physical I/O anyway.*

The secret of ideal index buffer allocation in an NSR environment under CICS is to allocate enough buffers to keep the index set in core plus one additional buffer for each string. The strings will share all the index set buffers while keeping the additional sequence set buffer for each string's exclusive use. The value of BUFNI will be

$$BUFNI = STRNO + \text{number of index set records}$$

We can use various formulas to calculate the value of BUFNI. First get a listing of the data set using the LISTCAT command of AMS. Find out if the data set is defined with the IMBED/NOIMBED or REPLICATE/NOREPLICATE options. Each combination of these index options requires a different formula.

IMBED and NOREPLICATE The value of BUFNI will be

$$BUFNI = \frac{HURBAI}{CISZI} + STRNO$$

where   HURBAI = High Used RBA for the index set of the index component. There will be more than one value of the high used RBA in the index listing. Take the value shown by EXTENT-TYPE X'00'. The other

16.4 INDEX BUFFERS (BUFNI)

values will have a number significantly higher than that. Ignore them.

CISZI = CI size for the index component, and
STRNO = Number of VSAM strings.

The result should be an integer number. If it contains a fraction, you probably used the wrong values in the listing. Also, without adding the STRNOs, the result you get should be between 0 and 20. If it is significantly larger than 20, you probably did not pick up the HURBA from the EXTENT-TYPE X'00'.

NOIMBED and NOREPLICATE

$$\text{BUFNI} = \frac{\text{HURBAI}}{\text{CISZI}} - \frac{\text{HURBAD}}{\text{CISZD} \times \text{(CI/CA)}} + \text{STRNO}$$

where HURBAI = High used RBA value of the index component,
       CISZI = CI size of the index component,
       HURBAD = High used RBA value of the data component,
       CISZD = CI size of the data component,
       CI/CA = Number of data CIs within each data CA,
       STRNO = Number of strings.

Values of all of the variables (except STRNO) are in the data set listing. Again, without adding the STRNOs, the result should be an integer between 0 and 20.

IMBED and REPLICATE Although REPLICATE is recommended for LSR buffer pool eligible data sets only, the following formula may be used if you used REPLICATE for an NSR environment:

$$\text{BUFNI} = \frac{\text{HURBAI}}{\text{CISZI} \times \text{(PHYRECS/TRK)}} + \text{STRNO}$$

where HURBAI = High used RBA for the index component as given in the EXTENT-TYPE X'00',
       CISZI = CI size for the index component,
       PHYRECS/TRK = Physical records per track for the index component as given by LISTCAT. This is, in fact, the number of index CIs per DASD track. For the index component, a CI is a physical record.

Again, excluding the STRNO value, the result should be between 0 and 20.

NOIMBED and REPLICATE Although REPLICATE is recommended for LSR buffer pool eligible data sets only, the following formula may be used if you REPLICATE for an NSR environment:

$$\text{BUFNI} = \frac{\text{HURBAI}}{\text{CISZI} \times (\text{PHYRECS/TRK})} - \frac{\text{HURBAD}}{\text{CISZD} \times (\text{CI/CA})} + \text{STRNO}$$

where HURBAI = High used RBA value for the index component,
 CISZI = CI size for the index component,
 PHYRECS/TRK = Number of physical records per DASD track for the index component,
 HURBAD = High used RBA value for the data component,
 CISZD = CI size for the data component, and
 CI/CA = Number of data CIs per data CA.

In this case too, the result excluding the STRNO should be between 0 and 20.

Considerations for KEYRANGES If you used the KEYRANGES parameter, the data set listing would not give you the correct value of the HURBA of the data component (HURBAD) directly. This value can be calculated as follows. Determine the number of key range groups for the data set. This value can be found in the command syntax of the DEFINE CLUSTER or DEFINE AIX parameters. Expect to find as many sets of space allocation values in the listing as there are key range groups. In the space allocation value of each group, subtract the value of the low allocated RBA from the high used RBA. Add all the values determined from each group; this gives you the value of HURBAD. Use this value of HURBAD in the formulas given above.

Index Levels and BUFNI You don't have to use the given formulas for a one- or two-level index; there is an easier way to determine the value of BUFNI for such data sets. First determine the number of index levels from the data set listing. If the number of levels is 1, the value of BUFNI will be the same as STRNO. If the number of levels is 2, the value will be 1 plus STRNO. Using the formulas will yield the same result. For three-level indexes, you must use the formulas to get the correct value of BUFNI.

Minimum Buffer Allocation for a Three-level Index All the formulas we have discussed so far give us a value of BUFNI that will generate the minimum possible I/O's for a randomly accessed data set. If, due to virtual storage constraint problems, you cannot allocate as many buffers as

16.4 INDEX BUFFERS (BUFNI)

calculated, the next best thing to do is to calculate BUFNI as follows (for a three-level index):

$$BUFNI = STRNO + 2$$

This value will ensure that there are no I/O's on the highest level of index. It will do I/O's only on the lower levels. Although this may not be the ideal solution, it will still reduce I/O's significantly.

Case Study: Suppose we have a KSDS defined with the IMBED and REPLICATE options. From the data set listing, we determine that the value of the high used RBA for the index (HURBAI) is 409,600 and the index CI size (CISZI) is 4096 bytes. The listing also reveals that the index component on the device has 10 physical records per track (PHYRECS/TRK). On the basis of an analysis of CICS shutdown statistics, the value of STRNO is determined to be 4. The value of BUFNI under ideal situations will be calculated as follows:

$$BUFNI = \frac{HURBAI}{CISZI \times (PHYRECS/TRK)} + STRNO$$

$$= \frac{409,600}{4096 \times 10} + 4$$

$$= 10 + 4 = 14$$

The file control table entry will be:

```
DFHFCT    TYPE=DATASET,
          DATASET=EMPLOYEE,
             :
             :
          STRNO=4,
          BUFNI=14,
             :
```

You will recall that if we leave out the BUFNI operand from the macro, the default value is the same as STRNO, which in this case is 4. That value will also give us the maximum number of I/O's per file request and thus the worst performance. However, if our environment has virtual storage constraint problems, the minimum suggested buffer allocation could be STRNO plus 2, which would be 6 in this example. Any value between 6 and 14 will further reduce the probability of I/O's on the index component.

16.4.1 Excess Index Buffers

What happens if we allocate more index buffers than the number calculated with the formulas? In the case study above, that would mean giving

BUFNI a value higher than 14. *Since VSAM does not do a look-aside of the sequence set records from the buffers, the excess index buffer thus allocated will have absolutely no positive performance impact on I/O's.* Therefore it is recommended that you not overallocate the index buffers.

16.5 DATA BUFFERS (BUFND)

The default value of the data buffers is calculated by CICS as follows:

$$BUFND = STRNO + 1$$

Under most circumstances, this default value is sufficient. It ensures the allocation of one data buffer for each string. The single extra buffer is used during CI and CA splits.

This buffer allocation will ensure that a file request, whether a random read or a sequential browse, does not get more than one data buffer. No matter how heavy the browse activity may be, it will not let that VSAM string steal the data buffers of other strings to do a read-ahead of data CIs for that request.

Case Study: In a previous case study, the number of strings required was 4. Therefore, the value of BUFND would be 4 + 1, or 5. The File Control Table entry would be:

```
DFHFCT    TYPE = DATASET,
          DATASET = EMPLOYEE,
          :
          :
          STRNO = 4,
          BUFNI = 14,
          BUFND = 5,
          :
```

Since this is also the default value, we can leave it out of the DFHFCT macro altogether.

16.5.1 Excess Data Buffers

If we allocate more data buffers than the default value, they cannot be uniformly allocated to all the strings. The string that happens to issue a browse request (READ NEXT) first will grab them all for the duration of the browse. This will help that particular task read more data records in a single I/O and thus perform better. As soon as that task releases these buffers, the next string for any browse request will get hold of these extra buffers. In a multitasking environment, you may not be able to control which task acquires those buffers. Also, from an application point of view, the read-ahead of extra data CIs may not be of any use to the application.

If the file is used for random requests only (no browses), these buffers will remain unutilized. Therefore, *the allocation of extra data buffers is not recommended*.

16.6 STRNO, BUFNI, BUFND INTERRELATIONSHIP

Strings, index buffers, and data buffers have a peculiar effect on each other. If index buffers are underallocated, the strings will be held by CICS tasks for a long time. This will cause string waits and necessitate allocation of extra strings. Allocation of extra strings will automatically allocate additional index and data buffers. Although this will reduce the string waits, it will not help file requests to execute faster. That is, although we are allocating more buffers and strings, we are not getting any improvement in I/O performance. Performance is achieved only by reducing the number of I/O's per file request. We can draw a very important conclusion from this: *Proper allocation of index buffers is the most effective technique for reducing I/O's and string requirements. Underallocation of index buffers will nullify the effect of extra strings and have no positive impact on performance. Therefore, for heavily accessed files, do not save on index buffers in an NSR environment.*

16.7 ALTERNATE INDEX CONSIDERATIONS

Since an alternate index is a KSDS in architecture, all the formulas and techniques discussed in this chapter apply to them as well. The calculations for strings, index buffers, and data buffers for alternate index paths can be done in the same way as for the KSDS. However, there is an extra consideration for base cluster strings. Let's take an example.

Example: We have an employee master file with Social Security Number as the prime key. From analysis, we see that it may have a maximum of two concurrent file requests through the prime key. So the value of STRNO for the base cluster will be 2. It has two alternate index paths defined on Employee Number and Employee Name alternate keys. We also determine that there are not many requests on the Employee Number alternate key. Therefore, one string will be enough for that alternate index path. However, most read requests are made through the Employee Name alternate key. We judge that it will require three strings for the Employee Name alternate index path. Since the file requests via an alternate index path will also use base cluster strings to access the base cluster records, the string requirement for the base cluster will be the sum total of the string requirements for its own requests plus the requests coming from the alternate index paths. Thus it will need 2 + 1 + 3, or 6, strings to give

```
DFHFCT      TYPE=DATASET,
            DATASET=EMPSSN,
                  .
                  .
            STRNO=6,
            BUFNI=10,
            BUFND=7,
                  .
                  .
DFHFCT      TYPE=DATASET,
            DATASET=EMPNUM,
            BASE=EMPSSN,
                  .
                  .
            STRNO=1,
            BUFNI=1,
            BUFND=2,
                  .
                  .
                  .
DFHFCT      TYPE=DATASET,
            DATASET=EMPNAME,
            BASE=EMPSSN,
                  .
                  .
            STRNO=3,
            BUFNI=3,
            BUFND=4,
                  .
                  .
                  .
                  .
```

Figure 16.4 Sample FCT coding for a base cluster and its two alternate index paths.

adequate performance. Note that extra base cluster strings will also need extra index and data buffers.

It has been my experience that one of the causes of poor performance of alternate indexes in a CICS environment is not giving consideration to the string requirements in a base cluster. *The string requirements for a base cluster must be equal to the cumulative total of its own string needs plus the string requirements of its alternate index paths.* Figure 16.4 gives sample coding of the FCT entries for the previous example.

Note the allocation of base cluster strings. The values of BUFNI and BUFND for the alternate indexes have been calculated using the formulas discussed previously along with their catalog listings.

16.7.1 BASE Parameter

In Fig. 16.4, note the coding of the BASE operand in the DFHFCT TYPE=DATASET macros for the alternate index paths. In this example,

16.7 ALTERNATE INDEX CONSIDERATIONS

the value of this operand is the same as for the DD name for the base cluster, which is EMPSSN. BASE is effective for data sets using NSR buffer pools only. *Although it does not cause any processing problems, the absence of this parameter may degrade the system performance.*

This parameter helps to calculate the value of BSTRNO in the ACB at the time of FCT assembly. BSTRNO represents the number of strings initially allocated for access to the base cluster of a path. If this parameter is not coded, BSTRNO value defaults to STRNO, which may not be adequate. This may allocate an insufficient number of strings for the whole group and require dynamic string allocation while CICS is up. This causes performance problems.

The parameter also allows data set name sharing, which allows VSAM to create a single control block structure for all the strings and buffers in the base cluster and alternate index paths. This also ensures read integrity between alternate index paths and the base cluster.

chapter **17**

CICS Environment—LSR

We discussed the use of NonShared Resource (NSR) buffer pools in the Chapter 16. Each VSAM file has a set of data and index (for KSDS and AIX) buffers reserved exclusively for its own use. Under NSR, no VSAM file is allowed access to the buffers of another file. In other words, VSAM files *do not* share common buffers among themselves in an NSR environment. In an LSR environment, however, they *do* share the buffers. This kind of sharing comes with its own set of characteristics, advantages, and problems, which are the subject matter of this chapter.

17.1 WHAT IS LSR?

LSR buffers were discussed in some detail in Section 4.1.7 of Chap. 4. In LSR buffer pools, VSAM files share the use of common buffers. There can be many LSR buffer pools, varying in size from ½K to 32K. Each pool can have a multiple number of buffers allocated to it. The determination of which buffer pool will be used for a particular VSAM file is dependent upon its index and data CI sizes. *If a file has a different CI size for index and data components, it will use different LSR buffer pools for each component.*

Figure 17.1 is a graphic representation of an example of LSR buffer pools. Note that the index component of one file (e.g., file E) may use the same buffer pool as the data component of another file (e.g., file F).

17.1 WHAT IS LSR?

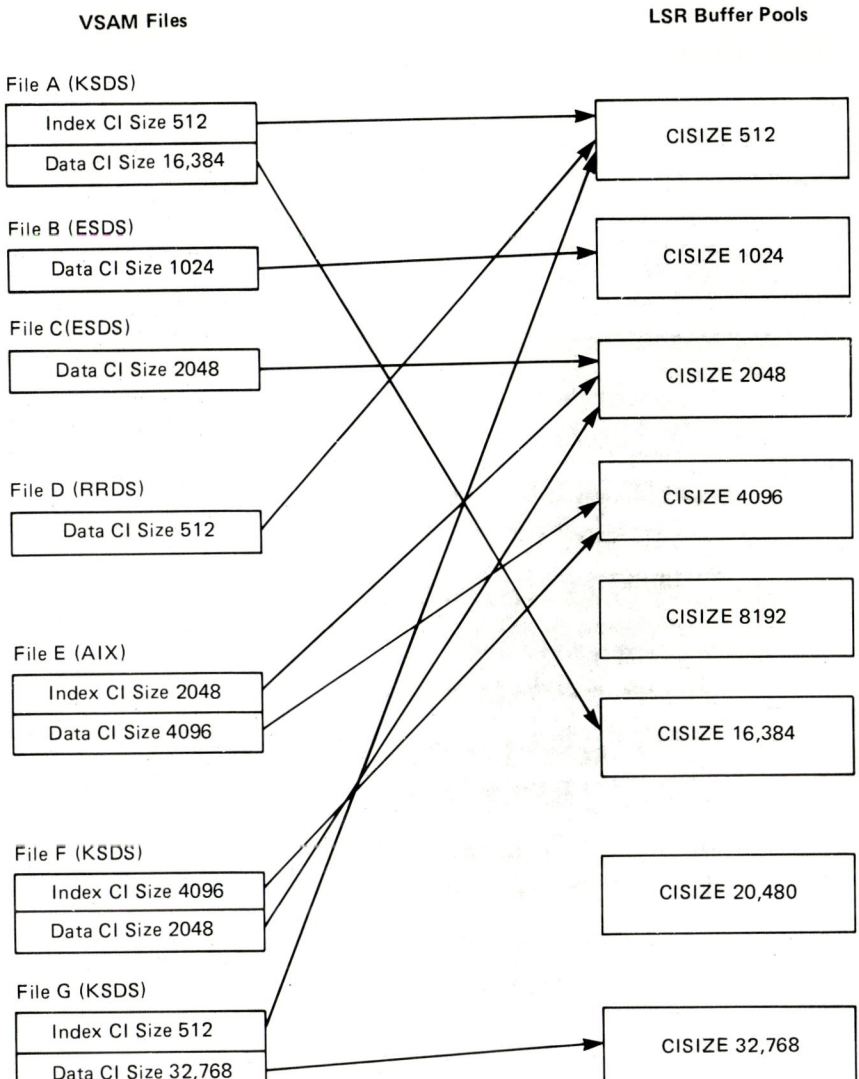

Figure 17.1 An example of different VSAM files using different LSR pool buffers in a CICS environment. The CI size of the index or the data component determines which LSR buffer pool it belongs to.

The buffer pool sizes supported by CICS are ½K, 1K, 2K, 4K, 8K, 12K, 16K, 20K, 24K, 28K, and 32K. A given buffer size may or may not be defined in CICS. For example, in Fig. 17.1, since no file is using the buffer pool of size 20,480 bytes (20K), it can be taken out to conserve virtual storage without affecting any processing or performance.

A buffer pool of a particular size if defined, may have a minimum of 3 and a maximum of 32,768 buffers. For example, depending upon your requirements, each buffer pool in Fig. 17.1 may have anywhere from 3 to 32,768 buffers in it. If a buffer size for a particular data set is not defined, the next larger buffer size will be used. For example, if we have a data component of a KSDS with a CI size of 6144 bytes, it will use the LSR buffer pool of 8192 bytes. Clearly, this results in an unnecessary waste of buffer space and should be avoided.

LSR and NSR can coexist within the same CICS/VS region; i.e., some VSAM files can have their exclusive NSR buffers, while others may be part of an LSR buffer pool. Beginning with release 1.7 of CICS/VS, LSR is the default for VSAM files, although you can override this and make them NSR files. Remember that the same VSAM file cannot use both the NSR and LSR buffers simultaneously in a CICS/VS region.

It should be noted that LSR is not a CICS specific feature. LSR is a VSAM buffering option that may be used in CICS/VS, IMS/VS, or batch jobs. The LSR buffer pools are created by the issuance of the BLDVRP macro. Although batch programs may use this feature, they seldom do.

17.2 LSR CHARACTERISTICS

LSR buffer pools have characteristics different from those of NSR buffers. You must be familiar with these differences if you are to make an intelligent decision regarding the choice of a buffer pool selection for a particular VSAM file.

17.2.1 Buffers Shared by Index and Data Components

In an LSR environment, no distinction is made between index and data components. The index component of one data set may share the same buffer pool as the data component of another (or the same) data set. The only determining factor is the CI size of a particular component (Fig. 17.1). This characteristic has the overall effect of not treating the index component CIs as the preferred CIs for buffers. The index CIs can be flushed out and replaced by data CIs on the basis of LRU algorithm. In the NSR environment, our fine tuning strategy included keeping the index set records in buffers to reduce I/O's. It is difficult to implement that plan in an LSR environment. However, since the index component may have CI sizes of only ½K, 1K, 2K, and 4K, this characteristic does not apply to LSR buffer pools of larger sizes. Buffer pools 8K to 32K in size will contain only data components CIs.

17.2.2 Less Virtual Storage

In an NSR environment, if the buffers of one data set are underutilized at a particular point in time and there are a lot of string waits on the file requests of another data set, there is no way for the inactive buffers to be

17.2 LSR CHARACTERISTICS

used to service the active data set I/O's. This kind of problem necessitates the allocation of additional strings and buffers for the active data set. In other words, *NSR requires you to provide for the allocation of strings and buffers for peak I/O activity.* If a data set does not have continuous peak activity, the resources will be underutilized most of the time. In an LSR environment, the peak I/O activity on one data set may be compensated for by low I/O activity on another data set within the same buffer pool. Because of this characteristic, the LSR technique usually requires fewer buffers than a purely NSR environment. This saves virtual storage. Although this may not seem to be a big advantage in an MVS/XA system, it provides relief in a virtual storage constrained environment like MVS/SP or DOS/VSE.

17.2.3 Buffer Look-Aside

In an NSR environment, VSAM will do a buffer look-aside before attempting a physical I/O for the following control intervals:

- The index set records of the index component
- The sequence set records and data CIs, provided the request is within the same VSAM string

Therefore, for all practical purposes, I/O's are saved only for index set records by using the proper buffering techniques. There may be many copies of the *same* sequence set record or data CIs because different tasks cannot share them. This not only results in increased virtual storage requirements but also increases I/O activity.

In an LSR environment, VSAM will do a buffer look-aside for every I/O request. It does not distinguish between index set, sequence set, and data component CIs. This is an excellent feature of the LSR technique, and it is used to reduce physical I/O's in a CICS/VS environment.

17.2.4 Sequence Set in Core

In previous chapters we discussed the fact that you incur a minimum of two physical I/O's on each file read request for a KSDS. This is true if the index set records are kept in buffers and therefore no I/O is performed to retrieve them. However, the sequence set records, even if they are in core, are not considered for a look-aside, and an I/O is always performed to read them from the DASD. *In an LSR environment, if the sequence set records are in core, no I/O is done to reread them.* Thus LSR is the only technique in CICS/VS to reduce I/O's on a sequence set of a KSDS. This feature is helpful for these data sets where most of the I/O activity is concentrated on a particular cylinder of a KSDS. LSR will keep one copy of the sequence set record pointing to all of the data CIs of a CA (cylinder in our case) rather than doing a physical I/O on each file request from different tasks.

17.2.5 MVS/XA Environment

CICS/VS, running under an MVS/XA environment, provides some additional features of LSR buffers. Beginning with release 1.6.1 of CICS/VS, the LSR VSAM buffers pools under MVS/XA reside above the 16-MB line, thus bypassing the virtual storage constraint imposed by 24-bit addressability. As a result, you have better control by having the ability to provide larger buffer pools than is permissible in a non-MVS/XA environment.

Beginning with release 1.7 of CICS/VS, you can have up to eight LSR pools. Each LSR pool is a different entity and may have its own set of buffers for different CI sizes. At the time of coding of FCT macros, you have to specify which LSR pool a particular data set should belong to. The default is LSRPOOL 1. This provides you with the opportunity to allocate a different LSR pool to different data sets depending upon their processing characteristics (Fig. 17.2). We will continue this discussion in more detail in Section 17.5.

Remember that non-MVS/XA systems still support only one LSR pool. Also, the IMS/DB buffers using VSAM data sets still reside below the 16-MB line and thus do not enjoy the virtual storage constraint relief. You do not have to use all the LSR pools in your system. For example, in Fig. 17.2 only LSR pools 1, 2, 3, 4, and 8 are being used.

17.2.6 No Read-Ahead in Browses

In the last chapter, we discussed that in NSR a browse request can get hold of surplus data buffers and perform a read-ahead of the data CIs in anticipation of future file requests. *In the case of LSR, a browse request (READ NEXT) will never retrieve more than one data CI even if surplus buffers are available in that pool.* This feature ensures that the tasks doing random I/O's will not suffer because of some other tasks doing sequential browses.

17.2.7 Alternate Index Support

Up until release 1.5 of CICS/VS, alternate indexes that were members of the upgrade set were not eligible for an LSR buffer pool. In release 1.6.1, this support was provided but was not part of the base product. CICS/VS 1.7 provides this support in the base product without any imposed restrictions. If virtual storage constraints are one of the reasons for discouraging alternate index clusters in your environment, the situation may be reconsidered in light of LSR support for them.

17.3 LSR PROBLEMS

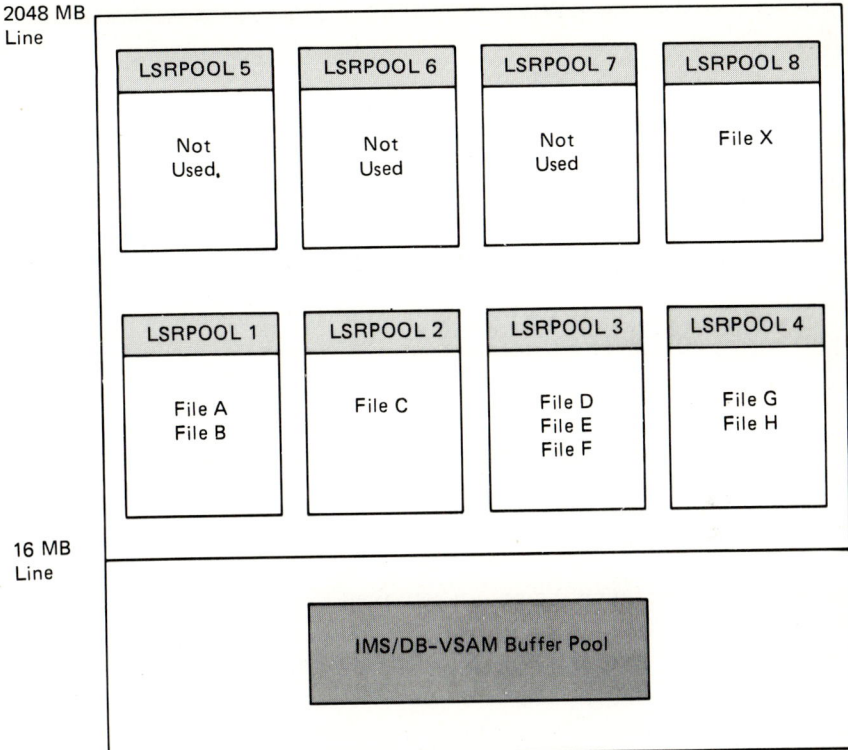

Figure 17.2 Buffer allocation for an MVS/XA and CICS/VS (release 1.7 or later) environment. There are up to eight native VSAM LSR pools residing above the 16-MB line. The IMS/DB VSAM pool is still below the 16-MB line.

17.3 LSR PROBLEMS

Because of their processing characteristics, LSR buffers may create some problems that must be analyzed for your particular environment. Some of these problems are solvable, while others are part of the design and may require you not to use LSR for a specific data set.

17.3.1 Lockout Possibility

Consider the scenario in Fig. 17.3. In an NSR situation, steps 1 to 3 will execute perfectly. In an LSR environment, a CICS task will hang. The reason for this problem is the following: The CIs that are accessed by a task are enqueued in an LSR buffer pool and dequeued when the task is finished or an explicit release request is issued. (In NSR, the CIs are enqueued only upon an update request, not for a read request.) In Fig.

> 1. A successful EXEC CICS STARTBR is issued for a KSDS.
> 2. Successive EXEC CICS READ NEXT requests are issued for the same data set.
> 3. The decision is made to update or delete the record retrieved in a READ NEXT operation. An EXEC CICS READ UPDATE (or EXEC CICS DELETE) is executed.

Figure 17.3 A sequence of events that will execute in an NSR environment but will hang the CICS task in an LSR situation.

17.3, the CI containing the record retrieved through READ NEXT is enqueued. The READ for UPDATE request is not executed, due to the enqueue. It waits for the queue to clear, not knowing that it is the same CICS task that is implicitly holding the CI. The update/delete request waits forever.

This problem can be alleviated by issuing an EXEC CICS ENDBR between steps 2 and 3. An explicit end browse will dequeue the CI and let the update request execute normally.

Since LSR is the default in CICS 1.7, you may be caught unaware in the deadlock situation. If CICS transactions that have been executing without any problem suddenly start hanging, check on whether the buffer pool has been changed from NSR to LSR.

17.3.2 Browses Monopolize Buffers

We already know that a browse request for an LSR file will not perform a read-ahead of the data CIs. Thus it would not require more than one data buffer at a time. However, during a long browse, if it has to read a number of data CIs one after the other, *it will not reuse the old data buffer for I/O*. This is due to the fact that the LSR buffers are invalidated on the basis of a least recently used (LRU) algorithm. Because of this characteristic, long browses can flood an LSR pool with data component CIs, thus flushing out the index component CIs of other files with the same CI size. This may nullify one of the major advantages of LSR—the ability to do a successful look-aside to reduce physical I/O's. Remember this while considering heavily browsed files as LSR candidates.

17.3.3 Slow CA Splits

If you are not familiar with the subject of CA splits, refer to Chap. 3. There are two reasons a CA split is adversely affected by LSR:

- CA splits cause a lot of physical I/O's to move massive amounts of data from one place to another. An NSR pool may give more buffers to VSAM for the duration of the split process and thus use chained I/O's to reduce real physical I/O activity. LSR would not allow chaining and uses only one buffer for CA splits.
- In a CA split, the newly acquired CA is formatted before the records are moved into it. *In an NSR environment, the formatting is done one track at a time, while in LSR it is done one CI at a time.* Let's take an example of an IBM 3380 where the CA size is one cylinder and CI size is 2048 bytes. In NSR, there will be 15 I/O's to format 15 tracks of the cylinder. In LSR, there will be 270 I/O's to format 270 CIs of the data component. In between the formatting of those 270 CIs, the read-write head can be stolen for the pending I/O's of other data sets on the same DASD.

Thus we see that files encountering an excessive number of CA splits may not be good candidates for LSR. However, you may use the techniques discussed in Chap. 12 to reduce the number of CA splits.

17.3.4 Increased Path Length

We know that in an LSR situation VSAM would do a look-aside of its buffers before attempting a physical I/O. We'd like to avoid an I/O if the required CI is in the buffers. However, this scanning of CIs in the buffers incurs extra machine instructions, thus increasing the path length. On an average, VSAM will scan half the buffers on a read-hit. On a read-miss, it scans all the buffers before resorting to a physical I/O. You may notice a slight increase in CPU activity with the use of LSR.

One way to reduce the path length in CICS/VS 1.7 (and later releases) and an MVS/XA environment is to use a multiple number of LSR pools (maximum of eight). Because VSAM will search only buffers of the pool to which the data set belongs, the spreading of data sets across multiple buffers could reduce the path length to one-eighth the value.

17.4 HOW TO DEFINE LSR IN CICS

CICS/VS 1.7 and Subsequent Releases When defining an FCT entry for a VSAM data set, we can determine whether it should be using NSR or LSR buffer pools. The following code will ensure that the data set uses NSR for buffering and not the LSR pool:

```
DFHFCT     TYPE = DATASET
           DATASET = ddname
             :
           LSRPOOL = NONE
```

If the data set is going to use the LSR pool and the environment is MVS/XA, you also have to determine the LSR pool number, which may vary from 1 to 8. Consider the following:

```
DFHFCT     TYPE = DATASET,
           DATASET = ABC,
             :
           LSRPOOL = 2,

DFHFCT     TYPE = DATASET,
           DATASET = XYZ,
             :
           LSRPOOL = 6,
```

In this case, data sets ABC and XYZ will belong to LSR pools 2 and 6, respectively. If the LSRPOOL parameter is not coded, the default is pool 1. In a non-MVS/XA environment, since there is only one LSR pool, you should not code any value but 1. However, if you do give a value between 2 and 8, it is ignored and defaults to 1. (Remember: Our discussion applies to CICS/VS 1.7 and subsequent releases only.) The values of BUFND and BUFNI in the DFHFCT TYPE = DATASET are not used by VSAM. It uses the values of buffer numbers from the DFHFCT TYPE = SHRCTL macro, which is discussed in Section 17.4.1. However, if that macro is not coded, VSAM uses the values of STRNO for LSR-eligible data sets to calculate the buffer pool. This is not a recommended procedure, and you must always code the TYPE = SHRCTL macro for proper buffer allocation.

CICS/VS 1.6.1 and Prior Releases In CICS/VS 1.6.1, there is only one buffer pool, whether the operating system is MVS/SP or MVS/XA. The LSRPOOL parameter does not exist. To make a VSAM file eligible for LSR, you code it as follows:

```
DFHFCT     TYPE = DATASET,
           DATASET = ddname,
             :
           SERVREQ = (SHARE, ......... ),
```

The value of the SERVREQ parameter of SHARE will put a data set in the LSR pool. Its absence means NSR buffers. The *keyword SHARE pertains to LSR only;* it has nothing to do with the sharing of VSAM files

17.4 HOW TO DEFINE LSR IN CICS

```
DFHFCT     TYPE=SHRCTL,
           LSRPOOL= number,
           BUFFERS=(size(count),size(count),.........)
           KEYLEN= number,
           RSCLMT= number,
           STRNO=  number
```
Figure 17.4 Syntax of the DFHFCT TYPE = SHRCTL macro.

with other regions, which is controlled by the SHAREOPTIONS parameter of DEFINE CLUSTER.

17.4.1. DFHFCT TYPE=SHRCTL Macro

This macro plays a major role in the allocation of LSR buffers. Figure 17.4 gives its complete syntax. You can code up to eight macro definitions to define each of the eight buffer pools in an MVS/XA environment. This macro should be coded after the last entry in the FCT that uses LSR buffer pools.

LSRPOOL This parameter identifies the buffer pool number in an MVS/XA environment. Its value may vary from 1 to 8. This value will relate it to the files that have the same number coded in the LSRPOOL parameter of the DFHFCT TYPE=DATASET macro. In a non-MVS/XA environment, the value can only be 1. A macro with any other value will be ignored, and its resources will not be merged with LSR pool 1.

BUFFERS This parameter identifies the size and the count of each buffer set within the pool. LSR supports only the following buffer sizes:

512	8,192	24,576
1,024	12,288	28,672
2,048	16,384	32,768
4,096	20,480	

If the CI size is other than these values, VSAM will use a buffer pool of the next higher size. The count value gives the number of buffers to be allocated for a particular buffer size. Its value may vary from 3 to 32,768. The following is an example of the coding of this parameter:

```
BUFFERS=(512(8),1024(4),2048(6),
         4096(12),8192(3), .......
```

This will allocate 8 buffers of ½K size, 4 buffers of 1K size, 6 buffers of 2K size, 12 buffers of 4K size, and 3 buffers of 8K size. Section 17.5 gives recommendations on how many buffers to allocate based on the monitoring of CICS shutdown statistics. Remember that these are the buffers that will be used by all the files that have the same LSR pool number coded on their TYPE = DATASET macro as the value of the LSRPOOL parameter in TYPE = SHRCTL macro.

KEYLEN This specifies the maximum key length of a data set in the buffer pool. If not coded, CICS will determine it for you, causing additional overhead. In a non-MVS/XA environment, this must also take into consideration the value required for any DL/I data bases. It is recommended that this value be coded at assembly time to eliminate CICS/VS overhead at execution time.

RSCLMT The value of this parameter specifies the percentage of resources to be allocated, as accumulated from parameter values specified for the data sets eligible for this LSR pool. *If BUFFERS and STRNO are both coded, RSCLMT is ignored.* It can have a value from 1 to 100. If BUFFERS or STRNO are not coded, VSAM sums up the maximum amount of resources required as defined by the TYPE = DATASET macros and reduces that value to the percentage figure coded for RSCLMT. For example, RSCLMT = 60 will allocate 60% of the resources after summing up the individual data set macro defined values. A value of 100 will allocate the maximum amount of resources. The default value is 50%.

STRNO This specifies the number of VSAM strings to be allocated for this buffer pool. Its value must be between 1 and 255. If this parameter is not coded, CICS calculates the total string requirements based on the individual data set macro definitions, and assigns STRNO a percent of that figure as coded or defaulted to in the RSCLMT parameter value.

17.4.2 Effect of Default Allocation

If the TYPE = SHRCTL macro is not coded, CICS calculates the resource allocation values of BUFFERS and STRNO based on an RSCLMT value of 50%. For most cases, this may not be an optimum value for buffers and VSAM strings. Also, for calculating resources, CICS takes into account only those files that have been allocated in the FCT. If it is not in the FCT, the file is not known to CICS. In that case CICS will be forced to calculate the pool resources on the basis of available information, which may not include all the LSR-eligible files. This may result in poor system performance. VSAM files may even fail to open in this situation. *It is therefore strongly recommended that you code TYPE = SHRCTL macros for each LSR pool and explicitly code BUFFERS and STRNO values in each one of them.* Monitor CICS/VSAM performance by means of CICS shutdown statistics (see Section 17.5.1), and alter the resource allocation if required.

17.4.3. LSR Guidelines

It bears repeating that you should explicitly code the values of BUFFERS and STRNO for each LSR pool TYPE=SHRCTL macro. The following procedure can be used to determine a starting value:

1. Calculate the values of required BUFNI, BUFND, and STRNO for each file as if the file is going to use NSR buffers (Chap. 16).
2. Classify the index and data buffer counts by CI size, and add them up for each CI size value.
3. Reduce the values of buffers and strings thus calculated by 50%. Use these figures as the starting values for BUFFERS and STRNO.

Although the above procedure gives you a good start, it must be monitored continuously for performance. Any excessive string waits reported in the CICS shutdown statistics indicates that the STRNO value for that LSR buffer pool should be increased. A low buffer look-aside to buffer read ratio will indicate low buffer allocation and poor usage of the buffer look-aside feature of LSR. These observations and their corresponding corrective measures will be discussed in the next section.

17.5 LSR RECOMMENDATIONS

LSR buffers can be very effective if their use is optimized by using the following techniques and recommendations.

17.5.1 Monitor via Statistics

CICS shutdown statistics are very helpful in determining the effective utilization of LSR buffers. CICS produces separate statistics for each LSR buffer pool. In addition, the statistics for each data set are reported as usual.

Data Set Statistics The individual data set shutdown statistics include the total number of file requests that waited for buffers and also the high water mark for such waits. Determine the index and data CI sizes for these data sets. If the total buffer waits is significant, find out whether the buffer waits occur more frequently for a particular CI size. If so, the buffer pool for that CI size needs more buffers. If there are no buffer waits for a particular CI size, you may be able to reduce the allocation of buffers for that CI size without affecting performance.

LSR Pool Statistics LSR pool statistics report total VSAM strings allocated, total number of string waits, and the high water mark for string waits. If the total number of string waits is high, the LSR buffers are not being used properly. You should gradually increase the value of STRNO until the waits are reduced to zero or some insignificant number.

LSR Buffer Statistics   LSR buffer statistics report the following:

- Buffer size
- Number of buffers allocated
- Number of buffer reads
- Number of successful look-asides
- Number of buffer writes

The number of successful look-asides is probably one of the most important features of using LSR. The higher this number, the better the utilization. You should expect to see a higher number of successful look-asides for buffers of 512, 1024, 2048, and 4096 bytes. Since only these buffer sizes belong to index components, a relatively high look-aside to buffer read ratio is desirable for performance reasons. If this ratio is low, you should increase the number of buffers allocated to reduce the chances of an index buffer being flushed out by an LRU algorithm.

17.5.2 Use Multiple LSR Pools

Since MVS/XA and CICS/VS 1.7 (or later release) provides you with up to eight separate LSR pools, you should use as many as possible to achieve better performance. Increasing the number of pools reduces the instruction path length for look-asides. The rules for allocating pools are as follows:

- Allocate a separate pool for each major application system.
- Put browse-intensive files in a separate pool. This will solve the problem of frequent buffer invalidations caused by lengthy browses.
- Put a small but very heavily used file in an LSR pool of its own.

An example of a small file whose use warrants a separate LSR pool is a security verification routine data set that is used by most of the CICS transactions. The allocation of enough buffers for such a data set can ensure that the sequence set of the index component is kept in core. This may further reduce physical I/O's on the index component. Thus a file request on the data set could be satisfied in a single I/O on the data component alone. Recall that NSR does not provide for keeping the sequence set in core.

17.5 LSR RECOMMENDATIONS

17.5.3 Use IMBED and REPLICATE

Unlike NSR, there is no way to ensure that the index set and sequence set buffers will stay in core in LSR. The only way to stay in memory is to be accessed more frequently and thus avoid the LRU algorithm. Since critical records may be flushed out by an LRU routine and heavy browse activity, we must ensure that it takes less time to read them back from the DASD. The IMBED and REPLICATE options of DEFINE CLUSTER and DEFINE AIX reduce the rotational delay for an I/O by repeating the index record many times on a track. *It is strongly recommended that all LSR-eligible data sets be defined with these options.*

17.5.4 Keep the Index and Data CI Sizes Separate

We know that LSR does not differentiate between index and data CIs. The index CIs are more critical for performance, because all file requests for a KSDS or AIX have to go through them. Since heavy browse activity can flush out index component records, it may be advisable to isolate the index components from the data components. One technique that is used in many CICS systems to segregate the index records from data CIs is to keep the CI sizes of the index and data components separate. The CI sizes of 512, 1024, 2048, and 4096 are not used for data CIs.

This technique has many negative side effects. Since the smallest data CI size would be 8192 bytes, it increases the buffer requirements. Many installations using this technique restrict index CI sizes to 512, 1024, and 2048 bytes and start data CI sizes at 4096 bytes. But then, since the largest possible index CI of 2048 bytes may not be large enough to contain pointers for all the data CIs in a data CA, this may result in underutilized DASD space and premature CA splits (refer to Chap. 9). Therefore this recommendation should be used with great caution.

17.5.5 Use LSR for Files with Heavy Look-Asides

Some files, by their very nature, make extensive use of the LSR look-aside feature and therefore are more suitable for LSR buffering.

Example 1: An ESDS data set in the load mode (EXEC CICS WRITE) is a prime candidate for buffer look-aside. If such a file used NSR buffers, there would be two I/O's per record add. The first I/O would be to read the CI from the DASD, and the second to write it back after record update. If LSR buffers are used, the I/O to read the CI from the DASD could be avoided if VSAM finds that CI in the buffers. Since a heavily accessed ESDS file will have a high probability of finding the last CI (used for record adds) in buffers, *the I/O's in* such a case can be cut in half. It is therefore recommended that you use LSR buffers for ESDS files which are used for new record additions.

Example 2: An invoice processing and printing transaction reads a particular VSAM record that keeps track of current invoice numbers. It picks up the current number to be used for invoice printing, adds 1 to that number in the record, and writes back the record. Another CICS task may pick up the currently updated invoice number and go through the same process.

If we used NSR buffers in this case, each record read would be one I/O on the data component, and the rewrite after update would be another I/O. Using LSR, the I/O for read might be eliminated by doing a look-aside on the data CI left in the buffers by a previous task. Successful look-asides will cut I/O's by half.

17.5.6 Combine Files with Nonuniform Activity

Some VSAM files are very active at times and unused at other times. These files will need a number of strings and buffers for the peak hours and very few the rest of the time. Using NSR for such applications would result in a waste of resources during nonpeak hours. VSAM files subject to this kind of activity should be combined in the same LSR pool as others that are subject to low I/O activity during the previous one's peak hours.

17.5.7 Use LSR Buffers for Low-Activity Files

Most CICS environments have data sets that are used infrequently throughout the day. These might include data sets that are accessed only during CICS startup or CICS shutdown or during occasional abnormal situations. You could allocate one string and its associated index and data buffers under NSR, but such files cannot fully utilize even a single string of VSAM. *It is recommended that LSR buffers be used to conserve virtual storage.*

17.5.8 DEFINE Buffer Pools for All CI Sizes

If a buffer pool for a particular CI size is not defined, it will use the next higher buffer pool and thus waste precious real and virtual storage. For example, let's say you have a VSAM data set with a CI size of 16K, but a 16K buffer was not defined when coding the DFHFCT TYPE = SHRCTL macro, and the next available buffer pool is, say, 20K. VSAM data sets with a size of 16K will use the 20K buffer pool, thus wasting 4K of real and virtual storage per buffer. This should be avoided.

17.5 LSR RECOMMENDATIONS

- The 512-byte buffer pool should have a buffer count that is an exact multiple of 8 (i.e., 8, 16, 24, 32, . . .).
- The 1024-byte buffer pool should have a buffer count that is an exact multiple of 4 (i.e., 4, 8, 12, 16, . . .).
- The 2048-byte buffer pool should have a buffer count that is an exact multiple of 2 (i.e., 2, 4, 6, 8, . . .).
- Buffer pools of 4096 and higher sizes do not have a 4K boundary problem.

Figure 17.5 Recommendations for buffer count for ½K, 1K, and 2K CI size LSR buffer pools.

17.5.9 Keep Buffer Pools on a 4K Boundary

LSR buffers are allocated on a 4K boundary. If the total space required by a buffer pool is not a multiple of 4K, VSAM rounds it up to the next 4K boundary. The excess space thus allocated is wasted. This feature should be considered when allocating 512-, 1024-, and 2048-byte buffers. For example, 9 buffers of 512 bytes will use the same space as 16 buffers of 512 bytes. In the first case, it will allocate 9 buffers in 4½K of storage but round it up to 8K. In the second case, it will allocate 16 buffers in 8K of storage. The recommendations in Fig. 17.5 give general guidelines to avoid this situation. Note that buffer pools of CI size 4K or more are always on a 4K boundary and do not have this problem.

appendix **A**

VSAM Terminology Glossary

Access Method Service (AMS) A multifunction service utility program that helps in performing various functions on VSAM files, non-VSAM files, VSAM catalogs, and ICF catalogs. These functions include allocations, deletions, loading, printing, alternate indexing, reorganizations, alterations, backups, and others.

AIXBLD feature A run-time PARM parameter option that causes the automatic building of all the alternate index clusters while the data records are being sequentially loaded into an unloaded base cluster.

alias of a catalog Another name for a catalog. It may be used as the first qualifier of a data set name, thus eliminating the need to code STEPCAT and JOBCAT DD statements and the CATALOG parameter within AMS commands.

ALTER command One of the Access Method Services commands that performs the alteration of many of the attributes and characteristics of a VSAM object (e.g., passwords, name, volumes).

alternate index A data set that contains alternate keys and one or more pointers to the data set records of a KSDS or an ESDS.

alternate index cluster A KSDS cluster consisting of an index and a data component, which keeps key-pointer pair records for an alternate index.

alternate key A key that provides access to a base cluster through field(s) other than the prime key.

backup A copy of a data set. It can be used to reconstruct the data set if necessary.

backup process The process of creating a backup copy of the data records in a data set. The REPRO and EXPORT commands of Access Method Services can be used to back up a VSAM data set.

Basic Catalog Structure (BCS) The first level of the two-level catalog structure of an ICF catalog. The second level is the VSAM volume data set (VVDS).

base cluster A KSDS, an ESDS, or an RRDS.

BCS (See **Basic Catalog Structure**.)

buffer look-aside The capability of VSAM to save an I/O to a DASD by verifying the existence of the same CI in its buffers.

buffer refresh The process of ignoring the existence of a CI in its buffers and rereading it from the DASD to preserve data integrity.

buffer space The amount of virtual storage required to allocate the index and the data buffers.

CA (See **control area**.)

cache High-speed buffer between a fast device and a slow device.

cache DASD controller A disk control unit with storage buffers of its own and capable of holding full tracks of DASDs to speed up I/O requests. IBM 3880 Models 13 and 23 are examples.

candidate volume A DASD that does not have VSAM data sets or VSAM space on it yet but is owned by a VSAM catalog and may be used for VSAM objects in the future.

catalog (See **master catalog** and **user catalog**)

catalog recovery area (CRA) An ESDS that exists on each volume owned by a recoverable VSAM (not ICF) catalog. It contains duplicates of the catalog entries and can be used to reconstruct a damaged catalog.

channel A very high speed (millions of bits per second) I/O medium that connects a locally attached device to the CPU. It is a processor in itself.

CI (See **control interval**.)

CIDF (See **control interval description field**.)

CIDF busy bit One bit of information in the 32-bit (4-byte) CIDF in a CI. Its value of 1 indicates a CI split in progress and prevents other tasks from accessing the same CI.

control area (CA) The building block of a VSAM data set. It consists of group of control intervals and is used for distributing free space and local reorganizations for a KSDS. The format information it contains (Software End of File) is used to help the VERIFY command correct the high used RBA information. One and only one sequence set record in a KSDS points to each data CA.

control area split The moving of half the records in an existing control area to a new empty control area because a record add or update cannot be accommodated in the existing control area. This results in two approximately half-full CAs instead of one full and one empty CA.

control interval (CI) A unit of data that is transferred between auxiliary storage and virtual storage. It contains records, free space, and control information.

control interval access Also called low-level access. A whole CI and not a logical record is processed as one logical entity.

control interval description field (CIDF) A field consisting of the last 4 bytes of a control interval. It contains information about the offset and the length of free space in the CI.

GLOSSARY

control interval split The movement of some records from an existing CI to another free CI in the same CA because a record add or update cannot be accommodated in the existing one. This results in two half-empty CIs instead of one full and one empty CI.

CRA (See **catalog recovery area**.)

cylinder An area of data storage on a disk device consisting of multiple concentric tracks. The read-write arm of the disk can access the data on a cylinder with one seek.

DASD (See **direct access storage device**.)

data buffer Area in virtual storage used to read a data CI from the DASD.

data component The part of the cluster or alternate index that contains the data records.

Data Facility/Extended Functions (DF/EF) An IBM program product for MVS environments that has enhanced the capabilities of VSAM. This product is a prerequisite for ICF catalogs.

data integrity Safety of data from unintentional damage or an out-of-synchronization condition.

data security Safety of data from unauthorized access, to protect against theft, unauthorized use, and destruction.

data set A major unit of the storage of information consisting of one or more data records. The term *data set* is synonymous with *file* in this book.

data transfer delay The delay caused by the transfer of data from the DASD over the channel to the buffers following a successful seek and rotational positioning.

DEFINE command An Access Method Services functional command used to allocate VSAM objects such as catalogs, clusters, alternate indexes, paths, and page data sets.

DELETE command An Access Method Services functional command used to delete VSAM and non-VSAM objects such as clusters, alternate indexes, and paths.

destage To transfer data from a DASD to a mass storage system.

direct access Access of data by its location without consideration of its placement relative to other units of data.

direct access storage device (DASD) A magnetic medium for data storage where access to particular data can be made directly without having to read the preceding data. An IBM 3380 is a DASD. Magnetic tapes are not DASDs because data can be accessed only sequentially.

dynamic allocation Allocation of a data set or a volume without the use of information contained in the JCL. Internally, it is done by SVC 99.

entry One or more records in a VSAM or ICF catalog containing information about a cataloged object.

entry name Same as a data set name.

entry sequence The order of storage of data records in an ESDS according to their physical arrival sequence rather than a key value.

entry-sequenced data set (ESDS) A data set whose records are stored and accessed in physical sequence without consideration of a key field.

ESDS (See **entry-sequenced data set**.)

exception exit A user-written program that takes control when an exceptional condition (e.g., an I/O error) occurs.

expanded memory Semiconductor memory in the IBM 3090 series of computers used for paging purposes.
extent Contiguous area on a DASD allocated for VSAM space or a data set.
fine tuning The art (and science) of achieving optimum performance using the available resources.
fixed-head cylinder A cylinder on a DASD with fixed read-write heads. The seek time is zero for data residing on a fixed-head cylinder.
free space Space left in a KSDS at the time of the initial or resume load to allow for record additions and updates later and to minimize or prevent CI and CA splits.
GDG (See **generation data group entry**.)
generation data group (GDG) entry An entry that allows multiple non-VSAM data sets to be related to each other by their relative generation numbers.
generation data set A data set that is a member of a generation data group.
generic key A left-justified set of one or more characters of a key that is a subset of the full key (e.g., for key ABC, generic keys are A and AB).
generic name A qualified data set name in which one qualifier (other than the first one) is replaced by an asterisk. The asterisk indicates that any value in that position is acceptable.
global resource serialization (GRS) Feature of MVS by virtue of which the ENQ and DEQ related information can be moved from the system queue area (SQA) to the GRS's own address space.
GRS (See **global resource serialization**.)
horizontal pointer A pointer in the sequence set of an index component that points to the next sequence set record so that access to top-level indexes becomes unnecessary for keyed sequential access.
IBM 3350 A disk device with 317 megabytes of storage capacity. It has 555 cylinders. Each cylinder has 30 tracks, each with a capacity of 19,254 bytes.
IBM 3380 A disk device with 630 megabytes of storage capacity per access mechanism (volser). It has 885 cylinders of 15 tracks each. Each track has a capacity of 47,968 bytes.
IBM 3380 (double-density) A disk device with 1260 megabytes of storage capacity per access mechanism (volser). It has 1770 cylinders of 15 tracks each. Each track has a capacity of 47,968 bytes. There are two models of the double-density IBM 3380: AE4 and BE4.
ICF (See **Integrated Catalog Facility**.)
index buffer Area in virtual storage required to read an index CI from the DASD.
index component An independent constituent of a KSDS, catalog, or alternate index that helps in establishing the sequence of records in the data component.
index entry Catalog entry for an index component.
index set The set of index records above the sequence set level.
Integrated Catalog Facility (ICF) The name of the catalog associated with the DF/EF or DFP program product.
interblock gap (IBG) A header that precedes every physical block on a DASD. Its value is 512 bytes for a VSAM file on an IBM 3380.
ISAM interface program (IIP) An interface program that makes it possible for a program written to process indexed sequential files to gain access to a KSDS.

GLOSSARY

job catalog A catalog allocated for a job by means of a JOBCAT DD statement.
key A field within a record that identifies a record or a set of records.
key compression A technique used to reduce storage requirements for an index that involves elimination of characters from the front and back of a key.
key of reference The prime or alternate key that is currently being used to access records in a base cluster. To the application program, the records in the base cluster seem to be sequenced on the key of reference.
key sequence The order in which records may be accessed in a sequence based on a key value within each record.
key-sequenced data set (KSDS) A data set whose records can be accessed in key sequence.
KSDS (See **key-sequenced data set**.)
LISTCAT command An AMS command used to list the attributes and statistics of a VSAM or non-VSAM object.
Local Shared Resource (LSR) buffer A set of VSAM buffers shared by one or more VSAM files.
LSR buffer (See **Local Shared Resource buffer**.)
master catalog A VSAM or an ICF catalog containing information and connector entries for user catalog, data sets, volumes, data spaces, etc. There is always one master catalog for an MVS system. It is established at initial program load time.
NonShared Resource (NSR) buffers A set of index and data buffers reserved exclusively for the use of a particular VSAM file and not shared with any other VSAM data set.
nonunique key An alternate key that points to one or more data records in a base cluster.
NSR buffers (See **NonShared Resource buffers**.)
object An entity created by VSAM such as a cluster, an alternate index, a catalog, a path, or VSAM space.
OPTIONAL file A read-only ESDS file that may not always be present when the program that requires it is executed. In the Cobol language, such a file is indicated in the SELECT statement by the use of the OPTIONAL clause.
page space An ESDS that acts as a paging data set for OS/VS2 systems.
password A combination of 1 to 8 characters assigned to a VSAM object at the time of its DEFINE to prevent unauthorized access to the object. It may be changed later through the ALTER command.
path A data set name referred to for accessing the records of a base cluster through an alternate index. A path can also be the alias of a data set name.
physical record A set of one or more 512-, 1024-, 2048-, or 4096-byte-long blocks that constitute a control interval. Each block is a physical record.
pointer An address or a key value used to locate a control interval or a record.
primary space allocation Initial allocation of space on a DASD reserved for a data set or VSAM space.
prime key A unique field in a KSDS used for sequencing, storage, and accessing of its data records.
PRINT command An AMS command used to print the records of a data set in character, hex, or dump format.
qualifier Each segment of a data set name separated from other segments by periods.

RBA (See **relative byte address**.)
RDF (See **record description field**.)
read-ahead Subject to the availability of surplus data buffers, the ability of VSAM to read multiple data component CIs ahead of time in a sequential browse operation.
record description field (RDF) One of the four components of a control interval. It is 3 bytes long and is contained in the space just preceding the control interval description field.
recoverable catalog A VSAM catalog defined with the RECOVERABLE parameter so that each volume maintains a catalog recovery area to contain duplicate information about the entries. The duplicate information is used for recovery upon catalog failure.
relative byte address (RBA) The displacement of a data record or a control interval from the beginning of the data set.
relative record data set (RRDS) A data set whose records are loaded into fixed-length slots and retrieved through the use of a relative record number.
relative record number (RRN) An integer number that identifies the relative position of a slot from the beginning of an RRDS.
reorganization The process of unloading and then reloading the contents of a KSDS in order to put its records into physical sequence.
REPRO command An AMS command used to copy records from one data set to another.
restore The process of recreating a data set from its backup copy after a system or application failure or problem.
reusable data set A VSAM data set whose high used RBA is reset to zero when opened as OUTPUT. Resetting the RBA logically deletes any existing records.
rotational delay The time it takes for the data on a particular track of a cylinder to reach the read-write head.
rotational position sensing miss After a successful seek, the failure of a DASD to transfer data because of the unavailability of a channel at that moment. The DASD control unit has to retry the I/O on the next revolution.
RPS miss (See **rotational position sensing miss**.)
RRDS (See **relative record data set**.)
RRN (See **relative record number**.)
secondary space allocation Space on a DASD that is allocated when the primary space allocation is used up.
seek time delay The time it takes for the read-write arm of a DASD to reach the desired cylinder.
sequence set The lowest level of the index component of a KSDS or an alternate index cluster that points to the data component CIs. Each record of a sequence set points to a full control area.
shared DASD A direct access storage device (e.g., a disk) that is accessible from more than one system (e.g., MVS) in twin-CPU or multi-CPU configurations.
shareoptions Attributes of a VSAM data set that control the concurrent sharing of its data by different programs running in the same CPU or different CPUs. The types of sharing can be at the read and/or update levels.
slot Space in a relative record data set where a record can be placed.

GLOSSARY

solid state device (SSD) A semiconductor DASD having no electromechanical moving parts and with extremely fast I/O service times.

spanned record A logical record whose length is greater than the control interval size, thus requiring it to span over more than one CI.

SSD (See **solid state device.**)

stage The movement of data from a mass storage system to a DASD.

step catalog A VSAM or an ICF catalog allocation that lasts for the duration of the job step and is identified by the STEPCAT DD statement.

string A set of control blocks and buffer resources required to execute a file request. It consists of VSAM control blocks, at least one index buffer (for KSDS), and at least one data buffer.

upgrade set A set of alternate indexes that are automatically updated and kept in synchronization when the base cluster to which they belong is updated.

user catalog A VSAM or ICF catalog that contains information about clusters, alternate indexes, paths, non-VSAM files, etc.

VERIFY command An AMS command used to close an improperly closed VSAM data set after a system or application failure. It sets the end-of-data (EOD) and end-of-key-range (EOKR) pointers in the catalog to the correct values.

vertical pointer A pointer in an index record that points to an index set or sequence set record at the next lower level.

VSAM space A storage area set aside on a DASD for exclusive use and management by VSAM.

VSAM volume data set (VVDS) An ESDS defined on each volume for storing the characteristics of the VSAM data sets residing on that volume. It is the second part of an ICF catalog, the first part being the basic catalog structure (BCS).

VVDS (See **VSAM volume data set.**)

appendix B

Access Method Services Command Summary for Cache DASD Controllers

Parameters	Abbreviation
LISTDATA	LDATA
COUNTS or STATUS	CNT or STAT
FILE(ddname)	—
VOLUME(volser)	VOL
UNIT(unittype)	—
DEVICE or SUBSYSTEM or <u>ALL</u>	DEV or SSYS
LEGEND or <u>NOLEGEND</u>	LGND or NOLGND
OUTFILE or OUTDATASET	OFILE or ODS
SETCACHE	SETC
FILE(ddname)	—
VOLUME(volser)	VOL
UNIT(unittype)	—
<u>DEVICE</u> or SUBSYSTEM	DEV or SSYS
<u>ON</u> or OFF	—

ACCESS METHOD SERVICES COMMAND SUMMARY

Parameters	Abbreviation
BINDDATA	BDATA
ESTABLISH or TERMINATE	EST or TERM
FILE(ddname)	—
VOLUME(volser)	VOL
UNIT(unittype)	—
LOWCCHH(cchh)	LCCHH
HIGHCCHH(cchh)	HCCHH
DEVICE or SUBSYSTEM	DEV or SSYS

appendix C

File Requests and I/O's

1. **KSDS with Default Buffer Allocation**

File request	Index level		
	One	Two	Three
READ	1	3	4
WRITE	2	4	5
REWRITE	2	4	5
DELETE	2	4	5
START	1	3	4
READ NEXT	0 or 1 or 2	0 or 1 or 2	0 or 1 or 2

FILE REQUESTS AND I/O'S

2. KSDS with Index Set CIs Kept in Core

File request	Index level		
	One	Two	Three
READ	1	2	2
WRITE	2	3	3
REWRITE	2	3	3
DELETE	2	3	3
START	1	2	2
READ NEXT	0, 1, or 2	0, 1, or 2	0, 1, or 2

3. ESDS—Number of I/O's

File request	Number of I/O's
READ	1
WRITE	1 or 2
REWRITE	2
READ NEXT	0 or 1
START BROWSE	1

4. RRDS—Number of I/O's

File request	Number of I/O's
READ	1
WRITE	2
REWRITE	2
DELETE	2
READ NEXT	0 or 1
START BROWSE	1

appendix D

CI/CA Splits and I/O's

1. Number of I/O's Without and With a CI Split

I/O's on KSDS update*	Without CI split	With CI split
Best case (index set in core)	3	6
Worst case (default buffers)	5	8

*Updates include record add, change, and delete.

2. I/O's for a CA Split with Various CI Sizes

Data CI size	Number of data CIs per CA*	Approximate number of I/O's on a CA split
512	690	1058
1,024	465	720
2,048	270	428
4,096	150	248
6,144	90	158
8,192	75	135
12,288	45	90
16,348	37	78
32,768	18	50

*It is assumed that CA is one cylinder in size, device is an IBM 3380, and sequence set is NOIMBEDed.

appendix E

Seek Time, Rotational Delay, and Data Transfer Delay for Selected DASDs

1. **Maximum, Average, and Minimum Seek Time**

IBM DASD	Maximum seek time, ms	Average seek time, ms	Minimum seek time, ms
3310	46	27	9
3330	55	30	10
3340	50	25	10
3350	50	25	10
3370	40	20	5
3375	38	19	4
3380 (single density)	30	16	3
3380 (double density)	31	17	3
2305	0	0	0
9335	37	18	4.5
9332	Approx. 50	23–25	3–5

2. Maximum and Average Rotational Delay

IBM DASD	Maximum rotational delay, ms	Average rotational delay, ms
3330, 3350, 9335, 3380 (single and double density)	16.8	8.4
3340, 3370, 3375	20.2	10.1
3310, 9332	19.1	9.6
2305	10	5

3. Data Transfer Delay for a 4K CI

IBM DASD	Data transfer rate, MBS	Data transfer delay for a 4K CI, ms
3310	1.03	4.0
3330	0.81	5.0
3340	0.89	4.6
3350	1.20	3.4
3370	1.86	2.2
3375	1.86	2.2
3380 (single density)	3.00	1.3
3380 (double density)	3.00	1.3
2305	1.50	2.7
9335	3.00	1.9
9332	2.60	2.1

appendix F

"Ideal World" I/O Times for Selected DASDs

IBM DASD	Average seek time, ms	Average rotational delay, ms	Data transfer delay for a 4K CI, ms	"Ideal world" I/O time, ms
3310	27	9.6	4.0	40.6
3330	30	8.4	5.0	43.4
3340	25	10.1	4.6	39.7
3350	25	8.4	3.4	36.8
3370	20	10.1	2.2	32.3
3375	19	10.1	2.2	31.3
3380 (single density)	16	8.4	1.3	25.7
3380 (double density)	17	8.4	1.3	26.7
2305	0	5.0	2.7	7.7
9335	18	8.3	1.9	28.2
9332	24	9.6	2.1	35.7

appendix G

DASD Storage Capacity

IBM DASD	Total capacity, MB	Cylinders per disk pack	Tracks per cylinder	Bytes per track
3350	317	555	30	19,254
3370	286	750	12	31,744
3375	410	959	12	36,000
3380 (single density)	630	885	15	47,968
3380 (double density)	1260	1770	15	47,968
9335	412	1963	6	36,352
9332	184	1349	4	37,888

appendix H

CI Sizes, Physical Block Sizes, IBGs, and DASD Utilization

1 Interblock Gaps (IBGs)

IBM DASD	IBG for each physical record, bytes
3330	135
3350	185
3375	384
3380	512

2 CI Size, Physical Block Size, and DASD Utilization

CI sizes	Physical block size	Effective DASD utilization, %			
		IBM 3330	IBM 3350	IBM 3375	IBM 3380
½K, 1½K, 2½K, 3½K, 4½K, 5½K, 6½K, 7½K	½K	79.1	73.5	57.1	50
1K, 3K, 5K, 7K	1K	88.3	84.7	72.7	66.6
2K, 6K, 10K, 14K, 18K, 22K, 26K, 30K	2K	93.8	91.7	84.2	80.0
4K, 8K, 12K, 16K, 20K, 24K, 28K, 32K	4K	96.8	95.7	91.4	88.8

appendix I

Storage Characteristics of FBA Devices (DOS/VSE Only)

FBA DASD	Number of FBA blocks per track	Number of tracks per cylinder	Number of FBA blocks per cylinder	Cylinders per volume
IBM 3310	32	11	352	358
IBM 3370	62	12	744	750
IBM 9335	71	6	426	1963
IBM 9332	74	4	296	1349

INDEX

Access Method Control Block (ACB), 50, 203
Access Method Data Statistics Block (AMDSB), 50
Access Method Parameter (AMP), JCL, 203–204, 206, 207, 208
  alternate index, 210, 212
  BUFNI, 32
  parameters, 216
  STRNO parameter, 45
  see also JCL
Access method processing time, 60, 64
Access Method Services (AMS), 4, 245
  cache-related commands, 84, 85–93, 252–253
  space allocation, automatic, 124, 127, 128, 130
Actuator, 57

Addressability constraints, 5–6
ALTER, 38, 52, 178, 179, 203
  alternate index, 211
  AMS, 158
  BUFFERSPACE, 213–214
  FREESPACE parameter, 164
Alternate index. *See* Index, alternate
Amdahl, 101
Applications, fine tuning, 10–11
Assembler H, 6

Backup, batch environment, 212
Base cluster
  FCT coding, 226, 227
  pointer, 190
Batch processing, fine tuning, 4; *see also* Buffer management, batch environment
Best fit algorithm, 132, 134, 135
Binary zeros, 113–115, 173

265

BIND, 100, 101
BINDDATA, 85, 87–89, 92, 96, 103, 180, 253
BLDINDEX, 171, 180–183
Block
  characteristics, various devices, 131
  FBA devices, various, listed, 263
  size
    physical, 76–77
    various DASDs, listed, 262
BLOCKS, 126, 131, 132
Bound track mode, 85
Browsing
  LSR buffer pools, 234
  no read-ahead, 232
  string allocation, 218
BSAM, cache I/O, 85
BSTRNO, 227
Buffer(s)
  allocation, BLDINDEX, 181–182
  data, 207–209
  defined, 201–202
  fine tuning, 5–6, 46–47
look-aside, 47, 49
  management, 199
  see also Index buffers; Local Shared Resources (LSR), buffer pools and I/O reduction; NonShared Resources (NSR), buffer management
Buffer management, batch environment, 201–212
  backup, 212
  buffers, defined, 201–202
  DASD–main memory transfer, 201, 202
  data buffer, 207–209
  default buffer allocation, 202
  DOS/VSE, 212
  ESDS, 201, 210
  index buffers, 204–207
    alternate index, 210–212

I/O reduction, 201, 202, 204, 206, 208
  KSDS, 201–203, 208, 210, 211
  reorganization, 212
  RRDS, 202
  specifying buffers, 202–204
BUFFERS, 237–239
BUFFERSPACE, 46, 47, 177–179, 213
  alternate index, 211–212
  batch environment, 202–203
BUFND, 46, 47, 108, 178, 182, 207–209, 236, 239
  alternate index, 210–212
  batch environment, 202–204
  NSR, 214, 216, 217, 224, 226
  and BUFNI and STRNO, 225
BUFNI, 29, 32, 46, 47, 51, 69, 148–149, 178, 236, 239
  alternate index, 210–212
  batch environment, 202–205
  cache I/O, 86
  index
    levels, 206, 222
    minimum, 207
  NSR, 214, 216, 217, 219–223, 226
  and BUFNI and STRNO, 225
  SHAREOPTION 4, 176
BUFSP, 46, 212
Bypass cache mode, 84

Cache, 55, 59
  and SSDs, 103
Cache Analysis Aid (IBM), 96
Cache DASD controllers, 80–96, 153
  AMS commands, 85–93
  cache ratios, 93–96
  channels and DASDs, 82
  command summary, 252
  configuration, 81–83
  and CPU, 80, 81
  I/O with, 83–84
  management modes, 84–85

INDEX

CAPERCENT, 187
Catalog(s)
  caching, 96
  and GDGs, 179–180
  ICF, 11–12, 76, 180
  OS, 180
  and space allocation, 132
  VSAM, 11–12
CATALOG parameter, BLDINDEX, 182–183
CCHH, 8
Channel, 57, 58, 59–60
  -attached, 9
  busy wait, 64
  and cache, 82
  command words (CCWs), 83, 84, 125
    DEFINE EXTENT, 84, 85
Channel-to-channel adapters/link (CTCs), 43, 67, 68
CICS, 52, 64, 67
  buffers, 199
  cache I/O, 84, 86, 88
  CI/CA splits and file sharing, 39–43
  CI size, 108, 110
  device busy/stolen seek, 144
  Dynamic Storage Area (DSA), 67
  and ERASE option, 175
  FCT, BUFNI parameter, 29
  IMS/DB, 153, 155
    buffers, 76
  index
    buffers, 148–149
    and sequence sets, 19
  Local Shared Resource (LSR), 19
    defining, 235–237
  performance, 105
  preformatting data sets, 167, 168, 170
  shutdown statistics, monitoring LSR buffers, 239
  STAGE, 100, 101
  VERIFY command, 127

WRITE, 22
see also NonShared Resources (NSR) *entries*
CICS/VS, 4, 24, 25, 35, 38
  buffers, 48, 49
  CIDF busy bit, 30, 32
  File Control Table, 32
    STRNO operand, 45, 46
  fine tuning, 5, 7–9
  flow, 7–9
  index
    and data buffers, 46
    putting in core, 21
  LSR
    buffer pools, 231–233, 235–238, 240
    defining, 235–236
  NONSPACE condition, 37
  secondary extents, 136
  secondary volumes, 137
  spanned records, 125
  strings, 44–45
CIDF, 29, 51, 173
  busy bit, 30, 32
CIPERCENT, 185
CISIZE/RECORDSIZE ratio, 158
CISPERCYL, 195
CISZ parameter, 112
CKD devices, 126
CLIST (TSO), 67
CLOSE, 99
Cluster, 15
Cobol, 6, 37, 38, 39
  buffers, 48, 203
  cache I/O, 92
  CLOSE, 99
  dynamic access, 207
  EXTEND file, 52
  loads, initial and resume, 156
  and macros, 67
  mixed mode access, 209
  OUTPUT file, 52
  preformatting data sets, 170

READ, 50, 62
secondary volumes, 137
sequential access, 207, 209
SPEED vs. RECOVERY, 172
Common Key Value, 133
Common Service Area (CSA), 5
Control area (CA)
and CI, and IMBED, 146
file architecture and I/O's, 13–16, 17–20
free, 52
cf. CI, 161–162
and FREESPACE, 156, 157
index, 15–16
and KSDS space estimation, 186–188
size, 158–159
see also Control interval (CI) entries; Data CA
Control area (CA) split, 24–25, 33–37
appearance of data set after, 34
and data CA size, 127
how it happens, 33
I/O's in, 33, 35–36
points of failure, 36
premature, 38
share option 4 and, 37
see also Control interval (CI)/control area (CA) splits
Control blocks, fine tuning, 50
Control data sets, caching, 96
Control interval (CI)
architecture, and DASD, 76–79
cache, 87
and data, index CI, 124
definition, 17
description field (CIDF), 14–15, 16
file architecture and I/O's, 13–16, 17–20
index, 15–16
free, 52
cf. CA, 161–162
and FREESPACE, 156, 157

and KSDS space estimation, 185–186, 187–188
sequence set, 29
size
data, 107–110
index, 110–124
see also Data CI; Index CI
Control interval (CI) split
appearance of data set after, 31
CIDF busy bit, 30, 32
how it happens, 25, 28–30
ideal index buffer allocations, 32
I/O's in, 29–30, 32–33
update without, 29–30
Control interval (CI)/control area (CA) splits, 24–43, 52
buffers, 208
CICS, 39–43
data buffers, 224
ESDS, not in, 24
file sharing, 38–43
and FREESPACE, 157–162, 164–168
indexes alternate, 24, 38
I/O generation, 24, 25
listed, 256
KSDS, 24, 26–27, 28, 30, 32, 37, 38, 40, 41, 42
LSR buffer pools, 235
minimization, 37–38
RRDS, not in, 24
and sizes, 107
and small index CI size, 112
see also Control area (CA) splits
Count Key Data (CKD) device, 131
COUNTS parameter, 93
CPU
and cache, 80, 81
cycles, 4
wait, 63–64
Cylinder
adjacent, 73
characteristics, various devices, 131

INDEX

data CA space utilization, 143
FBA devices, 263
fixed-head, 75–76
rotational, 73
CYLINDERFAULT, 100–101
CYLINDERS, 126, 130, 131
DASD, 4, 13, 14, 17, 70–79
  architecture, 70–73
  block size, physical, 76–77
  cache storage, 55
  characteristics, various devices, 131
    capacity, 260
    data CA space utilization, 143
    data transfer delay, 258
    effective utilization, 262
    FBA, 263
    ideal I/O times, 259
    interblock gaps, 261
    rotational delay, 258
    seek times, 257
  and CI architecture, 21, 22, 78–79
  configuration, 57–60
    control unit, 58–59
    disk drives, 57–58
  conserving space, 79
  controller, 57, 58
  control unit busy, 64
  cylinder
    adjacent, 73
    fixed-head, 75–76
  fast-, 60, 64
  interblock gaps, 77–79
  I/O delays, 73–76
    reducing, 74–75
  management (DASDM) software, 132, 133, 134
  cf. mass storage system (MSS), 97, 98
  read-write area, 72, 73
  seek, seek-time, 72–74
  and small index CI size, 112
  storage capacity, 76
  see also Cache DASD controllers;

Mass storage system (MSS);
Solid state devices (SSDs);
specific devices
Data buffers, 207–209
  excess, 224
  fine tuning, 45–46
  see also BUFND
Data CA, 51, 54
  file architecture and I/O's, 14–15
  size, 141, 127, 128
    and alternate index, 189–192
    and index CI, 124
    index utilization, testing for, 124
    space utilization, various DASDs, 143
Data CI
  and alternate index, 189–191
  file architecture and I/O's, 14–15
  and index CI, 124
  index utilization, testing for, 124
  LSR buffers, 241
Data Facility Data Set Services (DFDSS), 84
Data load technique, index utilization, testing for, 112–113
Data set
  activity, and freespace, 159–161
  allocation time
    batch environment, 202–203
    NSR, 213–214
  control blocks (DSCBs), 132
  parallel-processed, 133
  statistics, LSR buffers, 239
  see also specific types
Data transfer. See Transfer, data
DEFINE, 92
DEFINE ALTERNATEINDEX
  CISZ parameter, 112
  MSS, 99
DEFINE CLUSTER/DEFINE AIX, 89, 105, 136, 137, 139, 141, 153, 175, 176, 178, 222
  alternate index, 211–212

batch environment, 202, 206
BUFFERSPACE, 213
CISZ parameter, 112, 124
IMBED option, 19, 51
KEYRANGE parameter, 64
MSS, 99
NOIMBED option, 33, 35, 36
preformatting data sets, 168
REPLICATE option, 19, 51
SHAREOPTIONS, 237
SPANNED parameter, 125
SPEED vs. RECOVERY, 172–175
WRITECHECK vs. NOWRITECHECK, 176
DEFINE EXTENT CCW, 84, 85
DEFINE SPACE, 132
DEFINE USERCATALOG, 132
DELETE, 19, 20, 21, 175
  RRDS, 22
  string allocation, 218
DEQ, 39, 65, 66, 67
DESTAGEWAIT, 99–100
Destaging, 98
DEVICE, 87, 89
Device busy
  IMBED and NOREPLICATE, 144, 146
  wait, 64
DF/EF, 11
DFHFCT, 86, 214, 215, 219–220, 224, 226, 236, 237, 242
DFHRPL library, 67
DFP, 11
Direct access storage device. *See* DASD
DLBL, 46, 212
DOS/VSE, 43, 231
  block size, 77
  buffers, 212
    allocation, 46
    management, batch, 212
    NSR, 214, 215
  index utilization, testing for, 124

no MSS, 98
space allocation, 126
UNIQUE data sets, 127
Dynamic path reconnect, 60, 64
Dynamic Storage Area (DSA), CICS, 67

EDB, 137, 184
ENDBR, 218, 219
ENQ, 39, 65–68
ERASE vs. NOERASE, 175–176
ESDS, 3, 15, 17, 21–22, 183
  with alternate index, cf. KSDS, 38
  buffer management, batch environment, 201, 210
  cache I/O, 85
  CI/CA splits, 24
  file requests, listed, 255
  LSR buffers and look-asides, 241–242
  no index component, 51
  space estimation, 193–194
    alternate index, 189, 190, 192
    cf. ESDS, 193
  UPGRADE option, 38
ESTABLISH, 89
EXEC CICS ENDBR, 234
Execute Channel Program (EXCP), 63
EXPRECS, 188
Extend Data Block (EDB), 50, 137, 184
EXTEND file, 52
Extents, secondary, 127, 136–137
EXTENT-TYPE X'00', 114

Fast-DASD, 60, 64
Faster and fewer techniques, 68–69
FBA devices, 131–132, 138
  characteristics, listed, 263
File architecture and I/O's, 13–23
  CI and CA, 13–16, 17–20

INDEX   **271**

    data, 14–15
    index, 15–16
  ESDS, 15, 17, 21–22
  index, alternate, 22–23
    levels, 23
    speed vs. need, 23
    upgrade, 23
  KSDS, 13–22
  RRDS, 15–22
File Control Table (FCT), 43, 155
  buffers, NSR, 214, 216
  BUFNI parameter, CICS, 29
  coding, base cluster, 226, 227
  defining, NSR cf. VSR, 235, 237
  STRNO operand, CICS/VS, 45, 46
FILE parameter, 86
Files
  low-activity, 242
  nonuniform activity, use LSR, 242
  reorganization, and FREESPACE, 167
  requests and I/O's, listed, 254–255
  sharing
    CI/CA splits, 38–43
    CICS, 39–43
Fine tuning, 1, 3–12
  application design, 10–11
  batch jobs, 4
  buffer(s)
    data, 45–46
    index, 45–46
    look-aside, 47, 49
    LSR, 47, 48–49
    NSR, 47–48, 49
    refresh, 47
    space, 46–47
    see also Buffer *entries*
  control blocks, 50
  and virtual storage, 5–6
  DASD space utilization, 6–7
  defined, 4
  different environments, 11–12
  glossary, 44–53

  important features, listed, 50–53
  as ongoing process, 9–10
  on-line (CICS/VS) systems, 5, 7–9
    flow, 7–9
  read ahead, 49–50
  strings, 44–45
  tuning, principles of, 9
First available algorithm, 132–134
Fixed Block Architecture (FBA). *See* FBA *entries*
Fixed free space, 37
Fixed Link Pack Area (FLPA), 5
Formatting, internal, 38
FREESPACE, 37, 51–52, 105, 112–113, 156–171, 185–187
  alternate indexes, 171, 189–190
  CI and CA
    percent, 156, 157
    CA splits, 157–162, 164–168
  DASD space requirements, 160, 164, 167
  ESDS space estimation, 193
  factors affecting, 158–161
  file reorganization, 167
  fixed allocation, 161–162
  preformatting data sets, 167–170
  variable allocation, 162–166
  see also Space allocation *entries*
FROMKEY option, REPRO, 173, 174

Generalized Trace Facility (GTF), 60, 64, 97
Generation data groups (GDGs), 179–180
Global Resource Sterilization (GRS), 67–68
Global shared resources (GSR), IMS/DB, 153, 155
Glossary, 245–251
  fine tuning, 44–53
GRFACT, 188, 194

HARBA, 196–197
  space estimation, 196–197
HIDAM, 69
  fixed-head cylinders, 76
  IMS, 153
  SSDs, 102
Hierarchical Storage Manager (HSM), 98
  control data set, caching, 96
HIGHCCHH, 88, 92
High used relative byte address
    (HURBA), 37, 39, 50, 113,
    114, 115, 127, 166, 173, 175,
    196–197, 207
  data (HURBAD), 206, 222
  index (HURBAI), 220–223
  preformatting data sets, 170
  space estimation, 196–197
HISAM, 69
  fixed-head cylinders, 76
  IMS, 153

IBM 37 × 5, links, 43
IBM 2305, 60, 69
  emulation, 101
  cf. SSDs, 102
IBM 3090 (Sierra), 55, 59, 96, 97, 98
BIBM 3310, FBA, 131
IBM 3330, 98
  and cache, 80
  CI size, block size, 109, 110
  as CKD, 131
  and space estimation, KSDS, 186, 187
IBM 3340, 65
IBM 3350, 9, 83, 98
  as CKD, 131
  emulation, 101
  I/O speed, 63
  transfer rate, 61
IBM 3370
  FBA, 131
  KSDS allocation, 131

IBM 3375, CI size, block size, 109, 110
IBM 3380, 13, 33, 35, 36, 39, 57, 58,
    59, 69, 70–79, 83, 98, 142,
    144, 146, 153
  addressing, 89
  CI size, 110, 111
  as CKD, 131
  data buffers, 208–209
  data CI
    capacity, 113
    size, 124
  emulation, 101, 103
  ERASE option, 175
  FREESPACE, 157
  interblock gap, 109
  preformatting data sets, 167
  space allocation, 132
  space estimation, 190–193
    KSDS, 186, 187
    RRDS, 195, 197
  cf. SSDs, 102, 103
  transfer rate, 61
IBM 3850, 98, 109, 110
IBM 3880, 82, 83
IBM 4341, 59
IBM 9332, FBA, 131
IBM 9335, FBA, 131
ICF catalogs, 11–12, 76, 180
  caching, 96
IEHPROGM, 179
IMBED, 4, 68, 75, 105, 113, 114,
    115, 117, 124, 127, 128
  CI size, 110, 111
  DEFINE CLUSTER, 51
  and device busy, 146
  and space estimation
    alternate index, 189–192
    KSDS, 186, 187
  see also NOIMBED entries
IMBED and NOREPLICATE,
    141–146, 147
  increased DASD space requirement, 143

INDEX

index buffer, 204–205, 207
   NSR, 220–221
   and I/O performance, 143–146
IMBED and REPLICATE, 140, 146–150, 151
   DASD space requirement, 147
   index buffer, 205, 210
      NSR, 221, 223
   I/O performance, 147–150
   LSR buffers, 241
IMS
   cache I/O, 84, 86
      RECON data set, 96
   secondary index, 69
   SSDs, 102
IMS/DB
   fixed-head cylinders, 76
   performance, 105
   REPLICATE, 153–155
IMS/DC, 4, 24, 25
IMS/VS, 230
Index
   CA, 15–16
   clustering, 129
   component, 19
   FREESPACE, 52
   KSDS, 16, 17
      levels, 18
   record, 16, 50–51
   secondary, 69, 76
   separate from data, 51
   set, 25, 47
      KSDS, 18–19
      record (ISR), 140, 142, 143, 147, 149, 151, 153
      REPLICATE option, 51
   space allocation, 128–130
   speeding I/O, 68–69
Index, alternate, 38, 155, 171, 245
   buffers
      base processing, 212
      batch environment, 210–212
      dynamic open, 210–212
      NSR, 225–227

cluster, 245
CI/CA splits, 24, 38
file architecture and I/O's, 22–23
   levels, 23
   speed vs. need, 23
   upgrade, 23
FREESPACE, 52, 171
   as KSDS, 51
   LSR buffer pools, 232
   space estimation, 189–193
   upgrade set, 102
   UPGRADE vs. NOUPGRADE, 183
Index buffers, 204–207
   alternate index, 210–212
      NSR, 225–227
   batch environment, 204–207
   default allocation, 19–20, 53
   fine tuning, 45–46
   ideal allocation, 20–21, 32
   and NSR, 148–149
      excess, 223
   three-level, NSR, 222–223
   see also BUFNI
Index CI, 15–16, 50–51, 110–112, 141
   LSR buffers, 241
   small, implications, 112
   testing for index utilization, 112–124
      adjusting CA and CI sizes, 124
      binary zeros technique, 113–115
      data load technique, 112–113
      DOS/VSE, 124
      recommendations, 124
Inhibit cache loading mode, 85
Input data set, buffers, 208–209
Input/output (I/O), 50–53
   and cache, 83–84
   CI/CA splits and, 24–25, 29–30, 32–33
   listed, 256
   delays, and DASD, 73–76
      reducing, 74–75
   file requests, listed, 254–255

performance, and index allocation, 130
reduction, 199, 201, 202, 204, 206, 208
request
  KSDS, 19–21
  processing, 7, 9
  times, ideal, various devices, 259
  see also Buffer *entries*; File architecture and I/O's
Input/output (I/O) internals, 57–69
  access method processing time, 60, 64
  channel busy wait, 64
  CPU wait, 63–64
  DASD configuration, 57–60
    control unit, 58–59
    disk drives, 57–58
  DASD control unit busy, 64
  data transfer delay, 61–62, 63, 65
  device busy wait, 64
  faster and fewer techniques, 68–69
  queue, 63, 64
  read/write head selection delay, 60–61
  rotational delay, 61, 62, 63, 65
  RPS miss, 65
  seek time, 60, 62, 63, 65
  serializing I/O's, 65–68
Interblock gaps, 77–79, 109
  listed, 261
Intersystems Communications (ISC), 39, 43

JCL, 29
  buffers, 46, 203, 212
    allocation, 178, 179, 181
  cache commands, 86, 87
  freespace, 164
  REGION parameter, 202
  see also Access Method Parameter (AMP), JCL

Key
  alternate, 245
  compression, 51, 112
KEYLEN, LSR buffer pools, 238
KEYRANGES, 102, 162, 222, 126, 137–139
  DEFINE CLUSTER, 64
  index buffer, 206
KSDS, 3, 4
  allocation, IBM 3370, 131
  alternate indexes, 155
    cf. ESDS, 38
  buffers, 46
    batch environment, 201–203, 208, 210, 211
  cache I/O, 85, 86–87, 88–91
  CI/CA splits, 24, 26–27, 28, 30, 32, 37, 38, 40, 41, 42
  file architecture and I/O's, 13–22
  file requests, listed, 254, 255
  fixed-head cylinders, 76
  FREESPACE, 52
  HIDAM/HISAM, 153
  index, 16, 17
    CI, 112
    levels, 18
    set, 18–19
    three-level, configuration, 140, 141
  I/O requests, 19–21
  LSR buffer pools, 228–231, 241
  sequence set, 18–19
  space estimation, 185–189
    alternate index, 189, 190
    cf. ESDS, 193
  speeding I/O, 68, 69
  SSDs, 102
  strings, 44, 45
  see also FREESPACE

Least recently used (LRU) algorithm, 83, 84, 85, 87, 88, 96, 103, 149, 230, 234

IMS/DB, 153
LSR buffers, 240, 241
LEGEND option, LISTDATA, 93, 94–95
Libraries, test and production, mixing, 67
LIMIT parameter, 180
Linkage editor, 67
Links, 43
LISTCAT, 18, 24, 50, 62–63, 113–117, 120–121, 136, 159, 162, 165, 166, 196, 220
LISTDATA, 90–96
  cache DASD controllers, 252
  LEGEND option, 93, 94–95
  STATUS parameter, 93, 96
Local Shared Resource (LSR), 47, 69, 76, 147, 199
  CICS, 19
  file types recommended, 242
  IMS/DB, 153, 155
  and REPLICATE, 149–150
Local Shared Resource (LSR), buffer pools and I/O reduction, 228–243
  alternate index, 232
  buffers shared by index and data components, 230
  cache I/O, 88
  default allocation, 238
  defined, 228–229
  defining, in CICS, 235–239
  fine tuning, 47, 48–49
  graphic representation, 229
  KSDS, 228–231, 241
  look-aside, 231
  monitoring, 239–240
  multiple pools, 240
  MVS/XA cf. CICS/VS, 231–233, 235–238, 240
  no read-ahead in browse, 232
  cf. NSR, 213, 216, 228, 230–236, 240–242
  problems, 233–235
  recommendations, 239–243
    4K boundary, 243
    sequence set in core, 231–232
    statistics, 240
    virtual storage loss, 230–231
Locate mode, string allocation, 218
Lockout, LSR buffer pools, 233–234
Look-asides
  ESDS, 241–242
  fine tuning, 47, 49
  LSR, 231
LOWCCHH, 88, 92
LSRPOOL, 214–216, 237

Macros
  ACB, 203
  CLOSE, 99
  DEQ, 39, 65, 66, 67
  DFHFCT, 86, 214, 215, 219–220, 224, 226
  ENQ, 39, 65–68
  RELEASE, 39, 64, 66, 68
  RESERVE, 39, 64, 66–67, 68
Mass storage system (MSS), 97–101
  BIND, 100, 101
  CYLINDERFAULT, 100–101
  cf. DASD, 97, 98
  DESTAGEWAIT AMS parameter, 99–100
  STAGE, 100, 101
  storage capacity, 98
  see also Solid state devices (SSDs)
Memorex, 101, 102
Memory, expanded, 96, 97
  and SSDs, 104
Minimization, CI/CA splits, 37–38
Mixed-mode access
  data buffer, 209
  index buffer, 207
Move mode, string allocation, 218
Multiple loads, BLDINDEX, 181
MultiRegion Operation (MRO), 39

MVS, 5, 43, 124
  block size, 76
  buffer requirements, 46
  CI size, 109
  GDGs and VSAM catalogs, 179-180
  index CI size, 112
  MSS, 98
  space allocation, 126
  Systems Queue Area (SQA), 65, 66, 67
  UNIQUE data sets, 127
MVS/SP, CI, 16
MVS/XA, 60, 64
  buffers, NSR, 214, 215
  CI, 16
  LSR buffer pools, 231-233, 235-238, 240
  virtual storage constraint, 110

National Advanced Systems, 101, 102
NOERASE cf. ERASE, 175-176
NOIMBED, 33, 35, 36, 89, 92, 113, 114, 115, 121
  ESDS, 193
  RRDS, 195
  see also IMBED *entries*
NOIMBED and NOREPLICATE, index buffer, 205
  NSR, 221
NOIMBED and REPLICATE, 150-153, 153, 205
  DASD space requirement, 151
  index buffer, NSR, 221-222
  performance, 151, 153
NonShared Resources (NSR), 147, 148, 155
  and index buffer allocation, 148-149
NonShared Resources (NSR), buffer management, 199, 213-227
  alternate index considerations, 225-227

  BASE parameter, 226-227
  cf. KSDS, 225
  data buffers (BUFND), 214, 216, 217, 224, 226
  data set allocation time, 213-214
  DOS/VSE, 214, 215
  file control table and LSRPOOL operand, 214-216
  fine tuning, 47-48, 49
  index buffers (BUFNI), 214, 216, 217, 219-223, 226
  cf. LSR, 213, 216, 228, 230-236, 240-242
  MVS/XA, 214, 215
  STRNO allocation, 214, 216-219, 220, 221, 227
  STRNO, BUFNI, and BUFND interrelationships, 225
  where buffers reside, 214
NONSPACE condition, CICS/VS, 37
Nonuniform update activity determination, 164-166
NOREPLICATE, 89, 92, 113-114, 115
  NOIMBED and, 205, 221
  see also IMBED and NOREPLICATE
Normal cache mode, 84
NOSDESTAGEWAIT, 99, 100
NOSPACE, 137
NOUPGRADE, 23, 171
  cf. UPGRADE, alternate indexes, 183

Omegamon/CICS, 64, 65, 146
Omegamon/MVS, 60, 64, 65, 146
On-line systems, fine tuning, 5, 7-9
  flow, 7-9
OS
  catalogs, 180
  /VSI, CI, 16
OUTPUT, 52, 136
Output data set, buffers, 209

INDEX

Pageable Link Pack Area (PLPA), 5
Parallel-processed data sets, 133
Physical sequential (PS) data set, 76
PL/I, V5RI optimizer, 6
Pointer, base cluster, 190, 192
Preformatting data sets,
    FREESPACE, 167–170
Private area, 202
PROCLIB, 96
PTRLEN, 190, 192

QSAM, cache I/O, 85
Queue, 63, 64

RACF control data set, caching, 96
Random access
  data buffer, 208
  index buffer, 204–207
Random reads and data CI size, 108
RDF, 14–15, 16, 29, 51
READ, 19, 20, 21, 22, 50, 58, 62, 218
Read-ahead
  fine tuning, 49–50
  LSR buffer pools, 232
Read-hit, 83
  ratio, 83, 93, 96
Read-miss, 83
READ NEXT, 19, 20, 21, 22, 217, 218, 224, 232, 234
READ UPDATE, 234
Read-write area, DASD, 72, 73
Read/write head selection delay, 60–61
Read/write ratio, 93, 96
RECON data set, caching, IMS, 96
Record
  description field (RDF), 14–15, 16, 29, 51
  fixed cf. variable length, KSDS, 189
  index, 50–51

number, relative, 194, 195
size
  and data CI size, 109–110
  and spanned records, 125
  spanned, 125, 176–177
RECORDS, 126, 131
RECORDSIZE/CISIZE ratio, 158
RECOVERY vs. SPEED, 172–175
RECSCA, 188
RECSPERCI, RRDS, 195
RECSPERCYL, RRDS, 195, 196
REGION parameter, JCL, 202
Relative record number, 194, 195
RELEASE, 39, 64, 66, 68
Reorganization, buffer management,
    batch environment, 212
REPLICATE, 4, 69, 75, 105,
    113–114, 115, 128
  DEFINE CLUSTER, 51
  IMS/DB, 153–155
  and LSR, 149–150
  see also IMBED and REPLICATE;
    NOIMBED and REPLICATE
REPRO, 113, 164, 203
  FROMKEY option, 173, 174
  OUTDATASET cf. OUTFILE, 178
  preformatting data sets, 168, 170
  SKIP parameter, 173, 174
  SPEED vs. RECOVERY, 172
RESERVE, 39, 64, 66–67, 68
Resource Measurement Facility
    (RMF), 60, 64
REUSE, 127, 135–136, 180
REWRITE, 19, 20, 21
  ESDS, 22
  string allocation, 218, 219
RMF, 60, 64
Rotational delay, 61, 62, 63, 65
  DASDs and SSDs, 103
  IMBED and NOREPLICATE, 145
  various devices, listed, 258, 259
Rotational Position Sensing, 65, 102
  miss, 65

RRDS, 3
  buffer management, batch environment, 202
  CI/CA splits, 24
  file architecture and I/O's, 15-22
  file requests, listed, 255
  no index component, 51
  space estimation, 194-196
  RSCLMT, LSR buffer pools, 238

SEARCH, 58
Secondary extents, 136-137
  secondary volumes, 137
SEEK, 58
Seek, stolen, IMBED and NOREPLICATE, 144, 146
Seek time, 72-74, 60, 62, 63, 65
  DASDs and SSDs, 103
  IMBED and NOREPLICATE, 145
  various devices, listed, 257, 259
SELECT, sequential access, 207, 209
Sequence set, 25
  CI, 29
  core, LSR buffer pools, 231-232
  IMBED option, 51
  I/O, 52
  KSDS, 18-19
  records (ISR), 140, 142, 143, 144, 146
  and data CA, 51
Sequential access
  cache I/O, 85
  data buffer, 208-209
  index buffer, 207
Sequential processing, and small index CI size, 112
Sequential reads and data CI size, 108
Serializing I/O's, 65-68
SETCACHE, 85-87, 252
Shareoption, 47, 68, 176, 237
Shutdown statistics, CICS, monitoring LSR buffers, 239
Sierra. *See* IBM 3090 (Sierra)

SKIP parameter, REPRO, 173, 174
Software End of File (SEOF), 127, 173, 174
Solid state devices (SSDs), 101-104
  cache, 103
  capacity and performance, various models, 102, 103
  cf. DASDs, 102-103
  expanded memory, 104
  vendors, 101, 102
SORT/MERGE utility, 85
Space allocation
  fixed free space, 37
  recommendations, 138
  variable free space, 37-38
  see also FREESPACE
Space allocation parameters, 126-139
  CYLINDERS, 126, 130, 131
  data CA size, 127, 128
  FBA devices, 131-132, 138
  index space allocation, 128-130
  KEYRANGES, 126, 137-139
  RECORDS, 126, 131
  secondary extents, 136-137
    secondary volumes, 137
  TRACKS, 126, 131
  UNIQUE vs. SUBALLOCATION, 132-136, 138
Space, conserving, DASD, 79
Space estimation, 184-197
  ESDS, 193-194
  HARBA, 196-197
  HURBA, 196-197
  index, alternate, 189-193
  KSDS, 185-189
  RRDS, 194-196
Space utilization, fine tuning, 6-7
SPANNED parameter, DEFINE CLUSTER, 125
Spanned records, 125, 176-177
Speed, indexes, 23
SPEED vs. RECOVERY, 172-175
Splits. *See* Control area (CA) split;

INDEX

Control interval (CI) split;
Control interval (CI)/control
area (CA) splits
SSRs, 146, 151, 153
STAGE, 100, 101
Staging, 98
START, 19, 20, 21
START BROWSE, ESDS, 22
STATUS parameter, LISTDATA, 93, 96
Storage capacity
  mass storage system (MSS), 98
  various DASDs, listed, 260
Storage directors, 81
Storage Technology Corp., 101, 102
STRNO, 203, 206, 216-219, 236
  AMP, 45
  buffers, NSR, 214, 216-217, 220, 221, 227
  and BUFNI/BUFND, 225
  duration of string, 218
  fine tuning, 44-45
  LSR buffer pools, 238-240
  and string waits, 217
SUBALLOCATION vs. UNIQUE, 132-136, 138
SUBSYSTEM, 87, 89
System Queue Area (SQA), 5, 65, 66, 67

TERMINATE, 89
Terminology
  fine tuning, 44-53
  glossary, 245-251
TEST.KSDS1.CLUSTER, 114, 122-123
TEST.KSDS1.INDEX, 115, 118-119, 122-123
Time Sharing Option (TSO), 67
Tracks, 70
  characteristics, various devices, 131
  data CA space utilization, various models, 143

FBA devices, various, listed, 263
TRACKS, 126, 131
Transfer, data, 61
  DASDs and SSDs, 102, 103
  delay, 61-62, 63, 65, 74
  IMBED and NOREPLICATE, 145
  various devices, listed, 258, 259
Tuning principles, fine tuning, 9

UNIQUE data sets, 127
UNIQUE vs. SUBALLOCATION, 132-136, 138
UNIT, 86, 93
UNLOCK, 219
Updates, incomplete, 219
UPGRADE, 23, 155
  ESDS, 38
  vs. NOUPGRADE, alternate indexes, 183
Upgrade set, indexes, 23

Variable free space, space allocation, 37-38
VERIFY, 50, 127, 173, 175
VICS, secondary extents, 136
Virtual storage
  allocation map, 5
  constraint, 5
    and data CI size, 110
    relief (VSCR), 6
  LSR buffer pools, 230-231
  management, fine tuning, 5-6
Virtual volumes, 98
VOLUME, 86, 93
Volume Data Sets (VVDSs), 183
Volumes
  secondary, 137
  serial (volser) number, 57
  virtual, 98
Volume Table of Contents (VTOC), 132
  RESERVE macro, 67
  secondary extents, overhead, 136, 137

VSAM, 11
    catalogs, 11-12

WRITE, 19, 20, 21, 58, 219
    ESDS, 22

WRITECHECK vs.
    NOWRITECHECK
    DEFINE AIX, 176
    DEFINE CLUSTER, 176